Complete
Spanish

Juan Kattán-Ibarra

Advisory editor Paul Coggle

For UK order enquiries: please contact Bookpoint Ltd, 130 Milton Park, Abingdon, Oxon OX14 4SB. Telephone: +44 (0) 1235 827720. Fax: +44 (0) 1235 400454. Lines are open 09.00–17.00, Monday to Saturday, with a 24-hour message answering service. Details about our titles and how to order are available at www.teachyourself.com

For USA order enquiries: please contact McGraw-Hill Customer Services, PO Box 545, Blacklick, OH 43004-0545, USA. Telephone: 1-800-722-4726. Fax: 1-614-755-5645.

For Canada order enquiries: please contact McGraw-Hill Ryerson Ltd, 300 Water St, Whitby, Ontario L1N 9B6, Canada. Telephone: 905 430 5000. Fax: 905 430 5020.

Long renowned as the authoritative source for self-guided learning – with more than 50 million copies sold worldwide – the *Teach Yourself* series includes over 500 titles in the fields of languages, crafts, hobbies, business, computing and education.

British Library Cataloguing in Publication Data: a catalogue record for this title is available from the British Library.

Library of Congress Catalog Card Number: on file.

First published in UK 1998 by Hodder Education, part of Hachette UK, 338 Euston Road, London NW1 3BH as *Teach Yourself Spanish.*

First published in US 1998 by The McGraw-Hill Companies, Inc.

This edition published 2012

The *Teach Yourself* name is a registered trade mark of Hodder Headline.

Typeset by Integra Software Services Pvt. Ltd., Pondicherry, India.

Illustrated by Barking Dog Art, Sally Elford, Peter Lubach.

Printed and bound in Dubai for Hodder Education, an Hachette UK Company, 338 Euston Road, London NW1 3BH.

The publisher has used its best endeavours to ensure that the URLs for external websites referred to in this book are correct and active at the time of going to press. However, the publisher and the author have no responsibility for the websites and can make no guarantee that a site will remain live or that the content will remain relevant, decent or appropriate.

Hachette UK's policy is to use papers that are natural, renewable and recyclable products and made from wood grown in sustainable forests. The logging and manufacturing processes are expected to conform to the environmental regulations of the country of origin.

Impression number   10 9 8 7 6 5 4 3 2 1

Year   2014 2013 2012

Acknowledgements

The author wishes to thank Juan Luzzi for his assistance in the production of the manuscript. Thanks are also due to Angela Howkins for writing the culture notes and to the following people for their help with recordings: María Catalina Botello, Carlos Riera, Elsa Ochoa, Leonardo Sánchez Gorosito, Sarah Sherborne.

Every effort has been made to obtain permission for all material used. In the absence of any response to enquiries, the author and publisher would like to acknowledge the following for use of their material: *Revistas Quo*, *Mía*, *Blanco y Negro de ABC*, *Guía del Ocio*, diario *El Periódico*, *Oficina Municipal de Turismo del Ayuntamiento de Fuengirola*, *RENFE*, from Spain; diarios *El Mercurio* and *La Tercera*, from Chile.

Meet the author

I am an experienced teacher of Spanish and the author of a number of best-selling Spanish courses. I began my career teaching Spanish in the United Kingdom in 1975, at Ealing College in London, and also acted as an external examiner in Spanish for various London examinations boards.

My first Spanish course was published in London in 1978, in a writing career which has lasted until today, and I have written, or co-written, courses in the *Teach Yourself* series including *Complete Spanish*, *Perfect your Spanish*, *Get Started in Latin American Spanish*, *Complete Latin American Spanish*, *Essential Spanish Grammar*, *Speak Spanish with Confidence*, *Get Talking Spanish in Ten Days*, *Keep Talking Spanish* and courses for other publishers, including the BBC and McGraw-Hill. I am now a full-time author, and very much look forward to being your guide in the journey you are just about to begin into the Spanish language. **¡Vamos!**

Contents

BEGINNER

Welcome to Complete Spanish! Is this the right course for you? If you are an adult learner with no previous knowledge of Spanish and studying on your own, then this is the course for you. Perhaps you are taking up Spanish again after a break from it, or you are intending to learn with the support of a class? Again, you will find this course very well suited to your purposes. Whether you are new to Spanish or have already had experience of it, I will be guiding you through all the essentials of the language, starting with the most basic forms and moving on to more advanced ones, giving you all the tools you need to communicate with Spanish speakers wherever you are. Successful language learning means being able to handle a number of abilities whose relative importance is determined by your own needs. Among these is the ability to communicate orally with native speakers, being able to express yourself in Spanish and understand what people say. This course has all the necessary ingredients to achieve this aim, without neglecting other less urgent needs. In the notes below you will find more information on the nature and structure of this course as well as guidelines on how to use it. Good luck!

About this course

The language introduced in this course is centred around realistic everyday situations. The emphasis is first and foremost on using Spanish, but we also aim to give you an idea of how the language works, so that you can create sentences of your own.

The course covers all four of the basic skills – listening and speaking, reading and writing. If you are working on your own, the audio recordings will be all the more important, as they will provide you with the essential opportunity to listen to Spanish and to speak it within a controlled framework. You should therefore try to obtain a copy of the audio recordings if you haven't already got one.

USE IT OR LOSE IT!

Language learning is a bit like jogging – you need to do it regularly for it to do any good! Ideally, you should find a 'study buddy' to work through the course with you. This way you will have someone to try out your Spanish on. And when the going gets tough, you will have someone to chivvy you on until you reach your target.

Where can I find real Spanish?

Don't expect to be able to understand everything you hear or read straight away. If you watch Spanish-speaking programmes on TV or buy Spanish magazines you should not get discouraged when you realize how quickly native-speakers speak and how much vocabulary there is still to be learned. Just concentrate on a small *extract* – either a video/audio clip or a short article – and work through it till you have mastered it. In this way, you'll find that your command of Spanish increases steadily. See the **Taking it further** section at the back of the book for information on sources of authentic Spanish, including newspapers, magazines, websites and organizations linked to the Spanish-speaking world.

The structure of this course

The course book contains
▶ an introductory unit
▶ 25 course units with self-assessment tests at the end of each unit
▶ a reference section at the back of the book
▶ 2 CDs (which you really do need to have if you are going to get maximum benefit from the course).

The course units

The course units can be divided roughly into the following categories, although of course there is a certain amount of overlap from one category to another.

STATEMENT OF AIMS

You will be told what you can expect to learn, mostly in terms of what you will be able to do in Spanish by the end of the unit.

CULTURE NOTES

Read the opening cultural piece in English to find out more about Spanish life and pick up some key vocabulary. The discovery question that follows helps you to work out a language point for yourself.

PRESENTATION OF NEW LANGUAGE

You will find two or more dialogues which are recorded on the CDs and also printed in the book. Some assistance with vocabulary is also given. The language is presented in manageable chunks, building carefully on what you have learned in earlier units. Transcripts of listening comprehension exercises are at the back of the book.

KEY PHRASES AND EXPRESSIONS

New phrases and expressions with their English translation are listed in the How do you say it? section.

DESCRIPTION OF LANGUAGE FORMS

In the Language Discovery section you learn about the forms of the language, thus enabling you to construct your own sentences correctly. For those who are daunted by grammar, assistance is given in various ways.

PRONUNCIATION

 00.02

The best way to acquire a good pronunciation and intonation is to listen to native speakers and try to imitate them. But most people do not actually notice that certain sounds in Spanish are pronounced differently from their English counterparts, until this is pointed out to them. Specific advice on pronunciation is given in the Pronunciation Guide later in this introduction, and in the Pronunciation section in the first half of the course.

PRACTICE OF THE NEW LANGUAGE

In the Practice section you will be able to use the language that you have learned. Practice is graded, so that activities ('actividades' on the recording) which require mainly *recognition* normally come first. As you grow in confidence in manipulating language forms, you will be encouraged to **produce** both in writing and in speech.

HELPING YOU GET TO GRIPS WITH THE NEW LANGUAGE

To help you get to grips with the new language and with the activities in the practice section, you will find, at various points in the unit, the author's hints on how to deal with specific points as well as suggestions for further practise.

INFORMATION ON SPANISH-SPEAKING COUNTRIES

At different stages in the course, you will find relevant information about aspects of life and customs in the Spanish-speaking world. This information is given in English in the first part of the course, but later on in Spanish.

TEST YOURSELF

A **Test yourself** section at the end of each unit will help you to test what you have learned and allow you to judge whether you have successfully mastered the language in that unit and if you are ready to move on to the next one. If you are uncertain about how you performed with the test you will be able to check your answers in **the Key to the activities and to Test yourself** at the end of the book.

At the end of the book there are sections that you can use for reference:

▶ a 'taking it further' section
▶ a glossary of grammatical terms
▶ a grammar summary
▶ a list of irregular verbs
▶ transcripts of the listening comprehension exercises
▶ a key to the activities and to 'Test yourself' in each unit
▶ an index to the grammar.

How to use this course

Make sure at the beginning of each course unit that you are clear about what you can expect to learn.

Then have a look at the opening cultural note about an aspect of Spanish life and see if you can answer the discovery question.

Read any background information that is provided. Then listen to the dialogues on the audio recordings. Try to get the gist of what is being said before you look at the printed text in the book. Refer to the printed text and the key vocabulary in order to study the dialogues in more detail. If you want an explanation of new language points at this stage, study the relevant paragraphs in the Grammar section. All the dialogues include listening and reading activities and you can check your answers in the **Key to the activities**.

Don't fall into the trap of thinking you have 'done that' when you have listened to the audio a couple of times and worked through the dialogues and activities in the book. You may recognize what you hear and read, but you almost certainly still have some way to go before you can *produce* the language of the dialogues correctly and fluently. This is why we recommend that you keep listening to the recordings at every opportunity – sitting on the train or bus, waiting at the dentist's or stuck in a traffic jam in the car, using what would otherwise be 'dead' time. Of course, you must also be internalizing what you hear and making sense of it – just playing it in the background without really paying attention is not enough!

After you have gone through the dialogues, check the **How do you say it?** section for key phrases and expressions. Try covering up the English translations and producing the English equivalents of the Spanish. If you find that relatively easy, go on to cover the Spanish sentences and produce the Spanish equivalents of the English. You will probably find this more difficult. Trying to recall the context in which words and phrases were used may help you learn them better.

You can then study the grammar explanations in the **Language discovery section** in a systematic way. We have tried to make these as user-friendly as possible, since we recognize that many people find grammar daunting. But in the end, it is up to you just how much time you spend on studying and sorting out the grammar points. Some people find that they can do better by getting an ear for what sounds right, but others need to know in detail how the language is put together. At this stage you may want to refer to the relevant sections of the **Glossary of grammatical terms** and the **Grammar summary** for clarification and further information.

You will then be ready to move on to the **Practice section** and work through the activities following the instructions that precede them. Some of the activities in this section are listen-only activities. The temptation may be to go straight to the transcriptions in the back of the book, but try not to do this. The whole point of listening exercises is to improve your listening skills. You will not do this by reading first. The transcriptions are there to help you if you get stuck.

As you work your way through the activities, check your answers carefully in the back of the book. It is easy to overlook your own mistakes. If you have a study buddy it's a good idea to check each other's answers. Most of the exercises have fixed answers, but some are a bit more open-ended, especially when we are asking you to talk about yourself. We then, in most cases, give you a model answer which you can adapt for your own purposes.

Before you move on to the next unit go through the **Test yourself** section at the end of the unit and check your answers in the **Key to the activities and to Test yourself.** If you did well you can start a new unit, otherwise go back to any relevant points that may need revision until you feel confident that you have mastered them. **The Grammar summary** may also help you with this.

What kind of Spanish am I going to learn?

The language we have chosen for your *Complete Spanish* course is standard Spanish, which will allow you to communicate with speakers anywhere in the Spanish-speaking world. The audio recordings have been done mostly by speakers from Spain, but to get you acquainted with other accents, some have been recorded by people from Mexico and Argentina. Differences between Peninsular and Latin American Spanish are explained in some of the course units. The abbreviation *LAm* has been used to signal a Latin American term, but note that usage may differ from country to country so, with a few exceptions, only words used more widely have been given.

We hope you enjoy working your way through *Complete Spanish*. Don't get discouraged. Mastering a new language does take time and perseverance and sometimes things can seem just too difficult. But then you'll come back to it another day and things will begin to make more sense again.

Pronunciation guide

The aim of this pronunciation guide is to offer hints which will enable you to produce sounds recognizable to Spanish speakers. It cannot by itself teach you to pronounce Spanish accurately. The best way to acquire a reasonably good accent is to listen to and try to imitate native speakers. Listed below are the main elements of Spanish pronunciation and their approximate English equivalent. In addition to these, between Units 1–13 you will find further notes on some individual sounds and you will have a chance to practise them by imitating the speakers on the recording. Read the notes below, which include only those sounds which may cause difficulty to English speakers, and listen to and repeat the words that you hear.

VOWELS

a	like the **a** in *answer* (but shorter – British English; like the *u* in *but* – American English)	**Ana**
e	like the **e** in *red*	**Elena**
i	like the **ea** in *mean*	**Rita**
o	like the **o** in *cost*	**poco**
u	like the **oo** in *moon*	**luna**

CONSONANTS

b and **v**	in initial position and after **n** are pronounced the same, with lips closed, like the **b** in *bar*	**Barcelona, invierno**

b and **v**	in other positions the lips are slightly apart	**Sevilla, Alba**
c	before **a, o, u**, like the **c** in *car*	**coche**
	before **e, i**, like the **th** in *think* (in Latin America, southern Spain and the Canaries, like the **s** in *sink*)	**gracias, Valencia**
g	before **a, o, u,** like the **g** in *get*	**Málaga**
	before **e, i**, like the **ch** in *loch*	**Gibraltar**
gu	before **e, i**, like the **g** in *get*	**Guernica**
h	is silent	**Honduras**
j	like the **ch** in *loch*	**Jamaica**
ll	like the **y** in *yes*, but there are regional variants (in Argentina, more like the **s** in *television*)	**paella**
ñ	like **ni** in *onion*	**mañana**
qu	like the **k** in *keep*	**que**
r	between vowels or at the end of a word, like the **r** in *very*;	**caro, calor**
	in initial position, strongly rolled	**Roma**
rr	always strongly rolled	**Tarragona**
v	like **b** (see **b** above)	
w	(in foreign words) like Spanish **b** and **v** (see above) or English **w**	**wáter** **Taiwán**
x	between vowels, like the **x** in *box*; before a consonant, as above or as **s** in Peninsular Spanish; in a few words, like the **ch** in *loch*	**taxi** **México**
y	like the **y** in *yes* (in Argentina, more like the **s** in *television*)	**mayo**
z	like the **th** in *think* (in Latin America, Southern Spain and the Canaries, like the **s** in *sink*)	**Zaragoza, Cádiz**

The pronunciation of **c** before **i**, **e**, as in **gracias**, **Valencia**, and **z**, as in **Zaragoza**, **Cádiz**, both pronounced like an **s** in Latin America (as well as in parts of southern Spain and the Canaries), can be said to be the main difference in pronunciation between Latin American Spanish and that spoken in most parts of Spain.

(For the alphabet and how the letters are read see Unit 3.)

Stress and accentuation

a Words which end in a vowel, **n** or **s** stress the last syllable but one: **Inglaterra** *England*, **toman** *you/they take*, **Estados Unidos** *United States*.

b Words which end in a consonant other than n or s stress the last syllable: **Madrid**, **español** *Spanish*, **aparcar** *to park*.

c A written accent overrides the above two rules and the vowel with the written accent will be stressed: **allí** *there*, **invitación** *invitation*, **inglés** *English*, **difícil** *difficult*, **González**.

d A number of words are stressed on the third-from-last syllable, in which case the stressed vowel carries a written accent: **América** *America*, **histórico** *historical*, **rápido** *quick, fast*.

e One-syllable words do not normally carry an accent (see exceptions in *f* below): **dio** *he/she/you gave*, **fui** *I went/was*, **pan** *bread*, **¡ven!** *come!*

f A written accent is used to differentiate meanings between pairs of words which are spelt the same: **de** *of* – **dé** *give* (but **deme/nos** *give me/us*), **el** *the* – **él** *he*, **mi** *my* – **mí** *me*, **se** *(one/him/her/your) self* – **sé** *I know*, **si** *if* – **sí** *yes*, **te** *(for/to) you* – **té** *tea*, **tu** *your* – **tú** *you*.

g Many educated speakers and Spanish grammar books use accents to differentiate words such as **este/éste** *this/this one*, **ese/ése** *that/that one*. The Real Academia Española (the body which regulates the spelling and usage of the Spanish language) has ruled that an accent on these words is not required, unless there is ambiguity, which is rarely the case. In this book they have been used without accents.

h Question words carry an accent: **¿cómo?** *how?*, **¿cuál?** *which?*, **¿cuándo?** *when?*, **¿cuánto?** *how much?*, **¿dónde?** *where?*, **¿por qué?** *why?*, **¿qué?** *what?*, **¿quién?** *who?* Accents are also used in exclamations: **¡qué bonito!** *how pretty!*, **¡quién sabe!** *who knows?*

i Words ending in **án**, **én**, **és**, **ín**, **ón** in the singular lose this accent when a syllable is added to form the plural, thus following rule **a** above: **alemán/alemanes** *German/s*, **jabón/jabones** *soap*. Similarly, words ending in **án**, **és**, **ín**, **ón** in the masculine lose the accent in the feminine form: **alemán/alemana** *German* (m/f), **escocés/escocesa** *Scottish* (m/f).

Abbreviations

The following abbreviations have been used in this book.

(m) for masculine, **(f)** for feminine, **(sing)** for singular, **(pl)** for plural, **(inf)** for informal, **(adj)** for adjective, **(adv)** for adverb, **(esp)** for especially, **(LAm)** for Latin America, **(AmE)** for American English, **(SCone)** for Southern Cone: Argentina, Uruguay and Paraguay, **(Mex)** for Mexico, **(Arg)** for Argentina, **(QV)** and **(QVocab)** for Quick Vocab.

Antes de empezar
Before you start

In this unit you will learn how to:
▶ *greet people*
▶ *ask someone's name and say your name*
▶ *seek clarification and help*
▶ *say goodbye.*

CEFR: *Can establish basic social contact by using simple everyday polite forms of greeting and farewell (A1); Can introduce himself/herself (A1); Can ask for clarification and help (A1).*

Hello and goodbye

When you are in Spain, you will find that conversations start with a greeting and finish with a farewell. As you get into a taxi, go into a shop, order a meal ..., you will exchange a **buenos días** (*good morning*), **buenas tardes** (*good afternoon/good evening*) or a **buenas noches** (*good evening good night*) depending on the time of day. You can add **hola** (*hello*) to say **hola, buenos días** (*hello, good morning*).

Likewise, when it's time to get out of the taxi, leave the shop or restaurant ..., you will exchange a farewell. This could be the same **buenos días**, **buenas tardes** or **buenas noches**, or simply **adiós** (*goodbye*), or the two together, for example: **adiós, buenos días** (*goodbye, good morning*). Another way to say goodbye is **hasta luego** (literally *until later*), though it doesn't matter whether you are going to see the other person again or not. And you can add **adiós – adiós, hasta luego**.

a **If someone says to you buenos días, what are you going to say?**
b **What are you doing when you say adiós, hasta luego?**

1 Hola, ¿qué tal? *Hello, how are things?*

00.03

In Part 1 of this unit you'll learn to greet people. You'll hear people say hello to each other and you'll learn the Spanish words for good morning, good afternoon, good evening and good night.

1.1 **Look at the drawings first, then listen to the recording and try to imitate the speakers as you hear them.**

¡Hola!

Hola, buenos días.

Buenos días   Buenas tardes   Buenas noches

Note the pronunciation of the **r** in **tardes**. A good way to practise this sound might be for you to pronounce the first syllable **tar-** first and then the full word, **tardes**.

HOW DO YOU SAY IT?: GREETING PEOPLE

¡Hola!	*Hello! / Hi!*
Hola, ¿qué tal?	*Hello, how are things?/How are you?*
Buenos días.	*Good morning* (literally, *good days*)
Buenas tardes.	*Good afternoon/evening.*
Buenas noches.	*Good evening/night.*

Hola, used on its own, is familiar, but it may also be used in formal address when followed by other greetings, for example **hola, buenos días. Buenas tardes** is normally used after lunch and until early evening. After that use **buenas noches**.

1.2 Say it in Spanish!

1 At a party you see your friend Rosa. Say hello to her and ask her how are things.

2 It's 8.00 a.m. Greet the hotel receptionist at your hotel.

3 It's 2.00 p.m. Greet the waitress who'll be serving you lunch.

4 It's 9.00 p.m. Greet the barman before you order a drink.

2 ¿Cómo te llamas? *What's your name?*

In Part 2 of this unit you'll learn to ask someone's name and to say your name.

2.1 Listen to the expressions on the recording and try to imitate the speakers as you hear them.

HOW DO YOU SAY IT?: ASKING SOMEONE'S NAME AND SAYING YOUR NAME

 00.04

¿Cómo te llamas?	*What's your name?* (informal)
¿Cómo se llama (usted)?	*What's your name?* (formal)
Me llamo ...	*My name is ...* (literally, *I call myself*)
¿Y tú/usted?	*And yours?* (inf/formal) (literally, *And you?*)

Spanish makes a distinction between informal and formal address. The informal word for you when addressing one person is **tú**, and the formal one is **usted**, shortened in writing to **Vd.** or **Ud.**

Generally speaking, **usted** is used for talking to people one doesn't know, especially if there is a difference in age – for example a young person addressing someone much older, or a difference in status such as a person in a subordinate position talking to a superior.

Tú is used among friends, equals, for example people at work, and generally among younger people, even if they haven't met before. Within the family, the prevalent form is **tú**. Overall, the use of **tú** is very common in Spain today but less so in **Hispanoamérica** (the Spanish-speaking countries of Latin America), where people tend to be more formal, although there are regional differences.

Verb forms, like some other grammatical words, change depending on whether you are using informal or formal address (see examples above).

2.2 During an excursion, Elena meets José. They are both young, so they use informal language.

Elena	Hola, ¿cómo te llamas?
José	Me llamo José. Y tú, ¿cómo te llamas?
Elena	Me llamo Elena.

    1 What phrase does Elena use to ask José´s name?
    2 What phrase is used in the conversation to say *And you?*

2.3 Señor Salas, *Mr Salas*, meets señora Montes, *Mrs Montes*. They use formal language to address each other.

| Señor Salas | Buenas tardes. Me llamo Carlos Salas. ¿Cómo se llama usted? |
| Señora Montes | Me llamo Julia Montes. |

    1 What phrase does señor Salas use to ask señora Montes's name?
    2 Now find the Spanish for *My name is Julia Montes.*

¿Cómo te llamas? and **¿Cómo se llama usted?** translate literally *How do you call yourself?*, **te** *yourself* being informal and **se** the formal equivalent. Note also the final **-s** in the informal **¿Cómo te llamas?**

2.4 Say it in Spanish!

    1 At a party in a Spanish-speaking country someone comes up to you.
       – Hola, ¿cómo te llamas?
       – Say your name and ask his/her name, using the informal form.
    2 Now here is an older person.
       – Say your name and ask his/her name, using the formal form.

3 Perdón, no entiendo *I'm sorry I don't understand*

 00.05

In Part 3 you'll learn some key phrases for seeking clarification and help with your Spanish.

3.1 Listen to the recording and try to imitate the speakers as you hear them.

The word **entiendo** means *I understand*, but the word for *I*, which is **yo** is not needed, as the final **-o** of **entiendo** signals *I*. To say *I don't understand* place **no** before the verb: **No entiendo.**

HOW DO YOU SAY IT?: SEEKING CLARIFICATION AND HELP

Perdón (or **Perdone**), **no entiendo.**	*I'm sorry, I don't understand.*
¿Cómo dice? or **¿Cómo?**	*Pardon me?* (literally, *How do you say?*)
¿Puede repetir, por favor?	*Can you repeat, please?*
Más despacio, por favor.	*More slowly, please.*
¿Qué significa …?	*What does it mean/does … mean?*
¿Habla usted inglés?	*Do you speak English?*
Perdone, no hablo muy bien español.	*I'm sorry, I don't speak Spanish very well.*

An alternative expression for *I'm sorry* is **Lo siento.**

Listen to the audio again and pay special attention to the pronunciation of **per-dón**, **re-pe-tir**, **por fa-vor**. Note that the first **r** in **repetir** is strongly rolled while the second one is softer.

3.2 Say it in Spanish!

1 The hotel receptionist mentioned the word **habitación**. Ask what **habitación** means.

2 He's speaking too fast. Ask him to speak more slowly.

3 You didn't catch what he said again. Apologize and say you don't understand and ask him to repeat.

4 A cry for help! Apologize and say you don't speak Spanish very well. Ask whether he speaks English.

4 ¡Adiós! *Goodbye!*

 00.06

In Part 4 you'll learn to say goodbye.

4.1 Look at the drawings in your book and listen to and repeat the expressions you'll hear on the recording.

1 Adiós.

2 Adiós, buenas tardes.

3 Hasta luego.

4 Chao.

HOW DO YOU SAY IT?: SAYING GOODBYE

Adiós	*goodbye* (formal and inf)
adiós, buenos días/buenas tardes/noches	*goodbye, have a good morning/ afternoon/evening* (more formal)
hasta luego	*see you, bye* (formal and inf) (literally, *until later*)
chao (**chau**, in some countries)	*cheerio* (inf, especially LAm)

In some Latin American countries, **hasta luego is** considered formal.
Adiós also means *hello*, as a form of greeting when passing
by. Other ways of saying goodbye are **hasta
ahora** *(see you in a minute – literally, until
now)* and **hasta la vista** *(see you)*.

4.2 **Say it in Spanish!**

    1 It's Friday evening and you are saying
goodbye to your Spanish boss.

    2 You'll be seeing your Spanish friend
later on in the day. Say goodbye to
him/her.

    3 Say goodbye to your Latin American
friend.

Conversation: Check what you have learned

00.07

On a flight home from Spain, Helen meets Enrique.

**Complete the missing parts of their conversation and then listen to
the recording to check whether your answers were correct.**

Enrique	¿Cómo se _____ usted?
Helen	Me _____ Helen. Helen Thomas. ¿Y _____?
Enrique	Enrique Ramírez.
Helen	Perdone, no _____ ¿ _____ repetir, por favor?
Enrique	Enrique Ramírez.
Helen	No _____ muy bien español. ¿ _____ usted inglés?
Enrique	No, lo siento.

Once you have completed the conversation and checked your answers,
cover the text, listen to the dialogue a few times and then, using your
pause button, try to play first one part then the other.

 Test yourself

Choose an appropriate word from the list to complete each sentence.

1 te   **2** puede   **3** buenos   **4** más   **5** se
6 hablo   **7** buenas   **8** me   **9** tal   **10** luego

a _____ días.

b _____ noches.

c ¿Cómo _____ llama usted?

d ¿Cómo _____ llamas?

e _____ llamo Silvia.

f ¿ _____ repetir, por favor?

g _____ despacio, por favor.

h Perdone, no _____ muy bien español.

i Hasta _____ .

j Hola, ¿qué _____ ?

How well do you think you performed? If you are uncertain about any of your answers, check the relevant section of the unit again or check the answers in the Key to 'Test yourself'.

SELF CHECK

	I CAN...
○	. . . greet people
○	. . . ask someone's name and say my name
○	. . . seek clarification and help
○	. . . say goodbye.

Hablo español
I speak Spanish

In this unit you will learn how to:
▶ *say where you are from*
▶ *say your nationality*
▶ *say what languages you speak.*

CEFR: *Can ask and answer questions about themselves and other people (A1); Can write simple phrases and sentences about themselves and imaginary people (A2).*

Spanish regions

Spaniards tend to be proud of the region they come from, especially if they come from one of the regions that has its own language:

▶ **Cataluña**, **catalán**
▶ **País Vasco** (Basque Country or Euskadi in Basque), **vasco** (euskera)
▶ **Galicia**, **gallego**.

In their regions, these languages have equal status with the official language for the whole of Spain, the language we know as Spanish.

Spain is divided into 19 regions or **autonomías**. These include the Canary Islands, Balearic Islands and Spain's two dependencies in North Africa: Ceuta and Melilla. Each **autonomía** has its capital city and parliament, giving them a fair measure of independence. The capital city of Spain is Madrid, which is also the capital of the **autonomía** of Madrid.

Can you guess where in Spain these people say they are from?
a **Soy barcelonés.**
b **Soy madrileña.**
c **Soy malagueño.**
d **Soy valenciana.**
e **Soy canaria.**

Conversations

1 ¿DE DÓNDE ERES? *WHERE ARE YOU FROM?*

At an international conference, Eva meets Pepe. They address each other using the informal form.

01.01

1.1 **Listen to the dialogue several times and fill in the gaps in the bubbles opposite without looking at the printed dialogue. A key phrase here is** *Soy de ...* **(I'm from ...).**

Soy de __ ¿y tú?

Soy de __

Eva	¿De dónde eres?
Pepe	Soy de Madrid, ¿y tú?
Eva	Soy de Salamanca.

1.2 **Now read the dialogue and find the Spanish equivalent for** *Where are you from?*

Soy means *I am* while **eres** means *you are* (informal). **Yo** (*I*) and **tú** (*you –* informal) are not needed. See paragraph 3 of Grammar.

2 USTED ES ESPAÑOL, ¿VERDAD? *YOU ARE SPANISH, AREN'T YOU?*

usted es ... *(you are ...; formal).*

Señora Medina meets señor Arenas. The language here is formal, so some of the expressions differ slightly from those in Dialogue 1.

2.1 **Listen to the dialogue several times and say whether the following statements are true or false (verdaderos o falsos).**

1 Señor Arenas is Mexican.
2 He's from Mexico City.
3 Señora Medina is Spanish.
4 She's from Puebla.

Señora Medina	Usted es español, ¿verdad?
Señor Arenas	Sí, soy español, soy de Málaga. ¿De dónde es usted?
Señora Medina	Soy mexicana. Soy de Puebla.

2.2 **Now read the dialogue and answer the following questions:**

1 How does señora Medina ask señor Arenas whether he's Spanish?
2 How does señor Arenas ask señora Medina where she's from?

The word **¿verdad?,** literally *true* can be said to be the equivalent of English *is that right?* An alternative to this is **¿no?** Both are equally frequent.

 3 ¿HABLA USTED INGLÉS? DO YOU SPEAK ENGLISH?

Sí, ¿dígame?   *Yes, can I help you?* (literally, *tell me?*)
sólo   *only*

Señor Arenas is approached by Sarah, who is looking for someone who speaks English.

3.1 **Listen to the conversation several times and then answer the questions which follow. The key word here is *hablar*, to speak.**

1 Does señor Arenas speak English?
2 What languages does he speak?

Sarah	Perdone.
Señor Arenas	Sí, ¿dígame?
Sarah	¿Habla usted inglés?
Señor Arenas	No, lo siento, no hablo inglés. Sólo hablo español.

3.2 Now read the dialogue and find the Spanish equivalent for:
1 Do you speak ...?
2 I speak ...

4 ES DE BARCELONA *HE'S FROM BARCELONA*

In an email to a friend, Mercedes, from Perú, wrote about Eduardo, whom she met at the conference. What languages does Eduardo speak?

se llama ...	*his name is ...*
un poco de	*some* (literally, *a little of*)
catalán	*from Catalonia*

... se llama Eduardo y es catalán. Es de Barcelona. Habla catalán, español y un poco de inglés ...

How do you say it?

ASKING PEOPLE WHERE THEY ARE FROM AND REPLYING

¿De dónde eres (tú)/es (usted)?   *Where are you from?*

Soy de ...   *I'm from ...*

ASKING SOMEONE'S NATIONALITY AND REPLYING

¿Eres español/a?   *Are you Spanish?* (inf, m/f)

¿Es usted mexicano/a?   *Are you Mexican?* (formal, m/f)

ASKING PEOPLE WHETHER THEY SPEAK A CERTAIN LANGUAGE AND REPLYING

¿Hablas/Habla Vd. español?   *Do you speak Spanish?* (inf/formal)

Hablo (un poco de) español.   *I speak (some) Spanish.*

No hablo español, hablo inglés.   *I don't speak Spanish, I speak English.*

GIVING SIMILAR INFORMATION ABOUT OTHERS

Es ... (nationality)   *He/She is ...*

Es de ... (place)   *He/She is from ...*

Habla ... (language)   *He/She speaks ...*

 Language discovery

1 THREE TYPES OF VERBS

If you look up verbs – that is words like **ser**, *to be*, **hablar**, *to speak* – in a Spanish dictionary, you'll see that they fall into three main categories according to their endings:

-ar	hablar	to speak
-er	ser	to be
-ir	vivir	to live

2 REGULAR AND IRREGULAR VERBS

The majority of Spanish verbs are 'regular', that is, they change in a fixed way – for example for *person* (e.g. *I, you*) or for *tense* (e.g. *present, past*), but others show some variation, and so are called 'irregular'. In this unit you will learn some of the present-tense forms of two important verbs: **hablar** (*to speak*) and **ser** (*to be*). The first one is regular, the second irregular.

	hablar	to speak	ser	to be
(yo)	**hablo**	*I speak*	**soy**	*I am*
(tú)	**hablas**	*you speak* (inf.)	**eres**	*you are* (inf.)
(usted)	**habla**	*you speak* (form.)	**es**	*you are* (form.)
(él/ella)	**habla**	*he/she speaks*	**es**	*he/she/it is*

Note that the forms for **usted** (*you* – formal), **él** (*he*), and **ella** (*she*) are always identical. These same verb forms are used for *it*, as in 'it is', for which Spanish does not have a specific word, as the verb on its own is sufficient (see 3 below), e.g. **es español** (*it is Spanish*).

3 YO, TÚ, ÉL, ELLA … *I, YOU, HE, SHE …*

As the ending of the verb normally indicates the person one is referring to (e.g. *I, you*), words like **yo**, **tú** (*you* – informal), **él** (*he*), **ella** (*she*) are usually omitted, except for emphasis or contrast.

Soy español.   *I'm Spanish.*

Yo soy mexicano.   *I am a Mexican.*

Usted, *you* (formal) is very often kept, in speaking as well as in writing, for politeness and to avoid ambiguity (see 2 above).

4 ASKING QUESTIONS

As in English, there are different ways of asking questions in Spanish:
▶ By using the same word order as in a statement:

¿Usted es de Madrid?　　　*Are you from Madrid?*

▶ By starting your sentence with the verb:

¿Habla usted inglés?　　　*Do you speak English?*

▶ By placing the word **¿verdad?** or **¿no?** at the end of the statement:

Usted es español, ¿verdad?/¿no?　*You are Spanish, aren't you?*

▶ By using a question word:

¿Cómo te llamas?　　　*What's your name?*

Note that all questions in Spanish must carry two question marks, one at the beginning and one at the end of the sentence. Note, too, that all question words, e.g. **¿cómo?** (*how?*), **¿dónde?** (*where?*), carry a written accent.

5 SAYING 'NO'

To negate something in Spanish simply put the word **no** before the verb:

No soy español.　　　*I'm not Spanish.*

No hablo español.　　　*I don't speak Spanish.*

6 MASCULINE OR FEMININE?

Words for nationality, like other words used for describing people, e.g. **guapo/a**, *good-looking (man/woman)*, have *masculine* and *feminine* forms.

a　To form the feminine from a masculine word ending in **-o**, change the **-o** to **-a**:

Soy británico/(norte) americano/indio.　　*I'm British/American/ Indian (man).*

Soy británica/(norte) americana/india.　　*I'm British/American/ Indian (woman).*

Most Latin American countries use the word **norteamericano/a**, literally North American, instead of **americano/a**. A less common alternative is **estadounidense** (m/f) – *of/from the United States* ('de los Estados Unidos').

Some Spanish-speaking countries use the word **hindú** to refer to someone of Indian nationality. This word does not change for masculine and feminine (see below).

b To form the feminine from a masculine word ending in a consonant, add **-a** to the consonant:

Soy español/inglés/alemán. *I'm Spanish/English/German (man).*

Soy española/inglesa/alemana. *I'm Spanish/English/German (woman).*

Note the omission of the written accent in **inglesa** and **alemana** (see 'Stress and accentuation' in the introduction).

c Words denoting nationality or origin ending in **-a, -e, -í, -ú** remain unchanged.

Soy belga/árabe/paquistaní. *I'm Belgian/Arab/Pakistani.*

Note that words for nationality are not written with capital letters in Spanish.

7 'MÉXICO' OR 'MÉJICO'?

Mexicans spell their country's name **México** and their nationality **mexicano/a**, with an **x**, and this is the form adopted in this book. In Spain, you will sometimes find these spelt as **Méjico** and **mejicano**.

Pronunciation

 01.04

SPANISH VOWELS: 'A', 'E', 'O'

Spanish vowels are different from English vowel sounds, as they are generally short and do not change their quality or length, as do English vowels. Each vowel corresponds to one sound only. References to English below are an approximation to how Spanish should sound.

   a, as in 'Salamanca', like the 'a' in *answer* (British English) or the 'u' in *but* (American English)

   e, as in 'Pepe', like the 'e' in *yet*

   o, as in 'Antonio', like the 'o' in *cost.*

Listen to your recording and practise these sounds by imitating the speakers:

Se llama Ana, es española, de Granada. Habla español y un poco de francés.

Me llamo Eduardo, soy catalán, de Barcelona. Hablo español y catalán.

Spanish gives more or less the same value to each syllable, unlike English in which certain syllables are weaker than others. Compare the English word *comfortable*, with the Spanish **confortable** and practise saying the latter without shortening any of the syllables and giving each vowel more or less equal value, except for the stress, which in this word goes on **-ta**: **con-for-ta-ble**.

Practice

1 Palabra por palabra *Word for word*

How many of the countries listed below can you recognize? Match each country with the corresponding nationality and language.

País		Nacionalidad (m/f)		Idioma
a	Alemania	1	inglés/inglesa	A árabe
b	Francia	2	egipcio/a	B portugués
c	Rusia	3	brasileño/a	C inglés
d	España	4	francés/francesa	D francés
e	Inglaterra	5	ruso/rusa	E alemán
f	Brasil	6	alemán/alemana	F ruso
g	Egipto	7	español/a	G español

2 Soy española *I'm Spanish*

 01.05

2 Listen to Silvia, Cristóbal and Sofía introducing themselves, and fill in the table below with the nationality, city and language corresponding to each person.

Nombre Name	Nacionalidad Nationality	Ciudad City	Idioma(s) Languages
a Silvia			
b Cristóbal			
c Sofía			

3 Me llamo … *My name is …*

How would each of the following people introduce themselves? Follow the models in Activity 2, and look at the *How do you say it?* section and 6 in the Language Discovery section for other nationalities.

> **LANGUAGE TIP**
>
> María is a very common name in the Spanish-speaking countries, and is frequently used as the first part of a compound name (as in María Ángeles, above). Here María is abbreviated in writing to Ma.

    a Boris, Moscú.
    b Paco, Granada.
    c Ingrid, Berlín.
    d Marguerite, París.
    e Mark, Nueva York.
    f Ma Ángeles, Monterrey, México

4 Soy de Bogotá *I'm from Bogotá*

In an email to a correspondent, Ramiro, a student, gave some information about himself. Can you fill in the blanks with the missing verbs?

> *Querida Patricia:*
> _____ *Ramiro Fernández Salas y* _____ *colombiano.* _____ *de Bogotá. Aparte de español,* _____ *inglés y un poco de francés.*

> **LANGUAGE TIP**
>
> **Querido**, *dear* (to a man), and **querida**, *dear* (to a woman), are used for close relationships only. Note also that Ramiro, like all Spanish-speaking people, has two surnames (**apellidos**): **Fernández Salas**. The first surname is his father's, while the second is his mother's. The second surname is used in more formal and in official situations.

5 Ahora tú *And now you*

You are writing to a Spanish correspondent for the first time. Give similar information to that given by Ramiro in Activity 4.

Other than using the correct words in your writing you should pay attention to written accents. Spanish uses only one type of accent, as in the words **París, América, región**.

6 ¿Cómo se llama? *What's his name?*

During a visit to a trade fair in Barcelona, a visitor was asked to fill in this form, which is in Spanish and Catalan, the local language. How would you answer someone's questions about him?

Hora de su visita/Hora de la seva visita

☐	☐	☐	☑	☐	☐
Antes de las 8h.	De las 8h.a 11h.	De las 11h.a 14h	De las 14h.a 17h.	De las 17h.a 20h.	Después de las 20h.
Avant de les 8h.	De les 8h.a 11h.	De les 11h.a 14h.	De les 14h.a 17h.	De les 17h.a 20h.	Després de les 20h.

Fecha de su visita/Data de la seva visita: ......*23 de Julio*..............

Datos personales/Dades personals

Apellido/Cognom ...*Palma*............... Nombre/Nom ...*Guillermo*.........

Dirección/Adreça ...*Calle de Linares, 25*.................................

Ciudad/Ciutat ......*Córdoba*............ País/País ......*España*............

Gracias por depositar esta ficha en la urna
Mercès per depositar aquesta fitxa dins l`urna

el apellido	surname
la ciudad	city
el nombre	name
el país	country
la hora	time
la fecha	date

1 What's the visitor's surname?
2 What's his first name?
3 What city and country is he from?

7   Sólo hablo español *I only speak Spanish*

no hablo nada de ...   *I don't speak any ... (literally, I don't speak nothing of ...)*

pero   *but*

During a flight you talk to a Spanish-speaking person. Follow the guidelines below and complete your part of the conversation with him. He's using the polite form, so do likewise.

— *Ask his name.*

— **Me llamo Antonio. ¿Y usted?**

— *Reply, and ask where he's from.*

— **Soy mexicano, de Veracruz. Y usted, ¿de dónde es?**

— *Reply, and ask if he speaks English.*

— **No, lo siento, sólo hablo español. No hablo nada de inglés. Pero usted sí habla español.**

— *Say yes, you speak a little Spanish.*

> **LANGUAGE TIP**
> Note the use of **sí** (*yes*) in **Pero usted sí habla español** (*But you do speak Spanish*). This is emphatic.

 Test yourself

Match the sentences as appropriate.

a	¿De dónde eres?	**1**	No, mexicano.
b	Usted es española, ¿verdad?	**2**	No, de Granada.
c	¿Eres español?	**3**	No, soy argentina.
d	¿Usted es de Barcelona?	**4**	De Mallorca.
e	¿Habla usted inglés?	**5**	Sí, ¿dígame?
f	Perdone.	**6**	No, lo siento.
g	¿De dónde es Ramiro?	**7**	Sí, de Chicago.
h	¿Habla inglés María?	**8**	No, es argentina.
i	Carmen es chilena, ¿no?	**9**	Es de Málaga.
j	¿Eres norteamericano?	**10**	No, sólo habla español.

This test involves understanding some basic but important questions: asking where someone is from, what nationality someone is, and whether the person speaks a certain language. These are questions that you may have to answer at some stage. Check your answers in the Key to 'Test yourself' if necessary; otherwise go on to Unit 2.

SELF CHECK

I CAN...
... say where I am from
... say my nationality
... say what languages I speak.

2 ¿Cómo está?

How are you?

In this unit you will learn how to:

▶ *introduce yourself and others*
▶ *ask people how they are and say how you are*
▶ *ask people where they live and say where you live*
▶ *ask for and give telephone numbers and email addresses.*

CEFR: *Can introduce himself/herself and others (A1); Can ask how people are (A1); Can ask and answer questions about themselves and other people (A1); Can handle numbers (A1).*

Introductions

Introductions can be made in more than one way, as you will find out in this unit. As in English, the simplest is to say: *This is ...* and the name of the person. In Spanish, the word for *this* changes according to the person's sex: **Este es Juan** (*This is Juan*); **Esta es María** (*This is María*).

Generally speaking, Spaniards are tactile people so, if you are a woman, do not be surprised to receive **un beso** (*a kiss*) on each cheek. You can say: **Encantada** or **Mucho gusto**, two ways of saying: *Pleased to meet you.* If you are a man being introduced to another man, a handshake is the norm and, in less formal situations, a friendly pat on the shoulder as well. When being introduced to a woman, she may well expect you to give her a kiss on each cheek. You can say: **Encantado** or **Mucho gusto** (*Pleased to meet you*).

To ask: *How are you?*, you will say **¿Cómo está?** in a formal situation and **¿Cómo estás?** in an informal situation, to which the reply is: **Bien, gracias** (*Fine, thank you*).

a **What will a man do when he meets a male friend?**
b **What will he do when he meets a female friend?**

Conversations

1 MUCHO GUSTO *PLEASED TO MEET YOU*

At a fair, people introduce themselves and others and exchange greetings.

02.01

1.1 **Cristina spots someone she wants to meet. What do you think her question means, and how does she introduce herself? Listen and find out. Note that the language here is formal.**

Cristina	Perdone, ¿es usted el señor Peña?
Señor Peña	Sí, soy yo.
Cristina	Yo soy Cristina Dueñas. Mucho gusto.
Señor Peña	Encantado.

1.2 **What phrase is used in the conversation to say *Yes, it´s me.***

1.3 **Look at the vocabulary below, then read the dialogue and play, first Cristina's part, then señor Peña's.**

¿Es usted …?	*Are you …?*
Soy yo.	*It's me.*
encantado/a	*pleased to meet you* (said by a man/woman)
mucho gusto	*pleased to meet you* (invariable)

In this context **perdone** means *excuse me*. In other contexts it may mean *I'm sorry*:

Perdone, no hablo muy bien español. *I'm sorry, I don't speak Spanish very well.*

Perdone is the formal or polite form. The familiar form is **perdona**.

1.4 **How would you say the following in Spanish?**
1 Are you Mr Santana?
2 I am (your name). Pleased to meet you.

2 ¿CÓMO ESTÁ? *HOW ARE YOU?*

Raúl greets someone he knows and introduces his wife to her. The language in this dialogue is formal.

02.02

2.1 **How does Raúl greet his acquaintance, and how does she reply? Listen and find out.**

Raúl	Señora Silva, ¿cómo está?
Señora Silva	Muy bien, gracias. ¿Y usted?
Raúl	Bien, gracias. Le presento a María, mi mujer. Esta es la señora Silva.
Señora Silva	Encantada.
María	Hola, mucho gusto.

2.2 **Read the dialogue and find the expressions meaning *Let me introduce you to ..., This is Mrs ...***

presentar   *to introduce*
mi mujer/marido   *my wife/husband*

The word **la mujer** also means *woman* and it is the word normally used by most people in Spain. In more formal word contexts you may hear the word **la esposa** for which the masculine is **el esposo.** These are the forms commonly used by most Latin Americans.

3 ESTE ES RICARDO *THIS IS RICARDO*

mi novio/a   *my boy/girlfriend*
un/a compañero/a de trabajo   *fellow worker/colleague* (m./f.)
vivo (from **vivir** – *to live*)   *I live*

Ana introduces her colleague Ricardo to her boyfriend Fernando. The language here is informal.

24

3.1 Listen to the dialogue and focus attention on the informal equivalents of: *¿Cómo está?*, *¿Y usted?* and *Le presento a …* What are they?

Ana	Hola, Ricardo. ¿Cómo estás?
Ricardo	Bien, gracias. ¿Y tú?
Ana	Muy bien. Te presento a Fernando, mi novio. Este es Ricardo, un compañero de trabajo.
Ricardo	¡Hola!
Fernando	Hola, ¿qué tal?
Ricardo	¿Eres argentino?
Fernando	Sí, soy argentino, pero vivo en Madrid.

3.2 Read the conversation again and find the Spanish for:
1. a fellow worker/colleague
2. but I live in Madrid

3.3 Read the dialogue a few times, then give the Spanish for:
1. Let me introduce you to Luis/Luisa, my husband/wife. (**mi marido/mujer**) (inf)
2. This is Isabel, a colleague from work.

Le in Dialogue 2 and **te** in Dialogue 3, as in **Le/te presento …** translate *to you*. The first one is formal, the second one informal. Note that these come before the verb: <u>**Le/te** presento a Roberto</u>, literally *To you I introduce Roberto*.

4 *¿Cuál es tu número de teléfono? What's your telephone number?*

Antonio has met Clara and has given her his telephone numbers and email address, and now she gives him hers.

4.1 What's Clara's home number? And her mobile phone? Key words here are: la casa (*house, home*), el (teléfono) móvil (*mobile phone*), which in Latin America is el (teléfono) celular. Numbers 0 to 20 are in the Practice section.

¿cuál es ...? — *what is ...?*
el número de teléfono — *telephone number*
tengo/tienes (from **tener**) — *I/you have* (inf.)
arroba (@) — *at*
el punto — *dot*

Antonio	¿Cuál es tu número de teléfono?
Clara	El teléfono de mi casa es el 981 546 372.
Antonio	Y tu móvil, ¿cuál es?
Clara	Es el 696 00 19 82.
Antonio	¿Tienes correo electrónico?
Clara	Sí, sí tengo. Es claradiaz@hotmail.com

4.2 Read the dialogue and answer the following questions:
  1 How does Antonio ask Clara what her telephone number is, and how does she reply?
  2 What phrase does Antonio use to say 'Have you got an email address?'

Note the omission of **un/a** in **¿Tienes correo electrónico?** The omission of **un/a** occurs in a number of phrases with **tener** (to have), where the accompanying word is used in a general sense. Compare **Tengo coche** (I have a car) with **Tengo un coche grande** (I have a large car).

How do you say it?

INTRODUCING YOURSELF AND OTHERS

(Yo) soy ...	*I am ...*
Este/esta es ...	*This is ...* (man/woman)
Le/te presento a ...	*Let me introduce you to ...* (formal/inf)
Mucho gusto.	*Pleased to meet you.*
Encantado/a.	*Pleased to meet you* (said by a man/woman).

ASKING PEOPLE HOW THEY ARE AND SAYING HOW YOU ARE

¿Cómo está/s?	*How are you? (formal/inf)*
(Estoy) (muy) bien.	*I'm (very) well/fine.*

ASKING PEOPLE WHERE THEY LIVE AND SAYING WHERE YOU LIVE

¿Dónde vive/s?	*Where do you live? (formal/inf)*
Vivo en ...	*I live in ...*

ASKING AND GIVING TELEPHONE NUMBERS AND EMAIL ADDRESSES

¿Cuál es su/tu número de teléfono/correo electrónico?	*What's your telephone number/ email (address)? (formal/inf)*
Es el (93 541 26 70).	*It's (93 541 26 70).*
Es juliovera@hotmail.com.	*It's juliovera@hotmail.com.*
¿Tienes correo electrónico?	*Have you got an email address?*
Sí, tengo / No, no tengo.	*Yes, I have / No, I don't have one.*

 Language discovery

1 MASCULINE OR FEMININE?

▶ **El, la** (*the*) Nouns are words which denote a person (e.g. **secretaria**, *secretary*), a thing (e.g. **teléfono**, *telephone*) or an abstraction (e.g. **gusto**, *pleasure*). In Spanish, all nouns are either masculine or feminine, and the word for 'the' is **el** for masculine nouns and **la** for feminine nouns:

masculine	**el señor**	*the gentleman, Mr*
feminine	**la señora**	*the lady, Mrs*

▶ Nouns ending in **-o** are usually masculine, while nouns ending in **-a** are normally feminine.

▶ The endings of some nouns do not indicate whether they are masculine or feminine, so it is advisable to learn each word with its corresponding article (**el** or **la**):

masculine	**el nombre**	*name*
feminine	**la calle**	*street*

2 EL SEÑOR, LA SEÑORA/SEÑORITA

Note the use of **el** before **señor**, and **la** before **señora/señorita**, in indirect address:

¿Es usted el señor Martínez/la señorita Miranda?	*Are you Mr Martínez / Miss Miranda?*

But:

Buenas tardes, señora Vera.	*Good afternoon, Mrs Vera.*

In writing, **señor**, **señora** and **señorita** are often found in abbreviated form – **Sr.**, **Sra.** and **Srta.**, respectively.

3 DE *(OF)*

Note the use of **de** (*of*, *in*):

el teléfono de mi casa/oficina	*my home/office telephone number* (literally, *the telephone of my house/office*)
el teléfono de Carmen	*Carmen's telephone number* (literally, *the telephone of Carmen*)

4 AL *(TO THE)*, DEL *(OF THE)*

A + el becomes **al**, and **de + el** becomes **del**:

Te presento al señor Lira.	*Let me introduce you to señor Lira.*
El teléfono del señor Castro.	*Señor Castro's telephone number.*

5 UN, UNA *(A)*

The Spanish equivalent of *a*, as in *a colleague*, *a secretary*, is **un** for masculine and **una** for feminine:

un compañero de trabajo	*a male colleague*
una secretaria	*a female secretary*

6 MI, TU, SU … *MY, YOUR, HIS, HER …*

a The Spanish equivalent of *my, your, his, her, its, their*, is:

mi casa/apartamento	*my house/apartment*
tu piso/oficina	*your flat/office* (inf)
su teléfono/email	*your* (formal) *his, her, their telephone/email.*

These words agree in number (singular or plural) with the thing possessed, for example **mis cosas** (*my things*) (for plural forms see Unit 3). Note also that **su** (*your*) can be used to address one or more than one person formally.

b To say *our* use **nuestro**, and to say *your* when addressing more than one person informally, use **vuestro**. These words agree in number (singular or plural) and gender (masculine and feminine) with the thing possessed (see also Unit 3):

nuestra dirección	*our address*
nuestros socios	*our partners*
vuestra empresa	*your company*
vuestros amigos	*your friends*

Vuestro is not used in Latin America, where **su** is used in both formal and informal address, to address more than one person. A distinction is made, however, between **tu** and **su** (see above) when addressing one person.

7 SER AND ESTAR *(TO BE)*

There are two ways of saying *to be* in Spanish: **ser** and **estar**:

▶ Personal information such as where you are from, your nationality and who you are, are expressed with **ser**, e.g. **Soy Cristóbal** (*I'm Cristóbal*) (Unit 1).

▶ To ask people how they are and say how you are you need to use **estar**. **Estar** is an irregular verb, and its singular forms are:

(yo)	**estoy**	*I am*
(tú)	**estás**	*you are* (informal)
(usted)	**está**	*you are* (formal)
(él/ella)	**está**	*he/she/it is*

¿Cómo estás?	*How are you?*
Estoy bien.	*I'm fine.*

8 TENGO, TIENES … *I HAVE, YOU HAVE …*

Tener (*to have*) is an irregular **-er** verb, whose singular forms are:

(yo)	**tengo**	*I have*
(tú)	**tienes**	*you have* (informal)
(usted)	**tiene**	*you have* (formal)
(él/ella)	**tiene**	*he/she/it has*

¿Tienes (teléfono) móvil?   *Have you got a mobile phone?*

No, no tengo.   *No, I haven't got one.*

Note that the first person singular of **tener** is irregular, **(yo) tengo**, while the second and third the **-e** in the stem of the verb, **ten-,** changes into **-ie**, **tienes, tiene.**

9 -IR VERBS

The following are the singular present tense forms of **vivir** (*to live*), a regular **-ir** verb:

(yo)	**vivo**	*I live*
(tú)	**vives**	*you live* (informal)
(usted)	**vive**	*you live* (formal)
(él/ella)	**vive**	*he/she/it lives*

¿Dónde vive/s?   *Where do you live?*

¿En qué barrio/calle vives?   *Which area/street do you live in?*

Vivo en … / la calle …   *I live in … / on … street.*

Unlike English, in which words like *in* and *from*, are often placed at the end of a sentence – *Which area do you live in?, Where are you from?* – in Spanish such words must be placed <u>in front of</u> the sentence: **¿En qué barrio vives?, ¿De dónde eres?**

Pronunciation

02.05

SPANISH VOWELS 'I', 'U'

i, as in **oficina**, is pronounced like the 'ee' in *feet*.

u, as in **mucho gusto**, is pronounced like the 'oo' in *moon*.

Ñ (N + TILDE)

ñ, as in **señora**, is a separate letter of the Spanish alphabet and is pronounced nearly like the 'ni' in *onion*.

Practise with:

¿Usted es el señor Peña?
Soy Cristina Dueñas, de La Coruña.
Este es Raúl Núñez, de Madrid.
Esta es Alicia Zúñiga, de Logroño.
Mucho gusto.

 Practice

 1   ¿Ser o estar? *(translating 'to be')*

Mire   *look*

Alfredo meets Marisa, and señor Lira meets señorita Romero. Can you complete the conversations with the correct forms of *ser* and *estar*? The first exchange is informal and the other one formal.

a

    – Hola, ¿tú _____ Marisa Frías?
    – Sí, _____ yo.
    – Yo _____ Alfredo Ríos, de Sevilla.
    – Hola, ¿cómo _____?
    – Bien, gracias.

b

    – Buenos días. Usted _____ la señorita Romero, ¿verdad?
    – Sí, soy Mercedes Romero. ¿Usted _____ Alfonso Lira?
    – Sí, sí. ¿Cómo _____ usted?
    – Muy bien. Y usted, ¿cómo _____?
    – Bien, gracias. Mire, esta _____ María, mi mujer.
    – Encantada.

Check your answers and see whether you were able to distinguish between **ser** and **estar**. It is important that you do and learn each separate use right from the start. As you progress in the course you will learn other uses of these two verbs.

2 Fill in the gaps (a–g) with 'el', 'la', 'un', 'una' where necessary.

Sr. Ibarra	Perdone **a** _____ señora. ¿Usted es **b** _____ señora Santos, **c** _____ secretaria del señor Martínez?
Sra. Santos	Sí, soy yo.
Sr. Ibarra	Yo soy **d** _____ señor Ibarra, de Transibérica.
Sra. Santos	Mucho gusto **e** _____ señor Ibarra.
Sr. Ibarra	Le presento a Carmen, **f** _____ compañera de trabajo. Y este es Alfonso, **g** _____ amigo.
Sra. Santos	Encantada.

3 Una presentación *An introduction*

Señor Barrios is visiting your place of work, and you and your colleague John have been asked to meet him at reception. Follow the guidelines and fill in your part of the conversation, using the formal form.

– *Ask whether he is señor Barrios.*
– Sí, soy yo.
– *Say who you are.*
– Mucho gusto.
– *Say you are pleased to meet him and introduce your colleague to him.*

4 Ahora tú *And now you*

How would you introduce the following people to a friend? Look up the words in the Vocabulary and choose as appropriate, using the informal expression 'Te presento a ...'

   a tu marido/mujer
   b tu novio/novia
   c tu padre/madre
   d tu hermano/hermana

Now introduce each of the following people, using the expression 'Este/Esta es ...', as appropriate.

   e Gloria, una compañera de trabajo
   f Paul, un compañero de clase
   g Carlos, un amigo
   h Laura, una vecina

Padre (*father*) and **madre** (*mother*) normally become **papá** and **mamá** in direct address: **Hola papá/mamá** (*Hello Dad/Mum*). **Un compañero de trabajo** (*fellow worker*) is also **un/a colega** (*colleague*), a word ending in 'a' which can refer to a man or a woman.

5 ¿Dónde vive? *Where does he/she live?*

02.06

Ana, Julio and Silvia are being asked where they live. Listen and complete each sentence with information from the appropriate map below.

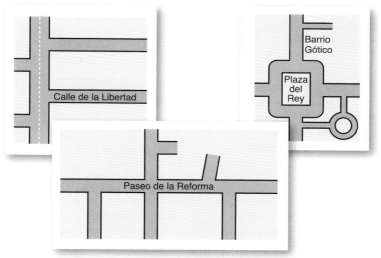

- **a** Ana vive en …
- **b** Julio vive en …
- **c** Silvia vive en …

02.07

6 Los números (*numbers*) 0–20

Listen and repeat each number as you hear it.

0 cero	6 seis	12 doce	18 dieciocho
1 uno	7 siete	13 trece	19 diecinueve
2 dos	8 ocho	14 catorce	20 veinte
3 tres	9 nueve	15 quince	
4 cuatro	10 diez	16 dieciséis	
5 cinco	11 once	17 diecisiete	

Note that **uno** becomes **un** before a masculine noun, e.g. **un amigo** (*a/one friend*).

7 ¿Qué número desea? *What number do you want?*

You will hear two conversations in which people request telephone numbers. Listen and write each number as you hear it.

  a Hotel Sancho: Teléfono …

  b Sr. Martín Ramos: Teléfono …

8 Ahora tú *And now you*

  a ¿Dónde vives?

  b ¿En qué barrio vives?

  c ¿En qué calle?

  d ¿Cuál es tu número de teléfono?

  e ¿Tienes teléfono en tu oficina/trabajo?

  f ¿Cuál es el número?

  g ¿Tienes extensión?

  h ¿Cuál es el número?

  i Y el número de tu móvil/celular (*LAm*), ¿cuál es?

  j ¿Tienes correo electrónico? ¿Cuál es?

> **LANGUAGE TIP**
> Telephone numbers in Spanish can be read out in single or double figures. For example, the telephone number 719 2015 can be read out as:
> **siete-uno-nueve-dos-cero-uno-cinco** *or* **siete-diecinueve-veinte-quince.**

9 Crucigrama *Crossword*

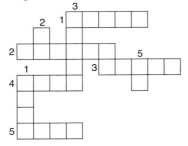

Horizontales (*Across*)

  1 ¿ _____ usted teléfono móvil?

  2 ¿(Tú) _____ teléfono en casa?

  3 Buenas tardes, señor Bravo. ¿Cómo está _____ ?

  4 (Yo) _____ en la Calle de la Rosa.

  5 ¿(Tú) _____ Gonzalo Martínez?

Verticales (*Down*)

1 Raquel _____ en Sevilla, en el barrio de Santa Cruz.

2 Te presento a _____ marido.

3 (Yo) no _____ teléfono en casa.

4 Perdone, señora, el teléfono de _____ oficina, ¿cuál es?

5 Y _____ extensión, Mónica, ¿cuál es?

Test yourself

How would you say the following in Spanish?

a I'm Pat Johnson.

b Pleased to meet you. (*the invariable form*)

c Pleased to meet you. (*said by a man/woman*)

d How are you? (*informal*)

e Let me introduce you to Mario. (*addressing someone formally*)

f This is Ana, a colleague from work.

g Where do you live? (*informal*)

h I live in London.

i What's your telephone number? (*formal*)

j Have you got an email address? (*informal*)

Learning a language well is being able to use its constructions more or less automatically, without resorting to translation, but at times this can be a valid exercise to bring home the differences between the two languages. Don't worry if you made some mistakes. Even if you did it's likely that people will understand you. Go back through the troublesome points before you proceed to Unit 3.

SELF CHECK

	I CAN. . .
○	. . . introduce myself and others
○	. . . ask people how they are and say how I am
○	. . . ask people where they live and say where I live
○	. . . ask for and give telephone numbers and e-mail addresses.

3 Quisiera una habitación

I would like a room

In this unit you will learn how to:
▶ *book into a hotel*
▶ *spell your name*
▶ *say where something can be done.*

CEFR: *Can make simple arrangements about places to stay (A2); Can spell his/her name and other personal details (A1); Can handle numbers and dates (A1).*

Accommodation

There is a wide range of **alojamiento** (*accommodation*) to choose from when travelling in Spain, from **la pensión** (*the guest house*) to **el hotel de cinco estrellas** (*the five-star hotel*) and **el parador**. Paradores are historical buildings such as castles, palaces or convents, turned into luxury hotels, though some are purpose-built in places of natural beauty such as **La Sierra Nevada** in the south of Spain. You can visit, have a drink or a meal without necessarily staying in them.

In Spain, you pay for **la habitación** (*the room*) and these are en-suite, **con baño** (*with bath*) except in the rarest of cases. **El desayuno** (*the breakfast*) is not usually included in **el precio** (*the price*). Indeed, smaller hotels tend not to have **un comedor** (*a dining room*).

a **What kind of room would you like?:** Quisiera una habitación doble.
b **What do you want to know?:** ¿El desayuno está incluido?

Conversations

 1 ¿PARA CUÁNTAS PERSONAS? *FOR HOW MANY PEOPLE?*

quisiera   **I would like**

¿para cuántas/os …?   **for how many …? (f/m)**

Julio, a hotel receptionist, is attending to some new arrivals.

 03.01

1.1   **Victoria is asking for a room, 'una habitación'. Does she want a single or a double room? How many nights does she want it for? Look at the vocabulary below, then listen and find out.**

Victoria	Buenas tardes. Quisiera una habitación, por favor.
Recepcionista	¿Para cuántas personas?
Victoria	Para una persona.
Recepcionista	Muy bien. Una habitación individual. ¿Para cuántas noches?
Victoria	Para seis noches.

1.2   **Go back to the conversation and then match the Spanish and the English.**

1 **Quisiera una habitación.**   **a** *A single room.*

2 **Para una persona.**   **b** *I´d like a room.*

3 **Una habitación individual.**   **c** *For six nights.*

4 **Para seis noches.**   **d** *For one person.*

 1.3   **Now read the dialogue and then play the parts of a hotel guest and the receptionist, using the following information.**
Número de personas: dos personas
Habitación: doble
Número de noches: tres

Try memorizing the word **quisiera** (*I'd like*). It is a polite way of saying what you want and you can use this in a number of contexts, for example when requesting something in a shop, buying tickets for a show, asking to speak to someone on the phone, etc.

2 ¿TIENEN HABITACIONES LIBRES? *HAVE YOU GOT ANY FREE ROOMS?*

libre	*free*
la cama	*bed*
hay	*there is*
claro	*certainly*
con	*with*
sin	*without*
el desayuno	*breakfast*
aparte	*separate*

Mario and his friend Luis are also trying to get a room.

 03.02

2.1 **What sort of room do they want? What facilities do the rooms have? Look at the vocabulary, then listen and find out. Note the use of plural verb forms such as: ¿tienen …? (*have you got …?*), son (*you are*), somos (*we are*), quisiéramos (*we would like*).**

Mario	Por favor, ¿tienen habitaciones libres?
Recepcionista	¿Cuántas personas son?
Mario	Somos dos. Quisiéramos una habitación doble, con dos camas.
Recepcionista	Sí, no hay problema.
Mario	¿Tienen baño las habitaciones?
Recepcionista	Sí, claro, baño, televisión y aire acondicionado.
Mario	¿Está incluido el desayuno?
Recepcionista	No, es sin desayuno. El desayuno es aparte.

2.2 **Go back to the conversation and find the Spanish for:**
1 Do the rooms have a bath?
2 Is breakfast included?

2.3 **Now read the dialogue and then play the parts of a hotel guest and the receptionist using the following information:**
Número de personas: 2
Habitación: doble/cama de matrimonio (*double bed*)
Servicios: baño, teléfono, aire acondicionado, televisión, minibar
¿Desayuno incluido?: sí

Two important things to note here are the endings **-mos** for *we*, and **-n** for *they*, as in **somos** (*we are*) and **son** (*they are*). These endings are important as you will need them not only when referring to the present, as in the dialogue above, but also when reference is to the future or the past.

3 TENEMOS UNA HABITACIÓN RESERVADA *WE HAVE A ROOM BOOKED*

reservado/a	*booked*
el nombre	*name*
se escribe (from **escribir** *to write*)	*it is spelled* (*written*)
el apellido	*surname*
quisiéramos	*we'd like*
cambiar dinero	*to change money*

Pat Johnson and a travelling companion have already booked a room.

03.03

3.1 Listen to the dialogue and focus attention on some of the key phrases:

a nombre de …	*in the name of …*
¿Cómo se escribe …?	*How do you spell (it) …?*
¿Dónde se puede cambiar …?	*Where can you change …?*

Pat	Buenas noches. Tenemos una habitación reservada.
Recepcionista	¿A qué nombre?
Pat	A nombre de Pat Johnson.
Recepcionista	¿Cómo se escribe su apellido?
Pat	J-o-h-n-s-o-n. Johnson.
Recepcionista	Muy bien. Sus pasaportes, por favor.
Pat	Aquí tiene.
Recepcionista	Gracias. Tienen la habitación treinta y cinco.
Pat	Quisiéramos cambiar dinero. ¿Dónde se puede cambiar?
Recepcionista	Pueden cambiar aquí mismo.

3.2 **Read the dialogue and give the Spanish for:**
  a We have a room booked.
  b In what name?
  c You have room thirty-five.
  d You can change right here.

3.3 **Now play Pat's part using and spelling your own name. You'll find the alphabet in Activity 7 and also in the recording.**

The word **reservada** (*booked* – from **reservar** *to book*) ends in **-a** because it refers to **la habitación**, which is a feminine word. Words of this kind have different forms for masculine and feminine and also for singular and plural:

Tenemos dos habitaciones reservadas.	*We have two rooms booked.*
Tenemos un coche reservado.	We have a car booked.

How do you say it?

BOOKING INTO A HOTEL

Quisiera una habitación individual/para una persona.	*I'd like a single room/a room for one person.*
Quisiéramos una habitación doble/para dos personas.	*We'd like a double room/a room for two people.*
¿Tiene/Tienen habitaciones libres?	*Have you got rooms available?*
Tengo/Tenemos una habitación reservada.	*I/We have a room booked.*

ASKING SOMEONE TO SPELL A NAME

¿Cómo se escribe su nombre/ apellido?	*How do you spell your name/ surname?*

| **¿Dónde se puede cambiar dinero/cenar?** | *Where can you/one change money/have dinner?* |
| **Pueden cambiar/cenar aquí mismo.** | *You can change/have dinner right here.* |

Did you notice the word **se** in **¿Dónde se puede cambiar dinero?** This is an important word which will help you to form impersonal sentences such as *Where can you have lunch/find a hotel here?* **¿Dónde se puede almorzar/encontrar un hotel aquí?**

Se is used with the form of the verb corresponding to *he, she*.

Language discovery

1 MORE THAN ONE

Most words form the plural by adding an **-s**. Nouns ending in a consonant add **-es**.

| **una persona** | *one person* | **cuatro personas** | *four people* |
| **una habitación** | *a room* | **dos habitaciones** | *two rooms* |

Note that the written accent on the vowel disappears after adding **-es**.

2 LOS, LAS *THE* (PLURAL)

The plural of **el** and **la** (*the*, sing.) are **los** and **las**, respectively:

| **el hotel** | *the hotel* | **los hoteles** | *the hotels* |
| **la llave** | *the key* | **las llaves** | *the keys* |

3 MIS, TUS, SUS ... *MY, YOUR ...*

When the object possessed is more than one, **mi**, **tu**, **su**, **nuestro/a**, etc., add an **-s**. Note that only **nuestro** and **vuestro** change for masculine and feminine. (See Unit 2.)

mi(s)	*my*	**nuestro/a(s)**	*our*
tu(s)	*your* (inf)	**vuestro/a(s)**	*your* (inf)
su(s)	*your* (formal) / *his/her/its*	**su(s)**	*your* (formal) / *their*

mis cosas	*my things*
sus pasaportes	*your* (formal) / *their passports*
vuestras maletas	*your* (inf) *suitcases*

4 ¿CUÁNTOS/AS? *HOW MANY?*

¿Cuántos? (*how many?*) becomes **¿cuántas?** before a feminine word:

| **¿Cuántos euros?** (m) | *How many euros?* |
| **¿Cuántas libras?** (f) | *How many pounds?* |

5 QUISIERA, QUISIÉRAMOS *I'D LIKE, WE'D LIKE*

Quisiera and **quisiéramos** are two special forms of the verb **querer** (*to want*), which are normally used in requests for extra politeness instead of **quiero** (*I want*), **queremos** (*we want*), which may sound a little abrupt. (For the full present tense forms, see Unit 5.)

| **Quisiera el desayuno en mi habitación.** | *I'd like breakfast in my room.* |
| **Quisiéramos hacer una reserva.** | *We'd like to make a reservation.* |

6 PODER *CAN, TO BE ABLE*

a Stem-changing verbs

A number of Spanish verbs, among them **poder**, undergo a vowel change in the stem (the infinitive minus **-ar**, **-er** or **-ir**) in certain forms, although their endings remain the same as for regular verbs. **Poder** changes the **-o** of the stem **pod-** into **ue** in all persons of the present tense, except the **nosotros/as** (*we*) and **vosotros/as** (*you* – informal, plural) forms. Such verbs are known 'technically' as stem-changing or radical-changing verbs. The symbol > next to a verb has been used to signal a vowel change, for example **poder** (**o>ue**). Some verbs change in a different way, for example querer (**e>ie**) (see Unit 5) and **tener** (**e>ie**, but irregular in the first person singular) (see Unit 2).

b Present tense forms

The following are the full present tense forms of **poder**, including the forms for **nosotros/as** (*we*) (m/f), **vosotros/as** (*you*) (informal, plural, m/f), **ellos/ellas** (*they*) (m/f), **ustedes** (*you*) (formal, plural). Note that **vosotros/as**, used to address more than one person in a familiar way, is not used in Latin America, where **ustedes** and the verb forms that go with it are used in both formal and informal address. This use is not restricted to Latin America, as it is also found in parts of southern Spain and the Canary Islands.

yo puedo	nosotros/as podemos
tú puedes	vosotros/as podéis
él/ella/Vd. puede	ellos/ellas/Vds. pueden

¿Dónde puedo cambiar dinero?	*Where can I change money?*
No pueden encontrar una habitación.	*They can't find a room.*
¿Qué podemos hacer?	*What can we do?*

7 SER *(TO BE)*, TENER *(TO HAVE)*: FULL PRESENT TENSE FORMS

In Unit 1 you learned the present tense forms of **ser** for **yo**, **tú**, **él**, **ella** and **usted**. In Unit 2 you learned the forms for **tener**. In this unit there are further examples of the uses of **ser** and **tener**, which include plural forms.

a Ser

yo soy	*I am*	**nosotros/as somos**	*we are*
tú eres	*you are*	**vosotros/as sois**	*you are*
él/ella/Vd. es	*he/she/it is/you are*	**ellos/ellas/Vds. son**	*they/you are*

¿Es con o sin desayuno?	*Is it with or without breakfast?*
¿Cuántas personas son?	*How many people are you?*
Somos cuatro.	*We're four.*

b Tener

yo tengo	I have	**nosotros/as tenemos**	we have
tú tienes	you have	**vosotros/as tenéis**	you have
él/ella/Vd. tiene	he/she/it has / you have	**ellos/ellas/Vds. tienen**	they/you have

Tengo una reserva a nombre de Ana Godoy.	I have a reservation in the name of Ana Godoy.
Tenemos la habitación noventa.	We have room ninety.
No tienen televisión por cable.	They don't have cable TV.

8 IMPERSONAL SENTENCES

To say *you* or *one*, as in *How do you spell it?*, use **se** followed by the third person of the verb:

¿Cómo se escribe su nombre?	*How do you spell your name?*
¿Dónde se puede aparcar?	*Where can you/one park?*
Aquí no se puede fumar.	*You can't smoke here.*

Pronunciation

 03.04

The pronunciation of **ll**, as in **apellido, calle**, varies from region to region, but it is pronounced by most Spanish speakers like the 'y' in *yacht*. In Argentina and Uruguay it is closer to the 's' in *pleasure*.

Practise with:
El Hotel del Valle en Valladolid es un hotel de tres estrellas y está en la calle de Mallorca.
¿Cómo te llamas?
Me llamo Estrella.
¿Y cómo te apellidas?
Ulloa. Estrella Ulloa.

It is important that you learn the sound represented by **ll** and that you are able to differentiate between this and **l**. Here are some words for you to practise this contrast. Don't worry about their meanings as it is the sounds that matter: **malla – mala, valle – vale, bella – vela, lloro – loro**.

Practice

1 Los números del 21 al 100 *Numbers from 21 to 100*

  03.05

 Listen and repeat each number as you hear it, and fill in the blanks with the missing ones.

21	veintiuno	31	treinta y uno	64	_____
22	veintidós	32	treinta y dos	70	setenta
23	veintitrés	36	_____	76	_____
24	veinticuatro	40	cuarenta	80	ochenta
25	veinticinco	42	cuarenta y dos	88	_____
26	veintiséis	45	_____	90	noventa
27	veintisiete	50	cincuenta	93	_____
28	veintiocho	53	cincuenta y tres	100	cien
29	veintinueve	59	_____		
30	treinta	60	sesenta		

For numbers 16 to 19 you combine **diez y** (**seis**, **siete** …) into a single word: **dieciséis**, **diecisiete**, and so on. Numbers **veintiuno** to **veintinueve** result from the combination of **veinte y** (**uno**, **dos** …). Beyond that, as in 35, 56, you use three separate words: **treinta y cinco**, **cincuenta y seis**. Note also numbers 70, **setenta** (from **siete**) and 90, **noventa** (from **nueve**).

2 ¿La habitación del señor Luis García, por favor? *Mr Luis García's room, please?*

03.06

Listen to these brief conversations and fill in the box with the room or office number of each of the people mentioned.

	Nombre	Habitación	Despacho
a Sr. García			
b Srta. Sáez			
c Sres. Silva			

3 Palabra por palabra *Word for word*

1.
2.
3.
4.
5.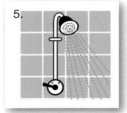
6.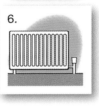

Below is a list of some of the facilities you might find in certain hotels. Can you match them with the drawings?

a la ducha
b el lavabo
c la calefacción
d el hilo musical
e el ascensor
f la piscina

4 *Say it in Spanish*

Play the part of the receptionist and the hotel guest in this dialogue.

Cliente/a:	Good evening. We'd like a double room with a bathroom, please.
Recepcionista:	For how many nights?
Cliente/a:	For five nights. Is breakfast included?
Recepcionista:	No, it's without breakfast. Breakfast is separate.
Cliente/a:	That's OK. Can you park in the hotel?
Recepcionista:	Yes, certainly. Your passports, please. (*Client hands in passports.*) Thank you. You have room seventy-eight.

5 Rellena con los verbos *Fill in the verbs*

Fill in the blanks in the following sentences with the appropriate form of 'tener' (*to have*) or 'ser' (*to be*).

a (Yo) _____ una habitación reservada.

b ¿ _____ (ustedes) una habitación individual?

c Los hoteles aquí _____ excelentes.

d (Ellos) _____ una reserva para dos noches.

e Carmen _____ la habitación 55 y nosotros _____ la 82.

f ¿Cuántas personas _____ (ustedes)? _____ dos, mi mujer y yo.

6 ¿Qué servicios tienen? *What facilities have they got?*

Now look at the accompanying table, which lists all the services you can expect to find in the different categories of hotels.

a What services would you find in a 3-star hotel?

b What extra service would you find in a 4-star hotel?

c Where would you find a safe-deposit box? And a fire exit?

Lo que tienen que tener					
	5★	4★	3★	2★	1★
Aire acondicionado	✓	✓	(1)	–	–
Teléfono en habitación	✓	✓	✓	✓	–
Bar	✓	✓	✓	–	–
Salidas de incendios	✓	✓	✓	✓	✓
Suites	✓	–	–	–	–
Caja fuerte individual	✓	✓	–	–	–
Superficies mínimas por habitación (en metros cuadrados)					
Doble	17	16	15	14	12
Individual	10	9	8	7	7
(1) En salón, comedor y bar					

7 El alfabeto *The alphabet*

03.07

Listen to the letters of the Spanish alphabet and try saying each as you hear them.

a	a	Ana	ñ	eñe	mañana
b	be	Bilbao	o	o	Colombia
c	ce	Cuba, gracias	p	pe	Perú
d	de	día	q	cu	que, quinto
e	e	Elena	r	erre, ere	perro, Río, París
f	efe	Francia	s	ese	Susana
g	ge	Gloria, Algeciras	t	te	Tarragona
h	hache	hasta	u	u	Murcia
i	i	Isabel	v	uve	Venezuela
j	jota	Juan	w	uve doble	Washington
k	ca	kilo	x	equis	taxi
l	ele	Londres	y	i griega	yo, Paraguay
m	eme	María	z	zeta	Cádiz
n	ene	no			

Ch and **ll** were considered separate letters of the alphabet but this is no longer the case. You may still find separate entries for them in some monolingual dictionaries, but most recent bilingual dictionaries treat **ch** within **c** and **ll** within **l**. Many speakers, however, still consider them as separate letters so you should be aware of their names:

ch	che	Chile
ll	elle	calle

8 ¿Cómo se escribe? *How do you spell it?*

A group of Spanish speakers arrive at your place of work and you need to spell their surnames to a Spanish person.

a **Aguirre**

b **Fernández**

c **Arredondo**

d **Bravo**

e **Collado**

f **Julián**

9 Ahora tú *And now you*

¿Cómo se escribe …?: tu nombre, tu apellido, el nombre de tu jefe/a (*boss*), profesor/a (*teacher*), el nombre de tu calle y barrio (*neighbourhood*).

Test yourself

Complete each sentence with an appropriate word from the list.

1 tengo
2 está
3 se
4 para
5 sin

6 quisiera
7 tiene
8 a
9 puede
10 dinero

a _____ una habitación, por favor.

b ¿ _____ cuántas personas?

c ¿ _____ una habitación libre?

d _____ una habitación reservada.

e ¿ _____ qué nombre?

f El desayuno, ¿ _____ incluido?

g Es _____ desayuno. El desayuno es aparte.

h ¿Cómo _____ escribe su apellido, por favor?

i Quisiéramos cambiar _____ .

j ¿Dónde se _____ cambiar?

Booking a hotel room is something you may have to do if you are travelling in a Spanish-speaking country. If you got the answers right, try going beyond the test and make up brief conversations using some of the language you learnt in this unit.

SELF CHECK

I CAN. . .
. . . book into a hotel
. . . spell my name
. . . say where something can be done.

4 ¿Dónde está?
Where is it?

In this unit you will learn how to:
▶ *ask and say if there is a certain place nearby*
▶ *ask for and give directions (1)*
▶ *ask and say how far away a place is.*

CEFR: *Can ask for and give directions referring to a map or plan (A2); Can understand instructions addressed carefully and slowly and follow short, simple directions (A1).*

Finding your way

Spanish towns and cities are full of interesting places to visit. If you want to know how to get to a particular place, you can ask: **¿Dónde está …?** (*Where is …?*), or if you are looking for a bank, for example, then ask: **¿Hay un banco por aquí?** (*Is there a bank nearby?*).

To understand the answer to your question, you need a few key phrases: **a la derecha** (*to the right*), **a la izquierda** (*to the left*), and **todo recto** (*straight on*), to point you in the right direction. If you are told: **Está a la final de esta calle** (*It's at the end of this street*), and you cannot see the end of the street, you may want to ask: **¿Está lejos?** (*Is it far?*), and be relieved to hear: **No, está cerca** (*No, it's near*).

Can you guess where these people want to get to:
a ¿Dónde está la catedral?
b ¿Hay una farmacia por aquí?
c ¿Hay un supermercado por aquí?
d ¿Dónde está el castillo?

Conversations

The main focus of the dialogues in this unit is asking for and understanding simple directions. Before you listen to the first conversation study the map and the list of places below. How many of them can you recognize?

1 ¿HAY UNA OFICINA DE CAMBIO POR AQUÍ? *IS THERE A BUREAU DE CHANGE NEARBY?*

primero/a	*first*
segundo/a	*second*
tercero/a	*third*
al lado de	*next to*
otro/a	*another one*
muchas gracias	*thank you very much*
de nada	*you're welcome*

04.01

1.1 Patricia, a tourist, is on calle Agustinas and San Martín, facing calle Morandé. What places is she looking for, and what phrase does she use in each question? Listen and find out. Key expressions here are:

hay	*is/are there? / there is/are*
por aquí	*nearby, near here*
¿dónde?	*where?*
a la izquierda	*on the left*
a la derecha	*on the right.*

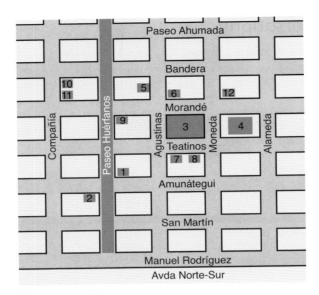

1 una oficina de cambio

2 un museo

3 una plaza

4 un aparcamiento

5 un restaurante

6 un banco

7 un hotel

8 una iglesia

9 un hotel

10 un banco

11 una oficina de turismo

12 (la oficina de) Correos

Patricia	Perdone, ¿hay una oficina de cambio por aquí?
Señor	Hay una en la calle Amunátegui, la primera calle a la izquierda.
Patricia	¿Y dónde hay un hotel?
Señor	Hay uno en la calle Teatinos, la segunda a la derecha, al lado de una iglesia. Hay otro en la calle Morandé, la tercera a la izquierda.
Patricia	Muchas gracias.
Señor	De nada.

1.2 **Now go back to the conversation and match the Spanish and the English.**

1 la primera calle a la izquierda   **a** *next to a church*
2 la segunda a la derecha   **b** *the first street on the left*
3 al lado de una iglesia   **c** *the third on the left*
4 la tercera a la izquierda   **d** *the second on the right*

1.3 **Read the dialogue a few times and then play first Patricia's part, then that of the person giving directions.**

1.4 **How would you say the following in Spanish? Look up the list of places again if necessary.**

1 Is there a bank nearby?
2 There's one on calle Bandera, the fourth (**la cuarta**) on the left, next to the tourist office.

The words for *first, second, third,* etc., **primero, segundo, tercero,** change the ending **-o** into **-a** when they refer to a feminine word: **el segundo hotel** but **la segunda calle.** This rule operates even when the word referred to is understood: **el segundo – la segunda,** *the second one.*

2 ¿DÓNDE ESTÁ? *WHERE IS IT?*

no (lo) sé (from **saber**)	*I don't know*
conozco (from **conocer**)	*I know*
lo siento (from **sentir, e>ie**)	*I'm sorry*
esta	*this* (f)
no hay de qué	*you're welcome*

Patricia is looking for the tourist office now. She's outside the post office, on calle Moneda and Morandé (number 12 on the map).

2.1 **Where's the tourist office and how far is it? Listen and find out. Key words and expressions here are:**

¿dónde está?	*where is it?*
lejos	*far*
cerca	*near*
al final de	*at the end of.*

Patricia	Por favor, ¿sabe usted dónde está la oficina de turismo?
Señor	Lo siento, no lo sé. No conozco muy bien la ciudad.
(Asking another passer-by)	
Patricia	Por favor, la oficina de turismo, ¿está muy lejos?
Señora	Está cerca. Al final de esta calle, a la derecha, a cinco minutos de aquí.
Patricia	Gracias.
Señora	No hay de qué.

2.2 **Read the dialogue and find the Spanish for**
   a ***Do you know ...?***
   b ***I don't know the city very well.***

2.3 **Look at the vocabulary below, then read the dialogue again and put the following sentences into Spanish. You may need to read the notes on 'saber' and 'conocer' in the Language Discovery section.**
   1 Do you know where the cathedral (**la catedral**) is?
   2 I'm sorry, I don't know. I don't know Granada very well.
   3 It is far. At the end of the street, on the left, is the bus stop (**la parada del autobús**).

3 ¿DÓNDE ESTÁN LOS SERVICIOS? *WHERE ARE THE TOILETS?*

sigue (from **seguir, e>i**) **todo recto**	*go straight on*
hasta el fondo	*to the end*
luego	*then*
tomar	*to take*
subir	*to go up*

Víctor is at a trade fair. At the information desk he asks where the toilets are.

04.03

3.1 **How does he ask where the toilets are? Can you guess what the answer means? Key words here are:**

los servicios	*toilets*
el piso	*floor*
el pasillo	*corridor*
la escalera	*stairs.*

Víctor	Por favor, ¿dónde están los servicios?
Empleada	Están en el primer piso. Sigue usted todo recto hasta el fondo, luego toma el pasillo de la izquierda y sube la escalera. Los servicios están enfrente del café.
Víctor	Gracias.

3.2 **Read the dialogue now and with the help of the key words and the vocabulary above, translate the answer into English.**

It is important that you become familiar with the various uses of **estar** and **ser**, both meaning *to be*. Look up **estar** in the Language discovery section and try building sentences of your own, including uses you have encountered in previous units. Then look at some of the previous units and do likewise with **ser**.

How do you say it?

ASKING AND SAYING IF THERE IS A CERTAIN PLACE NEARBY

¿Hay un banco por aquí (cerca)?	*Is there a bank nearby?*
¿Dónde hay un café/una panadería?	*Where is there a cafe/baker's?*
Hay uno/una en la calle ... / la primera (calle) a la izquierda/derecha/en la esquina.	*There's one on ... street / first (street) on the left/right/on the corner.*

ASKING FOR AND GIVING DIRECTIONS

¿Dónde está el museo?	*Where's the museum?*
Está al final de esta calle/ enfrente de ... / al lado de ...	*It's at the end of this street/ opposite ... / next to ...*
Sigue (Vd.) todo recto.	*Go straight on.*
Toma/Coge la primera calle.	*Take the first street.*
Sube/Baja por ...	*Go up/down ...*

Toma and **coge** (*you take*) – from **tomar** and **coger** – both mean the same in the context of directions. The second word is used frequently in Spain but it is a taboo word in some Latin American countries. **Tomar** is a standard word which will be understood everywhere.

ASKING HOW FAR A PLACE IS

¿Está cerca/lejos?	*Is it near/far?*
¿A qué distancia está?	*How far is it?*
Está cerca/lejos/a una hora/ cinco	*It's near/far/an hour/five minutes/*
minutos/cien metros de aquí.	*a hundred metres*
from here.	

 # Language discovery

1 HAY *THERE IS, THERE ARE / IS THERE?, ARE THERE?*

The single word **hay** (*there is/are*), an impersonal form from **haber** (*to have*) (auxiliary verb used in the Spanish equivalent of sentences such as 'I have gone'), can be followed by a singular or plural word, in statements or in questions.

Hay un supermercado en la esquina.	*There is a supermarket on the corner.*
Hay muchas tiendas cerca.	*There are many shops nearby.*
¿Hay una peluquería por aquí?	*Is there a hairdresser's near here?*
¿Hay sitios de interés en la ciudad?	*Are there any places of interest in the city?*

To ask where you can find something you are not sure exists, use the expression **¿dónde hay ...?**:

¿Dónde hay una gasolinera?	*Where's a petrol station?*

2 ¿DÓNDE ESTÁ/ESTÁN? *WHERE IS IT/ARE THEY?*

a To ask and say where a place is use 'estar' (to be) (see Unit 2).

¿Dónde está tu casa?	*Where's your house?*
Está detrás de la iglesia.	*It's behind the church.*
¿Dónde están los teléfonos?	*Where are the telephones?*
Están en la planta baja.	*They are on the ground floor.*

Here are some other expressions used to indicate location:

al otro lado de …	*on the other side of …*
delante de …	*in front of …*
entre … y …	*between … and …*
en la segunda planta *or* **en el segundo piso**	*on the second floor*
en la esquina	*at/on the corner*
en la calle (Santa Isabel) esquina a avenida (Duero)	*at the corner of (Santa Isabel) street and (Duero) avenue.*

Note that in Spain the word **el piso** means *floor* or *flat*. An alternative word for *floor* is **la planta**.

b To ask and say how far a place is use 'estar' with the preposition 'a'.

¿A cuántas horas/cuántos kilómetros está?	How many hours/kilometres away is it?
¿A qué distancia está?	*What distance is it from here?*
Está a casi una hora de aquí.	*It's almost an hour from here.*

c To say where you or others are, you may need other forms of estar, including plural forms. Here are the full forms of the present tense.

yo estoy	*I am*
tú estás	*you are*
él/ella/Vd. está	*he/she/it is/you are*
nosotros/as estamos	*we are*
vosotros/as estáis	*you are*
ellos/ellas/Vds. están	*they/you are*

¿Dónde estáis ahora?	*Where are you now?*
Estamos en casa de Pepe.	*We are in Pepe's house.*

3 USING THE PRESENT TENSE TO GIVE DIRECTIONS

There are two main ways of giving directions in Spanish, both equally common: one is with the present tense, the other with the imperative, a form of the verb which is introduced in Unit 23. The two forms are very similar, so being familiar with the present tense, you should be able to understand the other. The examples below correspond to the present tense (**usted** and **tú** forms).

Toma(s) el pasillo de la derecha.	*You take the corridor on the right.*
Sube(s)/Baja(s) la escalera.	*You go up/down the stairs.*
Gira(s) a la izquierda.	*You turn left.*

4 OTRO, OTROS *ANOTHER, OTHERS*

Otro agrees in number (sing or pl) and gender (m or f) with the noun it refers to:

otro mercado	*another market*
otra farmacia	*another chemist's*
otras tiendas	*other shops.*

Otro can replace a noun when this is understood:

Hay una frutería en la esquina y otra a la vuelta de la esquina.	*There's a fruit shop on the corner and another one round the corner.*

5 SABER, CONOCER *TO KNOW*

There are two ways of saying *to know* in Spanish: **saber** and **conocer**. The first refers to knowledge of a fact and ability to do something. The other indicates acquaintance with something, a person or a place. Both are irregular in the first person singular of the present tense, but regular in all other persons: **sé, sabes, sabe ...** etc.; **conozco, conoces, conoce ...** etc.

No sé dónde está.	*I don't know where it is.*
No sabe nadar.	*He/she doesn't know how to swim.*
Conozco muy bien el barrio.	*I know the area very well.*

6 ORDINAL NUMBERS

Ordinal numbers agree in gender (m or f) and number (sing or pl) with the noun they refer to. Here are ordinal numbers from first to tenth:

primero/a

segundo/a

tercero/a

cuarto/a

quinto/a

sexto/a

séptimo/a

octavo/a

noveno/a

décimo/a.

las primeras dos calles	*the first two streets*
el segundo semáforo	*the second traffic light*

Primero and **tercero** become **primer** and **tercer** before a singular masculine noun:

el primer/tercer piso	*the first/third floor.*

Pronunciation

 04.04

c before **a**, **o**, **u** – as in **c**asa, **c**onozco, **C**uba – is pronounced like the 'c' in *coast*.

c before **e**, **i** – as in **c**erca, **c**inco – is pronounced like the 'th' in *thin*.

z – as in pla**z**a, i**z**quierda – is also pronounced like the 'th' in *thin*.

Practise with:

¿Conoce usted la ciudad? No, no la conozco.

¿Hay una oficina de cambio por aquí cerca? Hay una en la plaza de Cádiz, a la izquierda, entre la oficina de turismo y la estación de metro.

c before **e**, **i** – as in **c̲erca**, **c̲inco** – is pronounced like the 's' in *sale*.

z – as in **pla̲za**, **i̲zquierda** – is also pronounced like the 's' in *sale*.

The pronunciation of **c** and **z** as the '**s**' in *sale* is not exclusive to Latin America, as it is also heard in parts of southern Spain and in the Canaries and it is totally acceptable. It is important that you are aware of the alternative sound, especially if you are in contact with Latin Americans.

  # Practice

 1 Rellena los espacios con hay o está(n) *Fill in the gaps with **hay** or **está(n)***

el/la más cercano/a	*the nearest one*
oiga	*excuse me* (literally, *listen*)
la lavandería	*launderette*

a ¿Dónde _____ una panadería, por favor?
La más cercana es la Modelo, a dos calles de aquí.

b Perdone, ¿la Telefónica _____ muy lejos?
A unos cinco minutos en coche.

c Oiga, perdone, ¿ _____ una lavandería por aquí cerca?
Sí, en la calle de Zamora, la tercera a la izquierda.

d Perdone, ¿sabe dónde _____ el mercado central?
Lo siento, no lo sé. No conozco bien este barrio.

e Los teléfonos, por favor, ¿dónde _____?
En la planta baja.

f ¿Dónde _____ un camping, por favor?
En la Avenida del Mar, la segunda a la derecha.

 2 Ahora tú *And now you*

la biblioteca	*library*

You are spending a few days in a Spanish city and you need to find your way around. How would you ask if there is one of the following nearby?

a un restaurante

b una librería

c una tienda de ropa

d una tienda de comestibles

And how would you ask where the following places are?

e la estación de autobuses

f la iglesia

g la biblioteca

h la Plaza Mayor

3 ¿Saber o conocer? *(translating 'to know')*

Martín is trying to find a hostal (less expensive family-run hotel). Fill in the gaps in the conversation with *saber* **or** *conocer,* **as appropriate, using the informal form.**

Martín	Perdona, ¿_____ (tú) dónde hay un hostal por aquí?
Chica	No (lo) _____. No _____ este barrio. _____ un hostal, pero está un poco lejos de aquí, en la calle de Los Olivos. ¿_____ (tú) la calle de Los Olivos?
Martín	No soy de aquí. No _____ la ciudad.

Did you get the answers right? If not, read the notes in the Language Discovery section again, and try remembering the equation **saber =** *knowledge of something,* **conocer =** *acquaintance with someone or something, including places.*

4 Entre el banco y la papelería *Between the bank and the stationer's*

You are working in a Spanish-speaking country and have been asked to look after some visitors who don't know your area. Study the map overleaf and answer their questions, using expressions from the following. First, look at the example.

al lado (de)

detrás (de)

a la derecha/izquierda

delante (de)

al final (de)

entre

enfrente (de)

en la esquina

Ejemplo: ¿Hay un restaurante por aquí?
Hay dos, uno enfrente y otro cerca de la parada de autobuses, entre el banco y la papelería.

a ¿Hay un aparcamiento por aquí cerca?

b ¿Dónde hay un banco?

c ¿Dónde está Correos?

d ¿Dónde hay un quiosco de periódicos?

e La parada de autobuses, ¿dónde está?

f ¿Dónde hay una agencia de viajes?

g ¿Hay una papelería por aquí?

h La Plaza de la Luz, ¿dónde está?

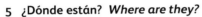

5 ¿Dónde están? *Where are they?*

 04.05

Where is each of the following? Listen and make a note of the directions and translate them into English.

a la avenida del Mar

c Correos

b la playa

d los teléfonos

Although it ends in **s**, the word **Correos** requires a singular verb as this is a short form for **la oficina de Correos** (*Post Office*), e.g.: **¿Dónde está Correos?** (*Where's the Post Office?*). Latin Americans normally call it **el correo**.

6 Ahora tú *And now you*

a ¿En qué calle está tu casa? ¿Y en qué barrio está?

b ¿Hay una parada de autobús o estación (de metro) cerca de tu casa? ¿A qué distancia está?

c ¿Qué tiendas hay en tu barrio?

d ¿Qué sitios importantes hay?

? Test yourself

1 How would you say the following in Spanish?
   a Is there a hotel nearby?
   b Where's a bank, please?
   c Do you know where the museum is? (*formal*)
   d Excuse me, the tourist office, please. Is it very far?
   e Where are the toilets, please?

2 What do the following directions mean?
   a Hay uno en la calle Lorca, la segunda calle a la derecha.
   b Está al final de esta calle, al lado de la iglesia.
   c Sigue usted todo recto hasta la Plaza Mayor.
   d Lo siento, no lo sé. No conozco la ciudad.
   e Están en la segunda planta, enfrente del café.

The first test above involves asking for simple directions while the second involves understanding some common directions. Check your answers in the Key to 'Test yourself' if necessary and go back through the unit again if you feel you need more practice, otherwise go on to Unit 5 in which you will find some useful language related to food and restaurants.

SELF CHECK

I CAN...
⚪ ... ask and say if there is a certain place nearby
⚪ ... ask for and give directions (1)
⚪ ... ask and say how far away a place is.

5 ¿Qué van a tomar?
What are you going to have?

In this unit you will learn how to:
▶ *ask people what they would like to eat or drink*
▶ *ask and say what's on the menu*
▶ *order food and drinks.*

CEFR: *Can understand and find specific information in a menu (A2); Can order a meal (A1); Can say what he/she wants (A1); Can ask people for things (A1).*

Eating out

Multinational and national **comida rápida** (*fast food*) outlets have populated the city centres of Spain, so look down the side streets to find the traditional bar or restaurant. But don't start looking before 1.30 p.m. for your midday meal or 8.30 p.m. for your evening meal. Bars and restaurants offer **el menu del día** (*the day's menu*) which is displayed with price for you to see before going in. You have a choice for **el primer plato** (*the first course*), **el segundo plato** (*the second course*), and **el postre** (*the dessert*), though you may swap dessert for coffee. **Pan** (*bread*) and **una bebida** (*a drink*): **vino** (*wine*), **cerveza** (*beer*), **agua mineral** (*mineral water*), for example, are included in the price.

La carta (*the menu*) lists dishes according to type: **sopas** (*soups*), **entremeses** (*hors d'oeuvres*), **verduras** (*vegetables*), **huevos** (*eggs*), **arroces** (*rice dishes*), **pescados** (*fish dishes*), **carne** (*meat*), **postre** (*dessert*). Vegetables are served separately and before the main dish.

Can you say which of these dishes is ...
a   a vegetable dish
b   a fish dish
c   a dessert?

sardinas a la plancha   ensalada mixta   peras al vino

Conversations

NEW EXPRESSIONS

Ángeles and her boyfriend Javier are having lunch in a restaurant.

How many of the words in the menu can you guess? Look up the rest of the vocabulary before you listen to the conversations which follow.

1 QUEREMOS EL MENÚ DEL DÍA
WE'D LIKE THE DAY'S MENU

el gazpacho	*cold soup made from tomatoes, peppers, cucumber, etc.*
¿qué van a tomar?	*what are you going to have? (formal, pl)*
patatas/papas (LAm) **fritas**	*chips, crisps*
beber	*to drink*
el agua (mineral)	*(mineral) water*

f Sopa
Gazpacho
Ensalada mixta
Guisantes con jamón

●

Paella
Merluza a la plancha con ensalada
Pollo con patatas
Cordero asado

●

Pan, vino, helado, flan, fruta

 05.01

1.1 Listen to the dialogue several times and, as you do, answer the following questions:

1 What is Ángeles having for lunch?
2 What is Javier having?
3 What is Ángeles having to drink?
4 What does Javier want to drink?

Camarero	Hola, buenas tardes. ¿Qué van a tomar?
Ángeles	Queremos el menú del día. Para mí, gazpacho de primero, y de segundo quiero merluza a la plancha con ensalada.
Camarero	¿Y para usted?
Javier	Yo, guisantes con jamón, y de segundo pollo con patatas fritas.
Camarero	¿Y para beber?
Ángeles	Agua mineral sin gas, para mí.
Javier	Yo quiero vino tinto.

1.2 Now read the dialogue and find the Spanish equivalent of *We want the menu of the day, For me ... , And for you?, As a first/ second course.* Then read the dialogue again a few times and, once you are familiar with it, try playing each one of the parts. Use the menu and the vocabulary above.

¿Qué van a tomar? (*What are you going to have?*) is used when talking to more than one person. If it is a single person, **van** becomes **va**: **¿Qué va a tomar?** Note also **el agua**: although this is a feminine word, because it begins with a stressed **a-** you must use **el** and not **la**. The word remains feminine, though.

 2 ¿ME TRAE OTRA AGUA MINERAL? *WILL YOU BRING ME ANOTHER MINERAL WATER?*

traer	to bring
el postre	dessert
un helado de (chocolate)	(a chocolate) ice cream
un poco más de	some more (*literally*, a little more of)
el flan	creme caramel
ahora mismo	straight away

 05.02

Javier calls the waiter to order something else.

2.1 What is each person ordering? Listen and find out.

Javier	Por favor, ¿nos trae un poco más de pan?
Ángeles	¿Y me trae otra agua mineral, por favor?
Camarero	Ahora mismo.
(*Ángeles and Javier order a dessert*)	
Ángeles	¿Qué tienen de postre?
Camarero	Hay flan, helados y fruta.
Ángeles	Un helado de chocolate, para mí.
Javier	Yo quiero un flan y un café.

2.2 What do you think the question '¿Qué tienen de postre?' means?

2.3 **Now read the dialogue and note the following two key phrases '¿Me trae ...?' 'Will you bring me ...?' (formal), '¿Nos trae ...?' 'Will you bring us ...?' (formal). Use them to say the following in Spanish and then try playing each one of the parts, varying what you order.**

1 Will you bring us some more wine?
2 Will you bring me another coffee?
3 Will you bring us the bill? (la cuenta)

Note the use of **me** (*me*) and **nos** (*us*) in **¿Me/nos trae ...?** (*Will you bring me/us ...?*). This construction differs from English in that Spanish places **me** and **nos** before the verb, and also in the use of the present tense form in Spanish instead of *Will you + verb* in English.

3 EN EL BAR *IN THE BAR*

el jamón serrano/de York	*cured/cooked ham*
el zumo/jugo (LAm)	*juice*
el calamar	*squid*
la naranja	*orange*

05.03

Silvia and her friends Paco and Gloria are having a snack in a bar.

3.1 **Listen and find out who is having each of the following.**

1 a portion or plate of mushrooms
2 black coffee
3 white wine
4 a beer
5 a cheese sandwich
6 crisps

Camarero	Hola, ¿qué van a tomar?
Paco	¿Qué quieres tú, Silvia?
Silvia	Quiero un café solo y un bocadillo de queso.
Paco	¿Y para ti, Gloria?
Gloria	Un vino blanco y patatas fritas.
Paco	Para mí, una cerveza y una ración de champiñones.

3.2 **Read the conversation and find the Spanish for:**

1 And for you ...? (*informal*)
2 For me ...

3.3 **Match each phrase on the left with an appropriate word on the right and use them to write a dialogue similar to the one above.**

1 un bocadillo de ...   **a** calamares
2 una ración de ...   **b** naranja
3 un zumo de ...   **c** jamón serrano/de York

How do you say it?

ASKING PEOPLE WHAT THEY WOULD LIKE TO EAT OR DRINK

¿Qué van/va(s) a tomar/ beber? *What are you going to have/drink?*

¿Qué quieren/quiere(s) tomar/ comer/beber? *What do you want to have/eat/ drink?*

¿Y para beber? *And to drink?*

ASKING AND SAYING WHAT'S ON THE MENU

¿Qué tiene/hay (de segundo/ de postre)? *What do you have/is there (as a second course/for dessert)?*

¿Qué tiene/hay para (beber/comer)? *What do you have/is there to (drink/eat)?*

Tengo/Tenemos/Hay (helados de fresa ...) *I/We have/There's (strawberry ice cream ...)*

ORDERING FOOD AND DRINKS

(Yo) quiero ... / Yo, ... / Para mí (una ensalada, un bocadillo, un agua mineral con/sin gas, un café solo / con leche, cortado, un té). *I want .../For me ... (a salad, a sandwich, a sparkling/still mineral water, a black/white coffee, coffee with a dash of milk, tea).*

 Language discovery

1 PARA *(FOR)*, CON *(WITH)*, SIN *(WITHOUT)* …: PREPOSITIONS

Words like **para**, **con**, **sin**, **de**, **a**, etc. are called prepositions. As in English, Spanish prepositions can have several uses and different meanings, and they don't always translate in the same way in English, as you can see from the examples below.

Para mí, una sopa.	*Soup for me.*
¿Y para beber?	*And to drink?*
con/sin gas	*with/without gas*
con leche/limón	*with milk/lemon*
de primero/segundo	*as a first/second course*
un helado de vainilla / un bocadillo de queso	*a vanilla ice cream/a cheese sandwich*
un poco más de pan/agua	*some more bread/water*
de postre	*for dessert*
pescado/carne a la plancha	*grilled fish/meat*

2 PARA MÍ, PARA TI, PARA USTED … *FOR ME, FOR YOU …*

In phrases such as *for me, for you, without him,* etc. words like *me, you, him* are called pronouns. In Spanish, as in English, prepositions are often followed by a pronoun. The forms of these pronouns are **mí** (for **yo**), **ti** (for **tú**) and subject pronouns for the rest of the persons, that is **él, ella, Vd., nosotros/as, vosotros/as, ellos, ellas, Vds.** Note the written accent on **mí**, to distinguish this from **mi** (*my*).

Una cerveza para mí, una Coca-Cola para ella y otra para él.	*A beer for me, a Coke for her and another one for him.*
¿Y para ti/usted?	*And for you?*

A special case is the use of **con** (*with*), which in combination with **mí** and **ti** gives **conmigo** *with me* and **contigo** *with you*.

Mí is another word for *me*, but unlike **me** (para 3 below), **mí** is used after prepositions, that is words such as **a, para, sin** – for example **a mí** (*to me*), **sin mí** (*without me*).

3 MAKING REQUESTS

Polite requests such as *Will you bring me/us some coffee?*, *Will you give me/us the bill?*, are often expressed in Spanish with the present tense preceded by **me** (*me*) or **nos** (*us*).

¿Me trae un cortado/un té con limón?	*Will you bring me a coffee with a dash of milk/a lemon tea?*
¿Nos trae un vaso/una botella de vino tinto?	*Will you bring us a glass/bottle of red wine?*
¿Me pasa la sal y la pimienta/ el azúcar?	*Will you pass me the salt and pepper/the sugar?*
¿Nos da la cuenta?	*Will you give us the bill?*

The verbs above are all in the formal **usted**. To make them informal, simply add **-s**:

¿Me pasas el aceite y el vinagre?   Will you pass the oil and vinegar?

In the spoken language, requests of this kind are usually expressed with a slightly rising intonation to make them more polite and to differentiate them from an order or command.

4 QUERER (E>IE) *(TO WANT)*: FULL PRESENT TENSE FORMS

Querer, like a number of other verbs, changes **e** into **ie** in the present tense, except in the **nosotros/as** and **vosotros/as** forms (see stem-changing or radical-changing verbs, Unit 3). Here are the full present tense forms:

yo quiero	I want
tú quieres	you want
él/ella/Vd. quiere	he/she/wants/you want
nosotros/as queremos	we want
vosotros/as queréis	you want
ellos/ellas/Vds. quieren	they/you want

Quiero la carta, por favor.	*I want the menu, please.*
¿Qué quieres tomar (tú)?	*What do you want to have?*

Note that **querer** also means *to love*:

Te quiero mucho.	*I love you very much.*

Tener (*to have*) also belongs to this category of verbs, except that **tener** is irregular in the first person singular: **tengo** (*I have*), **tienes** (*you have*, inf), **tiene** (*he/she/it has*), *you have* (formal), etc.

4 SAME WORD, DIFFERENT MEANING!

Just as in English, Spanish words related to food and meals can have different meanings in some regions. The standard words for the main meals are **el desayuno** (*breakfast*), **el almuerzo** or **la comida** (*lunch*) and **la cena** for the evening meal. But **el almuerzo** is a mid-morning snack in some places (for example Barcelona and Mexico City), while **la comida** refers to the evening meal in some Latin American countries. In Spain, **un sandwich** is a sandwich made from a tin loaf, and **un bocadillo** is one made with French bread. A number of Latin American countries use the word **sandwich**, without making a distinction between the two types of bread.

Pronunciation

 05.04

j – as in **J**avier, **j**amón, a**j**o – is pronounced like a strong 'h', or like the Scottish 'ch' in *loch*.

g before **e, i** – as in **Á**n**g**eles, **g**eneral, **G**ibraltar – is pronounced like Spanish **j** (see above).

g before **a, o, u** – as in **g**as, Die**g**o, se**g**undo – is pronounced like the 'g' in *government*. The same pronunciation occurs before **r** and **n**, for example **g**racias, i**g**norante.

g, in the combination **gue** and **gui** – as in **G**uernica, **g**uisante, is also pronounced like the 'g' in *government*. Here the **u** remains silent.

Practise with:

Para Javier, un bocadillo de jamón y un agua mineral con gas. Para Ángeles, un gazpacho, y de segundo pollo con guisantes y judías verdes. ¿Y para ti, Juan?

If you have difficulty in pronouncing **j** as the 'ch' in *loch*, don't worry, as this particular sound is softer in parts of southern Spain and Latin America where it is closer to the 'h' in *house*.

Practice

1 Una comida *A meal*

la lechuga	*lettuce*
el tomate	*tomato*

Raquel and her friend Francisca are having lunch in a restaurant. Fill in the gaps in the dialogue with one of these words: *a, con, de, sin, para*.

Camarero	¿Qué van a tomar?
Raquel	_____ mí, sopa _____ verduras _____ primero, y _____ segundo quiero cordero asado _____ arroz.
Camarero	¿Y _____ usted?
Francisca	Yo, una ensalada _____ lechuga _____ tomates, y _____ segundo quiero pescado _____ la plancha _____ puré.
Camarero	¿Y _____ beber?
Francisca	Dos aguas minerales y una botella _____ vino tinto.
Camarero	¿Quieren agua _____ gas o _____ gas?
Francisca	Una _____ gas y la otra _____ gas.

2 ¿Tú o usted? *(translating 'you')*

la servilleta	*napkin*

05.05

You are going to hear some people asking for things. Which of the requests are informal and which formal? Classify them accordingly, using *tú* for informal and *usted* for formal.

a _____
b _____
c _____
d _____
e _____
f _____

3 Un almuerzo informal *An informal lunch*

las fresas con nata/ crema (LAm)	*strawberries with cream*
el arroz con leche	*rice pudding* (literally, *rice with milk*)

On a visit to Spain you and your friend Pepe go out for lunch. Use the guidelines in English to fill in yours and Pepe's part of this dialogue with the waitress.

Camarera	¿Qué van a tomar?
Tú	*We want today's menu, please.*
Camarera	Aquí tienen.
Pepe	*I want a mixed salad as a first course, and as a second course I want a paella.*
Tú	*For me, soup, and as a second course I want roast lamb with mashed potatoes.*
Camarera	¿Y para beber?
Tú	*Red wine for me, please. And for you Pepe? What do you want to drink?*
Pepe	*I want a glass of white wine.*
Tú	*Will you also bring us a bottle of still mineral water?*
Camarera	Ahora mismo.
(Ordering dessert)	
Tú	*What do you have for dessert?*
Camarera	Tenemos melón, fresas con nata y arroz con leche.
Pepe	*I want strawberries with cream.*
Tú	*Rice pudding for me. And will you bring us two coffees and the bill, please?*

Did you notice the phrase **¿para beber?,** literally *for to drink*? In Spanish, words like **para**, **sin**, **a**, etc., which are known as prepositions, are always followed by the dictionary form of the verb, unlike English which uses the *-ing* form of the verb, e.g. **sin comer** (*without eating*).

4 En un bar *In a bar*

 05.06

What snacks do they serve in this Spanish bar? First, study the words in the menu board below, then listen to Ramón, Sofía and Clara placing their order. What is each one having? Fill in the table below with each order.

BAR LAS GAVIOTAS	
Tapas	**Bocadillos**
Champiñones	Jamón
Gambas	Queso
Calamares	Chorizo
Tortilla de patatas	Salchichón

	Para comer	Para beber
Sofía		
Clara		
Ramón		

5 Palabra por palabra *Word for word*

Here are some common words related to food and eating. Look them up and list them under the appropriate headings below.

cuchillo	lechugas	uvas	merluza	cerdo
piñas	pollo	manzanas	cordero	tenedor
atún	cuchara	ajos	cebollas	plato

Pescado	Carne	Verdura	Fruta	Utensilio

Can you add other words to each list?

6 ¡Que aproveche!/¡Buen provecho! *Bon appetit!*

se toma	*people take, it is taken*
ligero/a	*light*
el bollo	*bun*
la galleta	*biscuit*
la comida	*meal, lunch*
llevar (here)	*to contain*
el plato	*dish* (also *plate*)
el huevo	*egg*
la legumbre	*pulse*

The following passage describes the main meals in Spain and Latin America. How do eating habits compare with those in your country? Read and find out and say whether the following statements are true or false (*verdaderos o falsos*).

> En España, el desayuno es una comida ligera, que consiste normalmente en café y tostadas, bollos o galletas, pero en algunos países latinoamericanos – México por ejemplo – el desayuno es generalmente abundante. Aparte de café, un desayuno mexicano puede incluir fruta, huevos, y algún plato típico de la región.
>
> La comida o el almuerzo es la comida principal, se toma entre la una y las tres y consiste normalmente en dos platos, postre y café. El plato principal o segundo plato generalmente lleva carne o pescado. A la hora de la comida, españoles y latinoamericanos consumen muchas legumbres, verduras y frutas frescas.
>
> La cena se toma entre las nueve y las diez y es normalmente una comida ligera.

a En España se toma un desayuno muy abundante.

b En México se toma un desayuno ligero.

c La comida principal en España y Latinoamérica es el almuerzo o la comida.

d El primer plato normalmente lleva pescado o carne.

? Test yourself

Write meaningful sentences by putting the words in the right order.

a ¿tomar– van – qué – a?

b del – menú – queremos – día – el

c primero – mí – sopa – de – para

d asado – fritas – de – quiero – patatas – segundo – cordero – con

e ¿beber – y – para?

f tinto – dos – un – minerales – y – aguas – sin – vino – gas

g ¿poco – trae – de – me – pan – más – un?

h ¿de – tienen – qué – postre?

i bocadillo – un – cerveza – quiero – jamón – una – de – y

j ¿sal – me – la – por favor – pasa?

If you got most of the sentences right, it means you have now become familiar with some important Spanish constructions and also with how to use these when ordering food or drinks. You may wish to revise certain points, otherwise go on to Unit 6 in which you will learn a number of key expressions related to travel.

SELF CHECK

I CAN. . .
. . .ask people what they would like to eat or drink
. . . ask and say what's on the menu
. . . order food and drinks.

6 ¿A qué hora llega?
What time does it arrive?

In this unit you will learn how to:
▶ *ask and tell the time*
▶ *get travel information*
▶ *buy tickets.*

CEFR: *Can handle numbers, cost and time (A1); Can get simple information about travel using public transport (A2); Can buy tickets (A1); Can find specific information in timetables and advertisements (A2); Can catch the main point in short, clear messages (A2).*

Public transport

Getting about in Spain is not difficult. If where you are staying is on the outskirts of the city, you can use **el autobús** (*the bus*) to get to **el centro** (*the centre*). Madrid, Barcelona, Valencia, Sevilla, Bilbao and Palma de Mallorca also have **el metro** (*the underground*). In **la estación de autobuses** (*the bus station*; **la estación de guaguas** in the Canary Islands), you can get information on buses to outlying towns and inter city buses.

RENFE is the national rail network and there are also **cercanías** (*local rail networks*). **El precio del billete** (*the price of the ticket*) varies according to the type of train, the faster trains costing more. The fastest is **el AVE** (*the hi-speed train*). This high-speed network is expanding across Spain and Europe linking the major cities. It is an attractive alternative to **el avión** (*the plane*), which is another way to travel from one Spanish city to another.

Dos para el aeropuerto. Can you say:
a   How many people are travelling?
b   Where they want to go?

Conversations

NEW EXPRESSIONS

1 ¿QUÉ HORA ES? *WHAT TIME IS IT?*

 06.01

1.1 Listen to some people asking and telling the time and, as you do, look at the clock faces only and repeat each question and answer after the speakers several times. Note the two alternative questions:

¿Qué hora es?   *What time is it?*

¿Tiene hora?   *Have you got the time?*

a   Es la una   **b**   Son las cuatro y diez   **c**   Son las seis y cuarto

d   Son las siete y media   **e**   Son las diez menos cinco   **f**   Son las doce menos cuarto

1.2 Listen again several times while you read the phrases under each clock and say them aloud until you feel confident that you have learned them. Then look at the clock faces only, and practise asking and saying the time. You can then practise in a similar way with other times.

Compare the English *five to ten* and *a quarter to twelve* with the Spanish **las diez menos cinco**, literally *ten minus five* and **las doce menos cuarto**, literally *twelve minus a quarter*.

 2 QUERÍA HACER UNA RESERVA
I'D LIKE TO MAKE A RESERVATION

quería	*I'd like* (literally *I wanted*)
... que sale	*which leaves ...*

(11:30) de la mañana	*(11.30) in the morning*
por la tarde	*in the afternoon*
bueno (here)	*well then*
deme	*give me* (formal)

A tourist is making enquiries about rail travel to Seville.

 06.02

2.1 **Listen to the conversation several times and, as you do, answer the questions which follow. Key words and phrases in this dialogue are:**

sale (from **salir**)	*it leaves*
llega a ... (from **llegar**)	*it arrives in ...*
¿a qué hora ...?	*at what time ...?*

Note also the use of the 24-hour clock, with 1.00 p.m., for instance, becoming *las trece horas*, and fractions of a time like 6.45 p.m. expressed as **las dieciocho cuarenta y cinco**.

1 What time are the trains to Seville?

2 Does the tourist get *a single ticket*, **un billete de ida**, or *a return ticket*, **un billete de ida y vuelta**?

3 Is he travelling in tourist, business (**clase preferente**) or club class?

Turista	Buenos días, quería hacer una reserva para Sevilla, para el domingo.
Empleada	Pues, hay un tren que sale a las nueve y cuarto de la mañana, otro a las once y media, y por la tarde hay uno a las catorce treinta, otro a las dieciséis quince ...
Turista	El tren de las dieciséis quince, ¿a qué hora llega a Sevilla?
Empleada	A las dieciocho cuarenta y cinco. ¿Quiere un billete de ida o de ida y vuelta?
Turista	De ida.
Empleada	¿En clase turista, preferente o club?
Turista	¿Cuánto cuesta la clase preferente?
Empleada	Ciento veinticinco euros con cuarenta.
Turista	Bueno, deme clase preferente.

2.2 **Find in the conversation the phrases meaning:**

1 for Seville

2 for Sunday

3 in the afternoon

2.3 Read the dialogue several times and play, first the part of the traveller, then that of the booking clerk. Once you feel confident with it, put the following sentences into Spanish. (For the days of the week see Language Discovery, para 2.)

1 I'd like to make a reservation for Barcelona, for Saturday.
2 There's a train which leaves at 13.45, another one at 15.15 and another one at 17.20.
3 The 15.15 train, what time does it arrive in Barcelona?
4 I want a return ticket.
5 How much is the tourist class?
6 A hundred and thirty-five euros.

After **llegar** (to arrive), Spanish uses **a**:

¿A qué hora llega a Sevilla?   *What time does it arrive in Seville?*

Note also the use of **para** (*for*) to indicate direction:

una reserva para Sevilla   *a reservation for Seville*

More on **para** in paragraph 3 of the Language Discovery section.

3 ¿A QUÉ HORA HAY AUTOBUSES? *WHAT TIME ARE THERE BUSES?*

el autobús	*bus*
dentro de	*within*
tardar	*to take (time)*

EL VIAJE *THE JOURNEY*

*Here's a traveller – **un/a viajero/a** – wanting to go from Málaga to Ronda by bus.*

06.03

3.1 Listen to the dialogue a few times and, as you do, answer the following questions:

1 How frequent are the buses from Málaga to Ronda?
2 How long does it take to get to Ronda?
3 What time is the next bus and what time does it arrive in Ronda?
4 Does the traveller get a single or a return ticket?

Two things to notice in the dialogue below: **dentro de** (*within*), two words in Spanish, one word in English; **media hora** (*half an hour*), where Spanish does not use the equivalent of *an*.

Viajera	Por favor, ¿a qué hora hay autobuses para Ronda?
Empleado	Cada hora. El próximo sale dentro de media hora, a las nueve y cinco.
Viajera	¿Cuánto tarda el viaje?
Empleado	Una hora y media. Llega a Ronda a las once menos veinticinco.
Viajera	Deme un billete de ida y vuelta, por favor.
Empleado	Aquí tiene.
Viajera	¿Cuánto es?
Empleado	Son veintidós euros.

3.2 **Now read the dialogue and find the phrases which mean the following.**

1 every hour
2 How long does the journey take?
3 the next one leaves ...
4 How much is it?

How do you say it?

ASKING AND TELLING THE TIME

¿Qué hora es? / ¿Tiene hora?	*What time is it?/Have you got the time?*
(Es) la una/una y diez.	*(It's) one o'clock/ten past one.*
(Son) las once menos cuarto/veinte.	*(It's) a quarter/twenty to eleven.*
(Son) las dos y cuarto/y media.	*(It's) a quarter/half past two.*
(Son) las cinco de la mañana/ tarde.	*(It's) five o'clock in the morning/ afternoon.*

GETTING TRAVEL INFORMATION

¿A qué hora sale el tren/ autobús para (Bilbao)?	*What time does the train/ bus for (Bilbao) leave?*
Sale a las 2:00/dentro de una hora/media hora/cinco minutos.	*It leaves at 2.00/in an hour/half an hour/five minutes.*
¿A qué hora llega a (Madrid)?	*What time does it arrive in (Madrid)?*
Llega a (Madrid) a las 7:30.	*It arrives in (Madrid) at 7.30.*

BUYING TICKETS

Quería/Quisiera/Quiero dos billetes/boletos (LAm) **para …**	*I'd like/want two tickets for …*
un billete/boleto de ida/ida y vuelta	*a single/return ticket*
¿Cuánto cuesta/es?	*How much does it cost/is it?*
Son treinta euros con veinte (céntimos).	*It's thirty euros twenty (cents).*

Language discovery

1 LA HORA *THE TIME*

To tell the time use **ser** (*to be*): **es** for *midday*, *midnight* and *one o'clock* and **son** for all other times. Note that Spanish uses **la** (sing) or **las** (pl) *the* before the actual time:

Es mediodía/medianoche/ la una en punto.	*It's midday/midnight/ one o'clock sharp.*
Son las tres menos cuarto.	*It's a quarter to three.*

Some Latin American countries use expressions like:

es un cuarto para (las dos)	*it's a quarter to (two)*
son diez para (las seis)	*it's ten to (six)*

instead of **son (las dos) menos cuarto**, **son (las seis) menos diez**.

2 LOS DÍAS DE LA SEMANA *DAYS OF THE WEEK*

lunes	*Monday*
martes	*Tuesday*
miércoles	*Wednesday*
jueves	*Thursday*
viernes	*Friday*
sábado	*Saturday*
domingo	*Sunday*

Days are masculine in Spanish and are normally written with a small letter. They are preceded by **el** (sing) or **los** (pl) in phrases like the following.

el lunes	*on Monday*
para el martes	*for Tuesday*
los sábados	*on Saturdays*
todos los jueves	*every Thursday*

3 A, CON, DE, PARA, POR: *MORE PREPOSITIONS*

a

¿A qué hora llega a Madrid?	*At what time does it arrive in Madrid?*
A las dos y tres minutos.	*At three minutes past two.*

con

diez euros con cincuenta	*ten euros fifty*

de

Sale de Valencia a las cuatro de la tarde.	*It leaves Valencia at four in the afternoon.*
el tren de las seis	*the six o'clock train*
dentro de una hora	*within an hour*
un billete de ida/ida y vuelta	*a single/return ticket*

para

un billete para Zaragoza	*a ticket for/to Zaragoza*
para las nueve/hoy/el lunes	*for nine o'clock/today/Monday*

por

mañana/el domingo por la mañana/tarde/noche	*tomorrow/on Sunday morning/afternoon/evening*

4 QUE *THAT, WHICH, WHO*

To say *that* or *which* as in *There is a bus which/that leaves Barcelona at midday*, use the word **que**: **Hay un autobús que sale de Barcelona al mediodía.**

Que can also be used for people:

La persona que está allí es mi marido.	*The person who is there is my husband.*

5 QUERÍA *I'D LIKE*

An alternative to **quisiera** (*I'd like*) is **quería**, literally *I wanted*. The **nosotros/as** form is **queríamos** (*we'd like*), literally *we wanted*. These two forms correspond to the imperfect tense, a tense which will be covered in Units 17 and 18.

6 ¿CUÁNTO CUESTA/VALE? *HOW MUCH DOES IT COST?*, ¿CUÁNTO ES? *HOW MUCH IS IT?*

To ask how much something costs you can use **costar (o>ue)** (*to cost*), **cuesta** if you are enquiring about one thing only, and **cuestan** if there is more than one:

¿Cuánto cuesta el viaje/cuestan los billetes?	*How much does the journey cost/do the tickets cost?*

Valer (*to cost*) is used in a similar way:

¿Cuánto vale/n?   *How much does it / do they cost?*

When you are ready to pay for a service or something you bought use
¿Cuánto es? (*How much is it?*)

Pronunciation

06.04

q occurs only in the combination **que** and **qui**, and is pronounced like
[ke] and [ki].

Practise with:

¿A qué hora sale el avión para Quito?
Quiero un billete para el tren que sale a las quince treinta.
Queremos cambiar quinientos euros.

Practice

1   La hora en el mundo *The time around the world*

You need to make some
international phone calls from
Chile, where you have been sent
by your company. How would
you ask the operator what
the time is in the following
cities, and how would she/
he reply? Look at the table
opposite and ask and answer
using the twelve-hour clock and
expressions like 'de la mañana' /
'de la tarde'.

La Hora	
Cuando en Chile es mediodía en el resto del mundo es:	
Nueva York	12.00
Madrid	18.00
Londres	17.00
Roma	18.00
Tokio	01.00
San Francisco	09.00
México	10.00
Sao Paulo	13.00
París	18.00
Sidney	02.00

    a   Madrid
    b   Londres
    c   Tokio
    d   San Francisco
    e   São Paulo
    f   Nueva York

2 De Sevilla a Málaga *From Seville to Málaga*

You are now in Spain with a travelling companion and you want to take a train from Sevilla to Málaga. Check the timetable and answer your partner's questions using the 12-hour clock.

Origen

Sevilla Sta. Justa	7,50	12,20	17,30	18,40
La Salud	–	12,28	–	–
Dos Hermanas	8,01	12,35	17,41	18,51
Utrera (LL)	8,13	12,47	17,53	19,03
Utrera (S)	8,15	12,50	17,55	19,05
El Arahal	–	13,07	–	–
Marchena	8,39	13,18	18,19	19,29
Osuna	9,05	13,45	18,44	19,55
Pedrera	9,34	14,12	19,08	–
La Roda Andalucía	9,47	14,26	19,21	20,36
Fuente Piedra	–	14,37	–	–
Bobadilla (LL)	10,05	14,46	19,42	21,00
Bobadilla (S)	10,09	15,04	–	21,01
Málaga (LL)	10,58	16,17	–	22,03

a ¿A qué hora hay trenes para Málaga?

b ¿A qué hora llegan a Málaga?

The twenty-four hour clock normally used by officials at railway stations or airports is quite often converted by the public into the twelve-hour clock when passing on similar information to others. A phrase such as **las dieciocho treinta** can then become **las seis y media de la tarde**. Note that with the 24-hour clock the **y** is normally omitted.

3 Un recado *A message*

la salida   *departure*

la llegada   *arrival*

 06.05

María Luisa is being sent by her company overseas and her travel agent leaves a message, 'un recado', on her answerphone with details of her flight. Can you fill in the box below with the appropriate information?

Destino	Salida	Llegada	Presentación en aeropuerto
- - - - -	- - - - -	- - - - -	- - - - -

4 Números *Numbers*

06.06

Listen, tick the numbers that you hear, and then try learning them all.

100	cien	☐	800	ochocientos	☐
101	ciento uno	☐	900	novecientos	☐
200	doscientos	☐	1.000	mil	☐
299	doscientos noventa y nueve	☐	2.000	dos mil	☐
300	trescientos	☐	3.500	tres mil quinientos	☐
400	cuatrocientos	☐	10.000	diez mil	☐
500	quinientos	☐	100.000	cien mil	☐
600	seiscientos	☐	1.000.000	un millón	☐
700	setecientos	☐	2.000.000	dos millones	☐

▶ Note that **-cientos** becomes **-cientas** before a feminine plural noun :

doscientos euros   *two hundred euros*

doscientas libras   *two hundred pounds*

▶ The plural of **millón** is **millones**, and the word loses the accent.

▶ Years are read in the following way:

1985	**mil novecientos ochenta y cinco**
1999	**mil novecientos noventa y nueve**
2012	**dos mil doce**

5 Un programa de vacaciones *A holiday programme*

You have seen the following holiday advertisement in a Spanish paper and you phone a Spanish friend to tell him/her about it. How would you read the prices out loud?

EUROPA	
AMSTERDAM, 3 días	
Hotel 2*	desde **440** €
MALTA, 3 días	
Hotel 3*	desde **458** €
CAPITALES DE RUSIA, 7 días	
Hotel 4*	desde **1.590** €
AFRICA	
TWENDE (KENIA), 10 días	
Hotel 4*	desde **1.877** €
ASIA	
BANGKOK-BALI, 10 días	
Hotel 5*	desde **1.233** €
INDIA, 8 días	
Hotel 4/5*	desde **1.780** €
CHINA MILENARIA + GUILIN, 15 días	
Hoteles 5*	desde **2.593** €

6 El vuelo dura una hora *The flight lasts an hour*

While on business in Bogotá, Colombia, you decide to spend a weekend in the colonial town of Cartagena de Indias. Follow the guidelines and fill in your part of the conversation with the travel agent. Key words here are:

el vuelo	*flight*
el/la siguiente	*the next one*
la vuelta	*return*
último/a	*last.*

Tú	*Good morning. I'd like to make a reservation for Cartagena for Friday morning. What time are there flights?*
Empleada	Hay un vuelo a las ocho y cuarto, pero está completo. El siguiente es a las once y media.
Tú	*What time does it arrive in Cartagena?*
Empleada	A las doce treinta. ¿Para cuándo quiere la vuelta?
Tú	*For Sunday night. What time does the last flight leave Cartagena?*
Empleada	A las veintiuna quince.
Tú	*How much does the return ticket cost?*
Empleada	Cuatrocientos cincuenta mil pesos.
Tú	*It's all right. Give me a return ticket, please.*

Did you notice the phrase **¿para cuándo?** (*for when?*) in the dialogue above? **Para** is often found in time phrases such as this one. Here are some other examples: **para la semana próxima** (*for next week*), **para mañana** (*for tomorrow*), **para el sábado por la tarde** (*for Saturday afternoon*).

 Test yourself

1 **How would you say the following in Spanish?**

 a What time is it?

 b It's one o'clock.

 c It's a quarter past five.

 d It's half past seven.

 e It's a quarter to nine.

2 **Complete the following sentences with suitable words and phrases.**

 a Quería dos **(1)** _____ en clase turista **(2)** _____ Barcelona, por favor.

 b Hay un tren **(1)** _____ sale a las ocho treinta **(2)** _____ la mañana.

 c ¿Quiere de ida o _____ ?

 d '¿**(1)** _____ tarda el viaje?' – 'Tarda cuatro **(2)** _____ y media.'

 e ¿**(1)** _____ qué hora llega el tren **(2)** _____ Barcelona?

 f Quería **(1)** _____ una reserva **(2)** _____ el lunes **(3)** _____ la tarde.

Test 2 assesses your knowledge of words and phrases related to travel as well as of a few key grammatical words, among them the prepositions **a, de, para, por**. For a summary of the uses of **por** and **para** see paragraph 14 of the **Grammar summary** at the end of the book.

SELF CHECK

	I CAN. . .
○	. . . ask and tell the time
○	. . . get travel information
○	. . . buy tickets.

7 ¿Qué desea?
Can I help you?

In this unit you will learn how to:
▶ *buy food in a market*
▶ *buy groceries*
▶ *find out what things cost.*

CEFR: *Can deal with common aspects of everyday living such as shopping (A2); Can handle numbers, quantities and cost (A1); Can get an idea of the content of simpler informational material (A2).*

Going to the market

Every town and district in a city had **un mercado** (*a market*), a dedicated building open in the mornings with food stalls selling fresh produce. **El supermercado** (*the supermarket*) has seen many markets close or reinvent themselves as bijou shopping centres, but enough still operate. Some are tourist attractions, like the central market in Valencia with its beautiful nineteenth-century wrought ironwork and tiles.

In the market, you will find bigger and juicier fruit than anything you will get back home, so, if the season is right, why not ask for **un kilo de melocotones** (*a kilo of peaches*) or **medio kilo de uvas** (*half a kilo of grapes*). Try some of the local cheese, **un cuarto de kilo de este queso** (*a quarter kilo of this cheese*), and if you like olives, buy **cien gramos de estas aceitunas** (*100 grams of these olives*).

At the fruit and vegetable stall, you listen to the woman in front of you. What is she buying? What does she ask?
a un kilo de naranjas
b medio kilo de fresas
c dos tomates y una lechuga
d ¿Cuánto cuesta la piña?

Conversations

1 ¿CUÁNTO CUESTAN? *HOW MUCH ARE THEY?*

dar	*to give*
estos/estas	*these* (m/f)
medio	*half*
nada más	*nothing else*
el/la dependiente/a	*shop assistant*

Lola is doing her shopping in a Spanish market.

1.1 First, look at the list of fruit and vegetables below. How many of them can you guess? Look up the words you don't know.

Frutas

el albaricoque/damasco (LAm.)   el melocotón/durazno (LAm.)

la fresa	el limón	el melón	la naranja
la manzana	la piña	el plátano	la uva

Verduras

el ajo	la cebolla	la patata/papa (LAm.)
la coliflor	la lechuga	el pimiento (verde/rojo)
el pepino	el perejil	el tomate/jitomate (Méx)
la zanahoria		

The differences in vocabulary between Spain and Latin America in relation to fruit and vegetables are not restricted to those above and you will also find differences within Spain and within Latin America. A few words used in Spain as elsewhere, for example **tomate** actually originated in the New World.

07.01

1.2 Now listen to the dialogue several times. Can you say what and how much Lola is buying?

Dependiente	Buenos días. ¿Qué quería?
Lola	¿Me da un kilo de plátanos?
Dependiente	¿Algo más?
Lola	¿Cuánto cuestan estas naranjas?
Dependiente	Un euro con noventa el kilo.
Lola	¿Me pone un kilo y medio?
Dependiente	¿Alguna cosa más?
Lola	¿A cómo están estos tomates?
Dependiente	A dos euros veinte el kilo.
Lola	Póngame dos kilos ... ¡ah!, y me da una lechuga y dos kilos de patatas.
Dependiente	¿Quiere algo más?
Lola	No, nada más. ¿Cuánto es todo?
Dependiente	Son doce euros con noventa.

1.3 Now read the dialogue and find the expressions meaning

1 What would you like?
2 How much are these ...?
3 Anything else?
4 How much is it all?

Note the use of **poner** (*to put*) when asking for things that normally need to be weighed (to be put on a scale): **¿Me pone ...?** *Will you give me ...?* (literally, *To me you put ...*), **Póngame ...** *Give me ...* (literally, *Put me ...*). In the same context you may also hear the expression **¿Qué le pongo?** *What shall I give you?* (literally, *What to you I put?*).

 2 ¿ME DA UN CUARTO DE KILO? *WILL YOU GIVE ME A QUARTER OF A KILO?*

¿qué desea?	*can I help you?* (literally, *what do you wish?*)
este/ese	*this/that* (m)
esas	*those* (f)
aquel	*that* (m)
las aceitunas/olivas	*olives*
la mantequilla	*butter*

una lata	*a tin*
una barra	*a loaf*
media docena de ...	*half a dozen ...*
la mermelada	*jam/marmalade*
¿cuánto vale?	*how much does it cost?*
eso es todo	*that's all*

07.02

2.1 Listen to Lola buying some groceries now. What is Lola buying and how much?

Dependiente	Hola, buenas tardes. ¿Qué desea?
Lola	¿Me da un cuarto de kilo de ese queso?
Dependiente	¿Qué más?
Lola	Póngame ciento cincuenta gramos de aquel jamón ..., y medio kilo de esas aceitunas.
Dependiente	¿Algo más?
Lola	Un paquete de mantequilla ... una lata de atún ... una barra de pan ... y media docena de huevos. ¡Ah!, ¿tiene mermelada de naranja?
Dependiente	No, no tengo. ¿Alguna cosa más?
Lola	¿Cuánto vale este aceite de oliva?
Dependiente	Cuatro euros con noventa y cinco la botella de un litro.
Lola	Deme una.
Dependiente	¿Desea algo más?
Lola	Eso es todo. ¿Cuánto es?
Dependiente	Son veintidós euros con cuarenta.

2.2 Read the conversation again and then match the Spanish and the English.

1	un paquete	**a**	*a loaf*
2	una lata	**b**	*a packet*
3	una barra	**c**	*a bottle*
4	una botella	**d**	*a tin*

2.3 You ask a Spanish friend to do some shopping for you. Write a shopping list in Spanish using expressions from the dialogue and the words in brackets.

1 two hundred grams of cured ham (**jamón serrano**)
2 one kilo of sugar (**azúcar**)
3 one packet of chocolate biscuits (**galletas de chocolate**)
4 one tin of salmon (**salmón**)
5 a quarter of chorizo (**a spicy hard sausage**)
6 one loaf of wholemeal bread (**pan integral**)

How do you say it?

BUYING FOOD IN A MARKET

¿Qué quería/desea?	*What would you like?*
¿Qué le pongo?	*What shall I give you?*
Quería/Quiero un kilo de …	*I'd like/want a kilo of …*
¿Me da medio kilo de …?	*Will you give me half a kilo of …?*
¿Me pone un cuarto de kilo de …?	*Will you give me a quarter kilo of …?*
Póngame un kilo y medio.	*Give me one and a half kilos.*
¿Algo más/Alguna cosa más?	*Anything else?*
¿Qué más?	*What else?*
Nada más.	*Nothing else.*
Eso es todo.	*That's all.*

BUYING GROCERIES

Quería/Quiero …	*I'd like/want …*
¿Me da …?/Deme …	*Will you give me …? / Give me …*
una docena de …	*a dozen …*
doscientos gramos de …	*two hundred grams of …*
un paquete de …	*a packet of …*
una lata/botella de …	*a tin/bottle of …*
una barra de …	*a loaf of …*

¿Cuánto cuesta/vale?	*How much is it?*
¿Cuánto cuesta/vale este/esta ...?	*How much is this ...?* (m/f)
¿Cuánto cuestan/valen estos/estas ...?	*How much are these ...?* (m/f)
¿A cómo/cuánto está/están?	*How much is it/are they?*

Note that the phrase **¿Cuánto es?** (*How much is it?*) is not normally used to enquire about the price of something but rather to find out how much you need to pay after you have bought what you wanted. To find out what something costs use one of the phrases above.

 # Language discovery

1 ¿A CÓMO/CUÁNTO ESTÁ(N)?
HOW MUCH IS IT/ARE THEY?

When prices change from day to day, as may be the case with fruit and vegetables in a market (or foreign currency), you can use this construction with **estar**.

¿A cómo (or cuánto) está el perejil?	*How much is the parsley?*
¿A cómo (or cuánto) están los tomates?	*How much are the tomatoes?*
Está/Están a (dos euros).	*It is/They are (two euros).*

2 ESTE, ESE, AQUEL *(THIS, THAT):* DEMONSTRATIVES

a Words like **este** (*this*), **ese**, **aquel** (*that*) are known as demonstratives and they take different forms depending on whether the word they refer to is masculine or feminine, singular or plural. To refer to something which is more distant or far from you, Spanish uses **aquel**, which also translates *that* in English, but which is much less common than the other two forms.

Masculine/feminine singular		Masculine/feminine plural	
este melón	*this melon*	**estos melones**	*these melons*
esta lechuga	*this lettuce*	**estas lechugas**	*these lettuces*
ese pepino	*that cucumber*	**esos pepinos**	*those cucumbers*
esa naranja	*that orange*	**esas naranjas**	*those oranges*
aquel limón	*that lemon*	**aquellos limones**	*those lemons*
aquella manzana	*that apple*	**aquellas manzanas**	*those apples*

b   These words can also stand in place of a noun which is understood, in which case they are sometimes written with an accent: **éste**, **ésta**, **ésos**, etc. This written accent is now optional, so in this book we have used them without it.

Quiero este/esa.   *I want this/that one.*

c   Other useful words to learn in this context are the invariable forms **esto** (*this*), **eso** (*that*) and **aquello** (*that*), which are neuter – that is, they are neither masculine nor feminine.

Eso es todo.   *That's all.*

Perdone, ¿qué es esto?   *Excuse me, what's this?*

Quiero esto/eso.   *I want this/that.*

The last sentence will be useful if you want something but are not sure of the Spanish word for it.

Pronunciation

 07.03

Spanish does not make a distinction between **b** and **v**. The '**b**' in **barra** and the '**v**' in **vino** are pronounced in the same way, with lips closed, nearly like the '**b**' in **b**ig. More frequently, in other positions, as between vowels – for example **uva**, **cebolla** – the lips are slightly apart.

Practise with:

   Buenos días, ¿qué desea?
   Quería un kilo y medio de albaricoques ..., un kilo de uvas ..., dos cebollas ..., un pimiento verde ..., una docena de huevos ..., una barra de pan blanco ..., y una botella de vino blanco también, por favor.

The fact that English makes a distinction between **b** and **v** might interfere with your pronunciation of Spanish until you've had enough practice. Don't be discouraged about this, as you'll still be understood. Try listening to Spanish radio or television and focus attention on how they pronounce words containing **b** and **v** – for example **Barcelona**, **Valencia.**

Practice

1 Una lista de compras *A shopping list*

You and a Spanish-speaking friend are spending a few days in a small town. It is your turn to buy some food today and you need to prepare a shopping list. Complete each of the phrases which follow with the name of the appropriate product below.

1 un kilo de ...
2 una lata de ...
3 una barra de ...
4 medio litro de ...
5 media docena de ...
6 una botella de ...

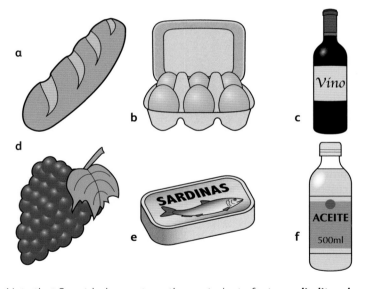

Note that Spanish does not use the equivalent of *a* in **medio litro de** (*half a litre of*) and **media docena de** (*half a dozen*). Notice also the use of **de** (*of*) after **docena**.

2 Ahora tú *And now you*

You are in a Spanish market doing some shopping. Follow the guidelines below, and fill in your part of the conversation with the stallholder.

Dependiente/a	Tú
¿Qué le pongo?	*Say you wanted one and a half kilos of tomatoes.*
¿Qué más?	*Ask how much the strawberries are.*
Tres euros el kilo.	*Ask him/her to give you one kilo.*
¿Algo más?	*Ask if he/she has green peppers.*
Sí, ¿cuántos quiere?	*Say you want four.*
¿Quiere algo más?	*Yes, you want some parsley, too.*
¿Qué más?	*That's all, thank you.*

3 Palabra por palabra *Word for word*

Each row below contains a word which is unrelated to the rest. Can you spot it? Some of the words will be new to you and you may need to look them up.

a queso, chorizo, aceitunas, plato, jamón, atún.

b harina, botella, arroz, azúcar, aceite, sal.

c ajo, judías verdes, espinaca, lata, guisantes, puerros.

4 ¿Cuánto es? *How much is it?*

07.04

A customer has done some shopping and is ready to pay. How much is the customer paying for each of the items below and what is the total? Listen and find out.

Note the use of the word **céntimo** (*cent*), normally used when the amount falls below one euro, as in **sesenta céntimos**, 0.60 €. Amounts which exceed one euro, for example 1.60 €, are usually expressed as **un euro con sesenta** or **un euro sesenta**.

a fresas

b manzanas

c naranjas

d uvas

e melón

f ajos

5 ¿Este o esta? *This (m/f)*

a Use 'este', 'esta', 'estos', 'estas', 'esto', as appropriate.

   i ¿Cómo se llama ... en español?

   ii ¿Cuánto cuestan ... galletas de chocolate?

   iii Quería dos botellas de ... vino.

   iv ¿Cuánto vale ... cerveza?

   v ¿Me pone un kilo de ... limones?

b Use 'ese', 'esa', 'esos', 'esas', 'eso', as appropriate

   i ¿A cómo están _____ patatas?

   ii Por favor, ¿me da una botella de _____ aceite de oliva?

   iii Perdone, ¿qué es _____ ?

   iv Póngame medio kilo de _____ melocotones.

   v ¿Cuánto vale _____ mermelada de naranja?

6 De compras *Shopping*

comprar	*to buy*
los alimentos	*food*
aun	*even*
la costumbre	*custom*
el pueblo	*small town, village*
cerrar (e>ie)	*to close*
abrir	*to open*
están abiertos/as	*they are open* (m/f)

The text which follows, which has no follow-up questions, is in Spanish, and it tells you a little about shopping habits among Spanish and Latin American people. Try to get the gist of what the passage says with the help of the key words above and your dictionary. As you read, focus attention on where people prefer to buy their food, and on opening and closing times for shops.

En España y en Latinoamérica la mayoría de la gente compra los alimentos en pequeñas tiendas de alimentación o de comestibles (*food shops*), y mercados. Esta costumbre es mucho más evidente en pueblos y ciudades pequeñas donde no hay supermercados. Pero aun en ciudades grandes, como Barcelona, Madrid, Valencia, donde hay muchos supermercados, la gente prefiere el contacto directo con el/la dependiente/a (*shop assistant*), o el/la tendero/a (*shopkeeper*).

Las tiendas normalmente abren entre 9:00 y 10:00 de la mañana, cierran al mediodía y abren nuevamente a las 3:00 o 4:00 de la tarde. En ciudades grandes muchas tiendas, especialmente los grandes almacenes (*department stores*), están abiertas todo el día.

The word **papa** (*potato*) is used in the Canary Islands and in the Spanish-speaking countries of Latin America. Peninsular Spanish uses the word **patata**, derived from **batata** (*sweet potato*). The term **papa** comes from Quechua, the language spoken by millions of indigenous people in the central Andean region.

 # Test yourself

Complete each sentence with a suitable word from the list.

1 póngame	**2** barra	**3** docena	**4** estos
5 paquete	**6** pone	**7** están	**8** cuánto
9 lata	**10** cuarto	**11** esas	**12** botella

a ¿ Me da un kilo de _____ tomates?

b ¿_____ cuestan los limones?

c ¿A cómo _____ las manzanas?

d _____ medio kilo de fresas.

e ¿Me _____ un pepino y dos pimientos?

f Quiero un _____ de kilo de jamón.

g Un _____ de mantequilla y una _____ de sardinas.

h Una _____ de huevos y una _____ de pan.

i Una _____ de aceite de oliva.

j Medio kilo de _____ aceitunas.

Are you ready to do your shopping now? Don't be discouraged if you can't remember some of the words for fruit and vegetables. That is less important than being able to handle some of the new constructions. And remember, you can always use **quiero** (*I want*) to say what you wish to buy, and the neutral **esto** (*this*) if you don't know the name of something: **Quiero esto**. It may not be quite what Spanish-speaking people normally say but it will help if you are stuck for words.

SELF CHECK

I CAN. . .
. . . buy food in a market
. . . buy groceries
. . . find out what things cost.

8 De compras
Shopping

In this unit you will learn how to:
▶ *buy clothes*
▶ *talk about size and colour.*

CEFR: *Can make simple purchases by stating what is wanted (A1); Can use simple descriptive language (A2); Can handle numbers (A1); Can understand phrases and expressions related to shopping (A2).*

Fashion

El Corte Inglés, Spain's largest department store with branches in every major city, started life in Madrid as a tailor's shop. **Zara**, **Mango** and **Desigual** are businesses that have crossed national frontiers to remind us of Spain's vibrant fashion industry in both **la ropa** (*clothes*) and **el calzado** (*footwear*).

Whether it is **una chaqueta verde** (*a green jacket*), **unos pantalones azules** (*blue trousers*) or **un jersey marrón** (*a brown jumper*), when you have seen something you like, you may want to ask **¿Dónde está el probador?** (*Where is the fitting room?*) or **¿Puedo probármelo?** (*Can I try it on?*). Study this question carefully in this unit as the bit underlined here changes depending on the gender of what you are asking to try on and whether it is singular or plural. Here, you're wanting to try on something masculine, **el jersey** (*the jumper*) perhaps.

What would you ask if you want to try on:
a **los zapatos** (*the shoes*): **¿Puedo probármelo?** or **¿Puedo probármelos?**
b **la camiseta** (*the T-shirt*): **¿Puedo probármelo?** or **¿Puedo probármela?**

Conversations

1 ¿PUEDO PROBÁRMELA? *MAY I TRY IT ON?*

ver	*to see*
en rojo	*in red*
pequeño/a	*small*
prefiero (from preferir e>ie)	*I prefer*
quedar	*to fit*
el probador	*fitting room*
llevar	*to take*

08.01

A customer is buying clothes for herself.

1.1 **Match the words and the items below, then listen to the conversation several times and say what clothes the customer is buying. Key words here are:**

la talla	*size*
el color	*colour*
probarse	*to try on.*

> 1 una chaqueta
>
> 2 unos calcetines
>
> 3 unos zapatos
>
> 4 un jersey/suéter (LAm)
>
> 5 unos pantalones
>
> 6 una camisa

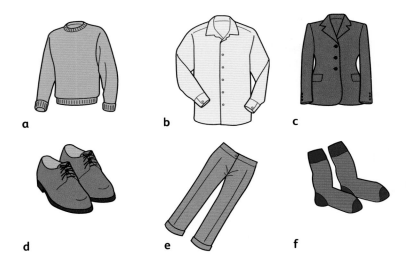

a   b   c

d   e   f

Clienta	Por favor, quisiera ver esa chaqueta.
Dependienta	¿Qué talla tiene?
Clienta	La cuarenta.
Dependienta	¿De qué color la quiere?
Clienta	La prefiero en rojo.
Dependienta	Aquí tiene una en rojo.
Clienta	¿Puedo probármela?
Dependienta	Sí, claro, el probador está al fondo.
(The customer comes back.)	
Dependienta	¿Qué tal le queda?
Clienta	Me queda un poco grande. ¿Tiene una más pequeña?
Dependienta	Sí, aquí tiene una de la talla treinta y ocho.
Clienta	*(Size 38 fits her well.)* Sí, esta me queda bien. Me la llevo.
Dependienta	¿Alguna otra cosa?
Clienta	Sí, quiero un jersey negro.

1.2 Look at the vocabulary below, then read the dialogue and try finding the phrases which mean the following. Note that they all refer to the jacket – 'la chaqueta' – which is feminine.

1 What colour do you want it?
2 I prefer it in red.
3 It's too big for me. (Literally, *it fits me big.*)
4 Have you got a smaller one?
5 This fits (me) well.
6 I'll take it.

¿Puedo probármela? (*May I try it on?* – literally, *May I try on myself it?*). The verbs here are **poder (o>ue)** and **probarse** (*to try something on*), in which **se** means *oneself*. **La** *it* stands for **la chaqueta**, a feminine word. Note that **me** and **la** have been added to the dictionary form of the verb.

2 ¿DE QUÉ COLOR? *WHAT COLOUR?*

gris	*grey*
blanco/a	*white*

 08.02

Another customer, this time a man, is buying clothes for himself.

2.1 What is he buying?

Cliente	Por favor, ¿tiene estos pantalones en la talla cuarenta y seis?
Dependiente	¿De qué color los quiere?
Cliente	Grises.
Dependiente	Un momento, por favor ... Sí, aquí tiene unos en gris.
Cliente	¿Puedo probármelos?
Dependiente	Sí, claro, el probador está al fondo, a la derecha.

(The customer comes back.) ¿Cómo le quedan?

Cliente	Me quedan muy bien. Me los llevo.
Dependiente	¿Desea algo más?
Cliente	Sí, quiero una camisa blanca, talla mediana.

Read the dialogue and answer these questions.

1 What size clothes does the customer wear?
2 Where's the fitting room?
3 What phrase does he use to say 'May I try them on?'
4 What phrase does the shop assistant use to say 'How do they fit?'
5 How does the customer express the following: 'They fit very well. I'll take them.'

How do you say it?

BUYING CLOTHES

Quiero/Quisiera/Quería ver ... esa chaqueta/esos vaqueros.	*I want/would like to see ... that jacket/those jeans.*
Quiero/Quisiera/Quería unos zapatos/unas sandalias.	*I want/would like some shoes/ sandals.*
¿Tiene esta camisa/este jersey en la talla ...?	*Have you got this shirt/sweater in size ...?*
¿Puedo probármelo/la(s)?	*May I try it/them on? (m/f)*
¿Quiere probárselo/la(s)?	*Would you like to try it/them on?*

TALKING ABOUT SIZE AND COLOUR

¿Qué talla (tiene)?	*What size (are you)?*
¿De qué talla?	*In what size?*
(La talla) cuarenta/pequeña (S)/mediana (M)/grande (L).	*(Size) forty/small/ medium/large.*
¿Cómo/Qué tal le queda(n)?	*How does it/do they fit?*
Me queda(n) (muy) bien.	*It fits/They fit (me) (very) well.*
Me queda(n) grande(s).	*It is/They are too big for me.*
¿Tiene uno/a(s) más pequeño/a(s)?	*Have you got a/some smaller one(s)?*
¿De qué color lo/la(s) quiere?	*What colour do you want it/them? (m/f)*
Lo/La(s) quiero/prefiero en rojo/azul/blanco.	*I want/prefer it/them in red/blue/ white.*
Quiero una camisa blanca/ un jersey negro.	*I want a white shirt/ black sweater.*

Language discovery

1 LO, LOS *IT, THEM*

To say *it* or *them* as in *I'll take it/them*, use **lo** for masculine and **la** for feminine. In the plural use **los** or **las**.

¿En qué color quiere el sombrero/la blusa?	*In what colour do you want the hat/blouse?*
Lo/La prefiero en negro.	*I prefer it in black.*
¿Y los pantalones/las medias?	*And the trousers/stockings?*
Los/Las quiero en azul.	*I want them in blue.*

These words, known 'technically' as direct object pronouns (see section 9 of the Grammar summary), normally come before the verb, translating literally as 'It/Them I prefer/want …etc.'. But in sentences with a main verb followed by an infinitive, they may be placed before the main verb (as above) or may be added to the infinitive, becoming one word with it. A sentence such as *I want to take it* may then be expressed as **Lo/la quiero llevar** or **Quiero llevarlo/la**.

(For a definition of the direct object, see 'Object' in the Glossary of grammatical terms and sections 9.1 and 9.2 of the Grammar summary.)

2 ME, TE/LE, NOS … *ME, YOU, US …*

You are already familiar with the use of **me** and **nos** in phrases such as **¿me/nos trae …?** (*will you bring me/us?*) (Unit 5), **¿me da …?** (*will you give me …?*) (Unit 7), **deme …** (*give me …*) (Unit 6). In this unit there are further examples of the use of **me** in a construction with **quedar** (*to fit*), in which **me** stands for *me* and *for me*. As with **lo(s)** and **la(s)** above, its position is normally before the verb.

Me quedan muy bien.	*They fit (me) very well.*
No me queda bien.	*It doesn't fit (me) well.*
Me queda grande.	*It's too big for me.*

The corresponding form for **tú** is **te**, and for **él/ella/Vd.** is **le**.

¿Qué tal te/le queda?	*How does it fit you/him/her?*
Te/Le queda corto.	*It's too short for you/him/her.*
La chaqueta te/le queda estupendamente.	*That jacket looks great on you/ him/her.*

For **nosotros/as**, **vosotros/as**, **ellos/ellas/Vds.** use **nos**, **os**, **les**, respectively.

¿Nos enseña esos cinturones?	*Will you show us those belts?*
Os quedan muy bien.	*They fit (you) very well.*
¿Les enseño otros?	*Shall I show you others?*

Me, **te**, **le**, **nos**, **os**, **les** are known as indirect object pronouns and you can find more information on them in Unit 9, and in sections 9.1 and 9.2 of the Grammar summary. For a definition of the indirect object, see the Glossary of grammatical terms.

3 ¿PUEDO PROBÁRMELO? *MAY I TRY IT ON?,* ME LO LLEVO *I'LL TAKE IT*

Me, like **te**, has other uses and meanings which do not correspond to those in 2 above. Sentences such as **¿Puedo probármelo?** and **Me lo llevo** can be learned as set phrases at this stage, but if you are interested in their grammar you can refer to the notes on reflexive pronouns in Unit 12.

4 LOS COLORES *COLOURS*

amarillo	*yellow*
azul	*blue*
blanco	*white*
gris	*grey*
malva	*mauve*
marrón	*brown*
naranja	*orange*
negro	*black*
rojo	*red*
rosa	*pink*
verde	*green*
violeta	*violet*

The following alternatives may be heard in some Latin American countries: **café** (*brown*), **rosado** (*pink*).

A note on pronunciation here: remember that the **double l** in **amarillo** is pronounced like the **ll** in **calle** or **paella**, nearly like the 'y' in *yes*. The **double r** in **marrón** and the **r** in **rojo**, **rosa** and **rosado** (LAm.) are strongly rolled, like a 'Scottish r'.

Some simple rules about colours:

a Colours are masculine in Spanish: **El negro te queda bien** (*Black suits you*).

b Colours ending in **-o** change for feminine and plural: **unas blusas blancas** (*some white blouses*).

c Colours ending in a consonant or **-e** change for plural but not for masculine and feminine: **los jerseys/las camisas azules** (*the blue sweaters/shirts*), **las faldas/los pantalones verdes** (*the green skirts/trousers*).

d Colours ending in **-a**, some of which correspond to names of things, are usually invariable: **los sombreros naranja/violeta** (*the orange/violet hats*).

e Like other words which describe things, colours normally follow the noun they describe (see 5 below): **unas bragas negras** (*some black panties*), **unos calzoncillos blancos** (*some white underpants*).

5 DESCRIBING THINGS: ADJECTIVES

a Position and agreement

Words which describe things, for example **grande** (*big*), **largo** (*long*), are called adjectives, and they normally come after the noun that they describe (see also 4e above). In Spanish, adjectives agree in *gender* (m/f) and *number* (sing/pl) with the word being described (see special rules for colours above): **un abrigo largo** (*a long coat*), **una camiseta pequeña** (*a small T-shirt*), **unos pantalones cortos** (*some short trousers*).

b Más + *adjective*

To say that you would like something bigger, cheaper, etc. place the word **más** before the adjective: **Busco unos calcetines más grandes** (*I'm looking for some bigger socks*), **¿Tiene un vestido más barato? Este es muy caro** (*Have you got a cheaper dress? This is too expensive*). (For more information on más + adjective see Unit 10.)

Practice

1 Quería ver ... *I'd like to see ...*

por supuesto	*certainly, of course*
estrecho/a	*tight*
ancho/a	*loose, loose-fitting*

08.03

Here is a brief exchange between a customer and a shop assistant. Listen to the dialogue a few times before you read it, then look at the words in the box and make up similar conversations, making all necessary changes. Try doing this without looking at the dialogue.

Clienta	Por favor, quería ver esas botas negras.
Dependienta	¿Estas?
Clienta	Sí, esas. ¿Puedo probármelas?
Dependienta	Sí, por supuesto. (Customer tries them on). ¿Qué tal le quedan?
Clienta	Me quedan grandes.

Two main things to be aware of before doing this exercise: is the word masculine or feminine, and is it in the singular or plural? That will determine which demonstrative you use (**este**, **esta**, etc.), which pronoun (**lo**, **la**, etc.) and whether **quedar** will be in the third person singular or plural.

Artículo	Color	Característica
a botas	negro	grande
b zapatos	marrón	pequeño
c camiseta	amarillo	ancho
d vestido	gris	estrecho

2 Find the opposite

Complete each sentence with the construction 'más' + adjective, using proper agreement between the adjective and the word this refers to.

Choose from: **pequeño, corto, ancho, barato, grande, largo**.

    a Esta falda me queda larga. ¿Tiene una ...?
    b Estas sandalias son muy caras. ¿Tiene unas ...?

c Esta blusa me queda grande. ¿Tiene una ...?

d Estos vaqueros me quedan cortos. ¿Tiene unos ...?

e Estos calcetines me quedan estrechos. ¿Tiene unos ...?

f Esta camisa es demasiado pequeña. ¿Tiene una ...?

3 Ahora tú *And now you*

las zapatillas	*trainers*
los guantes	*gloves*
precioso/a	*beautiful*
bonito/a	*nice, pretty*

You are buying some clothes and shoes for yourself. Use the guidelines below to reply to each question or statement.

The main thing to watch out for here is the position of **me**, **lo/s**, **la/s**, etc. Remember that these normally precede the verb, unless there is an infinitive (the dictionary form of the verb), in which case they can be attached at the end.

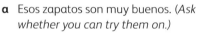

a Esos zapatos son muy buenos. (*Ask whether you can try them on.*)

b Ese cinturón marrón le queda muy bien. (*Say you'll take it.*)

c ¿Qué tal le quedan las zapatillas? (*Say they fit well. You'll take them.*)

d Estos guantes negros son preciosos. (*Say you'll take them.*)

e La camisa azul es muy bonita. (*Ask whether you can try it on.*)

f ¿Qué tal le queda el jersey verde? (*Say it doesn't fit well. You won't take it.*)

4 De compras *Shopping*

08.04

¿cuál/cuáles?	*which one/ones?*
pues, ... entonces	*well, ... then*

Carmen is buying some shoes for herself. Listen and answer the questions below. Note that the word for *size* when referring to shoes is **el número**, literally *number*.

  a What size shoes does she wear?

  b What colour shoes does she prefer?

  c What colours is she offered?

  d Which colour does she choose?

  e How do the shoes fit?

Can you think of other items of clothing not covered in this unit that you might want to know the Spanish for? Use your dictionary to look them up. You might find more than one word for them. A good dictionary will point out the differences between one word and another.

Test yourself

1 **Fill in the gaps in these sentences with a suitable word from the list.**

me   le   lo   la   los   las

  a Perdone, estas camisetas, ¿en qué color _____ tiene?

  b Estos pantalones son muy bonitos. ¿Puedo probar _____ ?

  c '¿Cómo (1)_____ quedan los zapatos, señor?' – '(2)_____ quedan muy bien.'

  d Esta camisa es muy elegante. (1) _____ (2)_____ llevo.

  e Perdone, este cinturón, ¿ _____ tiene en negro?

2 **How would you say the following in Spanish?**

  a I'd like to see those boots, please.

  b Have you got this shirt in size 16?

  c I prefer it (the shirt) in white.

  d May I try on these shoes?

  e This skirt is too big for me. Have you got a smaller one?

Words like **me, te, le, lo, la** are important, so if you are still uncertain about their use, go back through the relevant points in the grammar section of this unit again or study section 9 of the Language Discovery summary. Don't be discouraged if you still make a few mistakes, as that is quite normal. As you progress in the course you will gain more confidence and will probably be able to handle them.

SELF CHECK

I CAN. . .
. . . buy clothes
. . . talk about size and colour.

Queríamos alquilar un coche

We would like to hire a car

In this unit you will learn how to:

▶ *change money*
▶ *hire a car*
▶ *request a service on the phone.*

CEFR: *Can ask about things and make simple transactions (A1); Can handle numbers, cost and time (A1); Can ask for services (A1); Can find specific, predictable information in simple everyday material such as advertisements (A2).*

Changing money

To change money in **el banco** (*the bank*), look for the sign that says **CAMBIO** as not all banks have this facility and in some the opening hours are morning only. If a notice of exchange rates is not visible, you may want to ask: **¿A cuánto está el cambio?** (*What is the exchange rate?*) after saying **Quiero cambiar libras esterlinas a euros** (*I want to change pounds sterling into euros*). You tend to get a better rate for **billetes** (*banknotes*) than for **cheques de viaje** (*traveller's cheques*) when changing money.

If you look for **un cajero automático** (*a cashpoint*) to use your **tarjeta bancaria** (*bank card*), you don't need to worry about bank opening times. Or you can maybe use your **tarjeta de crédito** (*credit card*).

a **How much money do you want to change?** *Quiero cambiar doscientas libras esterlinas.*
b **How do you want to pay?** *¿Puedo pagar con tarjeta de crédito?*

Conversations

1 EN EL BANCO *AT THE BANK*

cambiar	*to change*
el cheque de viaje	*traveller's cheque*
el cambio	*exchange rate*
firmar	*to sign*

09.01

Ester is on holiday in Spain. Today she is changing some money at a bureau de change.

1.1 **What currency is Ester changing and how much? What is the rate of exchange for that currency? Listen and find out.**

Ester	Por favor, quisiera cambiar doscientos cincuenta dólares a euros. ¿A cuánto está el cambio? Tengo cheques de viaje.
Empleado	Está a setenta y nueve céntimos. ¿Me permite su pasaporte, por favor?
Ester	Aquí tiene.
Empleado	Muy bien, puede firmarlos. ¿Qué dirección tiene en Madrid?
Ester	Calle Salvador Nº 26, 2º, 4ª.

¿A cuánto está el cambio? (*What's the rate of exchange?* – literally, *At how much is the rate of exchange?*). An alternative to **¿cuánto?** here is **¿cómo?**, **¿A cómo está ...?** The use of **estar** here is due to the fact that rates of exchange tend to fluctuate.

1.2 **Find in the conversation the phrases for:**
   a May I have ...?
   b Here you are.

1.3 **Can you make sense of the following conversation which takes place in a South American country? Place the sentences in the right sequence and you'll get a dialogue on the same subject with some alternative expressions. The 'peso' is the currency in a number of Latin American countries, but the rate for the dollar is not the same in all countries.**

– Está a 540 pesos por dólar. ¿Cuánto quería cambiar?

– ¿Cuál es su dirección aquí?

– Tengo billetes. ¿A cómo está el cambio?

– Muy bien. ¿Tiene su pasaporte?

– Calle del Ángel, 842.

– ¿Tiene cheques de viaje o billetes?

– Sí, aquí tiene.

– Quería cambiar dólares a pesos.

– Cien dólares.

– ¿Qué desea?

 1.4 **Addresses in Spanish do not follow the same pattern as in English. What makes them different? Read and find out.**

Observa esta dirección: Salvador n° 26, 2°, 4ª. Salvador corresponde a la calle (*street*), 26 indica el número de la casa o edificio (*house or building number*), 2° corresponde al piso o planta (*floor*), y 4ª, 'cuarta', indica la puerta (*the door or flat number*). En avenida del Mar n° 150, 5° ('quinto'), B, 'B' indica la puerta B. En calle Rosas n°40, 6° ('sexto'), derecha, 'derecha' indica la puerta derecha. De manera similar, 'izquierda' indica la puerta izquierda. En cartas, las direcciones se utilizan normalmente en forma abreviada: C/ = calle; Avda. = avenida (*avenue*); P° = paseo (*walk, avenue*); dcha. = derecha; izq. o izda. = izquierda.

2 ALQUILANDO UN COCHE *HIRING A CAR*

el fin de semana	*weekend*
mediano/a	*medium size*
buen	*good* (before a *m, sing* noun)
de acuerdo	*fine, all right*
pagar	*to pay*
la tarjeta (de crédito)	*(credit) card*

 09.02

Pablo and a friend are hiring a car.

2.1 **First, look at the key words below, then listen to the dialogue several times and, as you do, say whether the following statements are true or false ('verdaderos o falsos'). Key words here are:**

alquilar	*to hire*
el alquiler	*hire charge*

el coche   *car*

recomendar (e>ie)   *to recommend.*

  a Pablo y su amigo quieren un coche para una semana.

  b Quieren un coche grande.

  c El seguro (*insurance*) obligatorio está incluido.

  d Los impuestos (*taxes*) están incluidos.

Pablo	Buenas tardes. Queríamos alquilar un coche para el fin de semana. Un coche mediano. ¿Qué nos recomienda?
Empleado	Pues, les recomiendo el Ford Fiesta.
Pablo	¿Cuánto es el alquiler?
Empleado	Para uno o dos días son diecinueve euros por día. El seguro obligatorio está incluido, pero los impuestos no. Es un buen coche. Se lo recomiendo.
Pablo	De acuerdo. ¿Podemos pagar con tarjeta?
Empleado	Sí, claro.

2.2 **Listen again a few times and fill in the gap in the following table with the car rate.**

Grupo	Modelo *Model*	KMS. ILIMITADOS 1–2 Días Por día/ *Per day*	3–6 Días Por día/ *Per day*	7+ Días Por día/ *Per day*
A	Ford Fiesta 1.1 Renault Clio		16 €	13 €
C	R. 19RL/Megane 1.4 A/C – Radio	25 €	19 €	15 €
D	Ford Escort 1.6 A/C – Radio	30 €	23 €	17 €
F	Seat Toledo 1.8 A/C – Radio	72 €	51 €	45 €
P	Renault Espace A/C 7 Pax. – Radio	92 €	79 €	67 €

Está incluido (*It is included*). The word **incluido** functions like an adjective (words like **negro**, **bueno**, etc.), so it must agree in number and gender with the noun it refers to, for example **La gasolina no está incluida** (*Petrol is not included*).

2.3 **Read the dialogue and find the Spanish for:**
  a What do you recommend (to us)?
  b I recommend (to you) ... (*formal, pl*)
  c I recommend it (to you). (*formal*)
  d Can we pay ...?

2.4 **Look at the car rental information now and use it to make up similar dialogues. Use words and phrases like 'pequeño', 'grande', 'económico', 'una semana', 'cinco días', etc.**

3 QUERÍA UN TAXI *I'D LIKE A TAXI*

enviar	*to send*
¿me dice (from decir) ...?	*will you tell me ...?*
en seguida	*straight away*
(gracias) a usted	*thank you*

 09.03

Sara phones for a taxi.

3.1 **Where does she want to go, and when does she want it for? Listen and find out.**

Empleado	Radio taxi, ¿dígame?
Sara	Hola, buenas tardes. Quería un taxi para ir al aeropuerto, por favor.
Empleado	¿Para qué hora lo quiere?
Sara	¿Me lo puede enviar ahora mismo?
Empleado	Muy bien. ¿Me dice su nombre y dirección, por favor?
Sara	Sara Moreno, calle Mistral 45, 3°, B.
Empleado	¿Su teléfono?
Sara	93 512 34 42.
Empleado	Pues, se lo envío en seguida.
Sara	Vale, gracias.
Empleado	A usted.

3.2 **What phrases are used in the conversation to say:**
  a Can you send it to me ...?
  b I´ll send it to you ...

3.3 It's 10 a.m. now and you want a taxi for 11 o'clock to go to Estación de Atocha (one of the main stations in Madrid). You are staying at calle de Los Cerezos 62, 5°, izquierda. Your phone number there is 91 412 30 88. Read the dialogue and then use the information to write a similar conversation between you and the taxi company attendant.

More uses of **para** in the dialogue above: **para ir** (*in order to go*), **¿Para qué hora ...?** (*For what time?*). Note also the emphatic use of **mismo** in **ahora mismo** (*right now*), as in **hoy/mañana mismo** (*today/tomorrow without fail*), **aquí mismo** (*right here*), **yo mismo/a** (*I myself*, m/f).

How do you say it?

CHANGING MONEY

Quería cambiar (dólares) a (euros).	*I'd like to change (dollars) into (euros).*
¿A cuánto/cómo está el cambio?	*What's the rate of exchange?*

HIRING A CAR

Quería/Queríamos alquilar un coche/carro or auto. (LAm)	*I/We would like to hire a car.*
para una semana/tres días/el fin de semana.	*for a week/three days/the weekend.*
¿Cuánto es/cuesta el alquiler?	*How much is the rental?*
¿Está incluido el seguro/IVA?	*Is insurance/VAT included?*
¿Va con gasolina o gasóleo?	*Does it run on petrol or diesel?*

REQUESTING A SERVICE ON THE PHONE

Quería un taxi/hacer un pedido/encargar algo para cenar.	*I'd like a taxi/to place an order/to order something for dinner.*
¿Para qué hora lo quiere?	*What time do you want it for?*

¿Me lo puede enviar ahora mismo/a las 9:00?	*Can you send it (to me) right now/ at nine?*
¿Qué dirección tiene?/ ¿Cuál es su dirección?	*What's your address?*
¿Me dice su nombre/dirección/ (número de) teléfono/(número de) habitación?	*Will you tell me your name/ address/telephone number/room number?*

In formal and official situations you may hear questions like the following: **¿su nombre/apellido/dirección/teléfono/email, por favor?** (*your name/surname/address/telephone number/email, please?*).

 ## Language discovery

1 ME, TE, LE …: INDIRECT OBJECT PRONOUNS

In Unit 8 you learned to use words such as **me** and **le/s** in phrases such as **¿Cómo le quedan?** (*How do they fit (you)?*), **Me quedan bien** (*They fit (me) well*). This unit brings in further examples of their use, which also include **nos**.

¿Me permite (from **permitir** *to allow*) **su pasaporte?**	*Will you let me have your passport? (literally, Allow me your passport.)*
¿Me dice su nombre?	*Will you tell me your name …?*
¿Me lo/la puede enviar …?	*Can you send it (to me …)?*
¿Qué nos recomienda?	*What do you recommend (to us)?*
Les recomiendo el Ford Fiesta.	*I recommend (to you) the Ford Fiesta.*

As explained in Unit 8, **me**, **te**, **le**, etc. are part of a set of words known 'technically' as indirect object pronouns, the full set being:

Singular	Plural
me *(to/for) me*	**nos** *(to/for) us*
te *(to/for) you* (informal)	**os** *(to/for) you* (informal)
le *(to/for) you/him/her/it*	**les** *(to/for) you/them*

Here are some further examples of their use:

¿Puede recomendarnos/sugerirnos un hotel/restaurante? (or ¿Nos puede recomendar/sugerir …?)	*Can you recommend/suggest a hotel/restaurant?*

| ¿Qué nos sugiere? | *What do you suggest?* |
| **Les sugiero el hotel/restaurante Don Sancho.** | *I suggest the hotel/restaurant Don Sancho.* |

2 ORDER OF OBJECT PRONOUNS

In a sentence with two object pronouns, one indirect, for example **me**, and the other direct, for example **lo** (see Unit 8), the indirect object pronoun must come first. The following examples illustrate this point:

¿Me puede enviar el taxi ahora mismo?	*Can you send me the taxi right now?*
¿Lo puede enviar ahora mismo?	*Can you send it right now?*
¿Me lo puede enviar ahora mismo? or **¿Puede enviármelo ...?**	*Can you send it to me right now?*

3 SE *IN PLACE OF* LE, LES

Le and **les** become **se** before **lo**, **la**, **los**, **las**, as shown in the examples below.

Le/Les recomiendo esta excursión.	*I recommend this excursion (to you).*
La recomiendo.	*I recommend it.*
Se la recomiendo.	*I recommend it (to you).*
¿Le/Les envío un taxi ahora?	*Shall I send a taxi for you now?*
¿Lo envío ahora?	*Shall I send it now?*
¿Se lo envío ahora?	*Shall I send it to you now?*

Practice

1 Cambiando dinero *Changing money*

09.04

la moneda	*currency*
la cantidad	*amount*
la corona sueca	*Swedish crown*
la libra (esterlina)	*pound (sterling)*

You'll hear three people changing money into euros. What's the rate for each currency and how much money is each person changing?

Moneda	Cambio	Cantidad
1	libras	
2	francos suizos	
3	coronas suecas	

2 Cambio *Change*

You are at a bureau de change in Mexico – 'una casa de cambio' – changing some money into pesos. Fill in the gaps in the conversation between you and the employee. You are staying at Calle Vergara 640, 6°, C.

la casa de cambio (LAm) (in Spain, **una oficina de cambio**)	*bureau de change*
el billete	*banknote*

Tú	_____ dólares a pesos.¿ _____?
Empleado	¿ _____ billetes?
Tú	No, tengo cheques _____
Empleado	_____ catorce pesos por dólar. ¿Cuánto quiere _____ ?
Tú	*Say you'd like to change two hundred dollars.*
Empleado	Muy bien.
Tú	Y el cambio _____ la libra, ¿ _____?
Empleado	La libra _____ veintiún pesos.
Tú	*Say you'd like to change a hundred and eighty pounds.*
Empleado	¿ _____ dirección _____ en México?
Tú	_____ .

La moneda oficial, *official currency*, de México es el peso. El peso es también la moneda oficial en Argentina, Chile, Colombia, Cuba, República Dominicana y Uruguay. Otras monedas latinoamericanas son: el boliviano en Bolivia, el colón en Costa Rica, el dólar en Ecuador, el colón y el dólar en El Salvador, el quetzal en Guatemala, la lempira en Honduras, el córdoba en Nicaragua, el balboa y el dólar en Panamá, el guaraní en Paraguay, el sol en Perú, y el bolívar en Venezuela.

3 Con cheque *By cheque*

cuándo	*when*
a ser posible	*if possible*
en efectivo	*cash*

Fill in the gaps in this conversation with one of the following pronouns: lo, me, le.

Clienta	Quería alquilar un coche pequeño. ¿Cuál _____ recomienda Vd.?
Empleado	_____ recomiendo este. Es pequeño y económico. ¿Para cuándo _____ quiere Vd.?
Clienta	Quisiera llevar _____ mañana a ser posible. ¿Puedo pagar el alquiler con cheque?
Empleado	Sí, puede pagar _____ con cheque, con tarjeta de crédito o en efectivo.

4 Ahora tú *And now you*

You and a travelling companion want to hire a car. What questions would you ask to get the following replies? Some of the questions allow more than one alternative.

a ¿Un coche económico? Les recomiendo este.
b El alquiler cuesta treinta euros por día.
c Sí, el seguro obligatorio está incluido.
d No, los impuestos no están incluidos.
e Va con gasolina.
f Sí, claro, pueden pagar con tarjeta de crédito.
g Sí, por supuesto, lo pueden llevar ahora mismo.

Claro and **por supuesto** certainly, of course, have the same meaning, the second expression being more emphatic than the first. Spanish seems to make more use of such words than English, especially **claro** which is sometimes repeated for more emphasis: **Sí, claro, claro.**

5 ¿Cómo se dice? *How do you say it?*

el periódico	*newspaper*
dar	*to give*

It is your last day at your holiday hotel and you phone reception to request certain things for you and your partner. Use the 'nosotros' form for verbs and pronouns.

a We'd like breakfast in the room, please. We are in room 12.

b Can you send it to us right now? We want one tea and one coffee, a pineapple juice and an orange juice, and wholemeal bread, please.

c Can you send us an English newspaper?

d We'd also like a taxi to go to the airport.

e The plane leaves at 12.30. We want it for half past ten.

f (You are ready to leave and you want the bill.) Will you give us the bill, please? We'd like to pay with a credit card.

6 Crucigrama *Crossword*

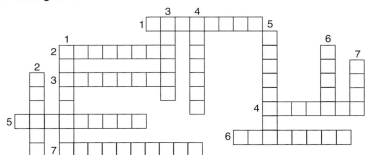

Horizontales (*Across*)

1 Puede pagar con cheque o en _____ .

2 Queremos _____ un coche.

3 (Yo) _____ llevarlo mañana.

4 ¿Puedo pagar con _____ de crédito?

5 El seguro y los impuestos no están _____ .

6 Va con _____ .

7 Le _____ este coche. Es estupendo.

Verticales (*Down*)

1 ¿Cuánto cuesta el _____ de este coche?

2 ¿A _____ está el cambio del dólar?

3 ¿Puede _____ los cheques, por favor?

4 Quería _____ cien euros.

5 ¿Tiene cheques o _____ ?

6 ¿Puedo pagar con cheques de _____ ?

7 ¿Hay una _____ de cambio por aquí? (LAm)

? Test yourself

Put the words in the right order to make up meaningful sentences:

a ¿está – cambio – a – el – cuánto?

b ir – taxi – queríamos – para – un – la – a – estación

c ¿lo – qué – hora – quiere – para?

d ¿mismo – enviar – lo – ahora – puede – me?

e ¿nombre – dice – su – me?

f lo – en seguida – envío – se

g coche – fin de semana – alquilar – quería – un – el – para

h (1) excelente – un – es – coche (2) se – recomiendo – lo

i doscientas – quería – euros – a – libras – cambiar

j ¿tiene – qué – Barcelona – en – dirección?

An important point in this test is the correct use of pronouns such as me, se, la, los, and their position within the sentence. Did you get them right? If you are uncertain about their use, check the Language Discovery notes in the unit again or study section 9 of the Grammar summary.

SELF CHECK

I CAN...
○ . . . change money
○ . . . hire a car
○ . . . request a service on the phone.

10 ¿Cuántos años tienes?

How old are you?

In this unit you will learn how to:

▶ *talk about yourself and your family*
▶ *describe places*
▶ *make comparisons.*

CEFR: *Can ask for and provide personal information (A2); Can describe his/her family (A2); Can describe places, a job or study experience (A2); Can write about everyday aspects of his/her environment (A2).*

Family life

Family structure has changed a lot in Spain and **los padres divorciados** (*the divorced parents*) and **la madre soltera** (*the single mother*) are as common as elsewhere. But **la familia** (*the family*) remains the most important social unit and extends beyond **los padres** (*the parents*) and **los hijos** (*the children*) to **los abuelos** (*the grandparents*), **los tíos** (*the uncles and aunts*), **los primos** (*the cousins*) and all the relations through marriage. Family members often live close to one another so family gatherings can be quite big affairs.

City dwellers whose family roots are in the country will talk about **mi pueblo** (*my village*). Even though no family member lives there any more, they may have a holiday home there or, at the very least, return in the summer for **la fiesta del pueblo**, another excuse for a big family reunion.

 What is Luis telling you: Soy hijo único pero tengo muchos primos.

Conversations

1 TENGO DOS HIJOS *I HAVE TWO CHILDREN*

10.01

los hijos	*children*
los padres	*parents*
los hermanos	*brothers and sisters*
joven	*young*
el/la hermano/a	*brother/sister*
el/la más pequeño/a	*the youngest*

Pablo and her new colleague María talk about themselves and their families.

1.1 **Listen to the conversation several times and say whether the statements which follow are true or false ('verdaderos o falsos'). Note the use of 'tener' (*to have*) to talk about someone's age.**

a María has an eight year old daughter and a six year old son.

b Pablo is single.

c He lives with his family.

d He has two younger brothers.

Pablo	Estás casada, ¿verdad?
María	Sí, estoy casada. Tengo dos hijos. El mayor, Gonzalo, tiene ocho años y la menor, Laura, tiene seis. Tú estás soltero, ¿no?
Pablo	Sí, vivo con mis padres y mis hermanos.
María	Eres muy joven. ¿Cuántos años tienes?
Pablo	Tengo veintidós años.
María	¿Cuántos hermanos tienes?
Pablo	Tengo dos, un hermano y una hermana. Yo soy el más pequeño.

1.2 **Now read the dialogue and say how the following is expressed:**

a You're married, aren't you?

b You are single, aren't you?

c I'm twenty-two years old.

d the eldest/the youngest.

To ask someone how old he or she is use **tener** (*to have*): **¿Cuántos años tienes?** (*How old are you?* – literally, *How many years do you have?*).

To say how old you are use **tengo**: **Tengo cuarenta años** (*I'm forty years old*).

nuevo/a	*new*
el/la tuyo/a	*yours* (inf)
ruidoso/a	*noisy*
buenos acabados	*high finish*
equipado/a	*fitted*
reformado/a	*converted*
el aseo	*toilet*
jto. (junto a)	*next to*

10.02

Pablo and María describe their homes and neighbourhoods.

2.1 **Here are some words you may need when talking about the place where you live and your neighbourhood. How many of them can you recognize? Check their meaning before you listen to the dialogue and answer the questions below:**

el baño   el barrio   la calefacción   la cocina   la habitación   el piso   el salón

Note also the following expressions: **¿Qué tal ...?** (*What is ... like?*), **más ... que** (*more ... than*), **tan ... como** (*as ... as*).

   a How does María describe her flat?
   b How does she describe the area where she lives?
   c How does Pablo describe his own flat?

Pablo	¿Qué tal tu nuevo piso?
María	No está mal. Tiene cuatro habitaciones, un gran salón, cocina equipada, dos baños y mucho sol.
Pablo	Es bastante grande. ¿Y qué tal el barrio?
María	Es muy bueno y es más tranquilo que el centro.
Pablo	Mi barrio es bastante ruidoso y el piso no es tan grande como el tuyo, pero es muy cómodo. Tiene tres habitaciones, un salón, una cocina grande, calefacción individual ...

To say what a place is like use **ser**: **Es pequeño/a** (*It is small*), **Son modernos/as** (*They are modern*). **Ser** is also used to say what someone is like: **Eres muy joven** (*You are very young*). In the question **¿Qué tal (es) tu nuevo piso?** the verb **ser** is understood.

2.2 **Read the dialogue and say which of the flats advertised below fits in:**

   a María's description
   b Pablo's description

RONDA
SAN ANTONIO

2 hab. salón, cocina y aseo.

200.000 €

GENOVA
V. MONTSERRAT

Luminoso, sol, 3 hab. salón, gran cocina, baño nuevo, calef. indiv. buenos acabados.

280.000 €

GRACIA
T. VIDALET

Todo reformado, alto, mucho sol, gran salón, 4 hab. cocina equip. y 2 baños.

330.000 €

COLLBLANCH
JTO METRO

Muy tranquilo, sol, 3 hab. gran salón, coc. y baño completo.

250.500 €

La casa, **el piso**, **el apartamento**. Peninsular Spanish uses three main words to describe a dwelling: **la casa** (*house* or *home*), **el piso** (*flat* or *apartment*), and **el apartamento**, used to name a smaller flat or apartment, such as holiday apartments. The word for a flat or apartment in Latin America is **el departamento**, or **el apartamento** in some regions. **La habitación** means *room*, but it is also used to designate *bedroom*: **esta es mi habitación** (*this is my bedroom*). A more specific word for bedroom is **el dormitorio**: **un piso de dos dormitorios** (*a two-bedroom flat*).

How do you say it?

TALKING ABOUT YOURSELF AND YOUR FAMILY

a Marital status

¿Estás/Está Vd. soltero(a) o casado(a)?	*Are you single or married?*
Estoy soltero(a)/casado(a)/ divorciado(a)/separado(a).	*I'm single/married/ divorced/separated.*

b Family

¿Tienes/Tiene Vd. hijos/ hermanos?	*Have you got children/brothers and sisters?*
¿Cuántos hijos/hermanos tienes /tiene Vd.?	*How many children/brothers and sisters do you have?*
Tengo un(a) hijo(a)/un(a) hermano(a).	*I have one son/daughter/one brother/sister.*

c Age

¿Cuántos años tienes/tiene Vd.?	*How old are you?*
¿Qué edad tienes/tiene Vd.?	*What age are you?*
Tengo veintidós (años).	*I'm twenty-two (years old).*
Él/Ella tiene ocho años.	*He/She is eight years old.*

d Describing places

Es un piso muy/bastante grande/bueno/cómodo.	*It's a very/quite a large/good/ comfortable flat.*
Tiene dos habitaciones/baños.	*It has two rooms/bathrooms.*

e Making comparisons

Es más tranquilo/caro que el centro.	*It's quieter/more expensive than the centre.*
No es tan grande/pequeño como el tuyo/el de María.	*It's not as large/small as yours/ María's.*

 Language discovery

1 EXPRESSING MARITAL STATUS: 'ESTAR' AND 'SER'

Marital status, **el estado civil**, is normally expressed with **estar**, which signals a state. But to define someone as being a single, married or divorced person, use **ser**. Words denoting marital status change for gender (m/f) and number (sing/pl).

Está casada con Víctor.	*She's married to Victor.*
Todavía está soltero.	*He's still single.*
Están divorciados.	*They're divorced.*
Es una mujer casada/un hombre casado.	*She's a married woman/He's a married man.*

2 EXPRESSING AGE

Age, **la edad**, is expressed with **tener**, but to define someone as being young, old, etc., use **ser**.

Tengo cuarenta años.	*I'm forty years old.*
¿Cuántos años/Qué edad tiene tu padre/madre?	*How old/What age is your father/ mother?*
Es una persona muy joven/mayor.	*He/She's a very young/old person.*

3 WORDS FOR RELATIVES

The masculine plural form of words referring to people such as **el padre** (*father*), **el hijo** (*son*), **el hermano** (*brother*) can refer to members of both sexes: **los padres** (*parents*), **los hijos** (*children*), **los hermanos** (*brothers and sisters*). Likewise with **el tío** (*uncle*), **el primo** (*cousin*), **el nieto** (*grandson*), **el suegro** (*father-in-law*). Note that **los parientes** means *relatives*.

A good way to increase your vocabulary is to look up words classified according to theme. Here are some more words for relatives in Spanish. What do they mean?: **el/la cuñado/a**, **el/la abuelo/a**, **el yerno**, **la nuera**, **el padrino**, **la madrina**, **el/la ahijado/a**.

4 DESCRIBING

a   To describe something or someone in terms of its or his/her characteristics, use **ser**.

Es un barrio excelente.	*It's an excellent area.*
Son pisos caros.	*They are expensive flats.*
Eres muy joven.	*You are very young.*

b   To describe something or someone in terms of a state or condition at a certain point in time, use **estar**.

La casa está limpia/tranquila.	*The house is (looks) clean/is quiet (now).*
María está contenta con su piso.	*María is happy with her flat.*

5 MAKING COMPARISONS

a   To say that something is smaller, more expensive, etc. than something else, or that someone is prettier, more intelligent, etc. than someone else, use **más ... (que).**

Madrid es más pequeño que Londres.	*Madrid is smaller than London.*
Este barrio es más caro.	*This area is more expensive.*
Rebeca es más guapa que Elsa.	*Rebeca is prettier than Elsa.*
Eva es más inteligente.	*Eva is more intelligent.*

Más is not needed with irregular forms:

Este hotel es mejor/peor.	*This hotel is better/worse.*
Cristina es mayor/menor que yo.	*Cristina is older/younger than I.*

Más joven (*younger*) is also correct when reference is to adults.

Mayor can also be used to refer to size:

Buenos Aires es más grande/ mayor que Santiago.	*Buenos Aires is bigger than Santiago.*

b   To say that something is the cheapest, the most comfortable, etc., or that someone is the nicest, the most efficient, etc., use **el/la/los/las más** + *adjective*.

Este hostal es el más barato/cómodo.	*This boarding house is the cheapest/most comfortable.*
Sara es la más simpática/ eficiente.	*Sara is the nicest/most efficient.*

Más is not needed with irregular forms:

Mi apartamento es el mejor/peor.   *My apartment is the best/worst.*

Elvira es la mayor/menor de todas. *Elvira is the oldest/youngest of all.*

Mayor can also refer to size:

México es el mayor país de habla hispana.

or

Es el más grande de los países   *Mexico is the largest Spanish-*
de habla hispana.   *speaking country.*

c   To say that something or someone is as interesting as, as quiet as something or someone else, use **tan ... como.**

Nueva York es tan interesante   *New York is as interesting as*
como Londres.   *London.*

Delia es tan tranquila   *Delia is as quiet as her sister.*
como su hermana.

Pronunciation

 10.03

rr, as in **ba<u>rr</u>io**, **pe<u>rr</u>o**, is strongly rolled.

r, after **n, l** and **s** – for example **En<u>r</u>ique**, **al<u>r</u>ededor** (*around*), **Is<u>r</u>ael** – and at the beginning of a word – for example **<u>R</u>onda**, **<u>r</u>osa** – is also strongly rolled, and is pronounced like **rr**.

r, between vowels, as in **ca<u>r</u>o**, **pe<u>r</u>o**, is much softer and closer to the English 'r' in *very*.

Practise with:

Enrique y Rosa viven en un barrio muy caro de Tarragona.

Sara vive en Gerona.

Ramón y Carmen tienen un apartamento en Sanlúcar de Barrameda.

It is important that you are able to produce the two sounds above – the strongly rolled **rr** and **r** and the softer one – as these can differentiate meanings. Practise with the following pairs of words: **perro – pero, cerro – cero, carro – caro, parra – para, correa – Corea.**

Practice

1 Mi familia y yo *My family and I*

contar (o>ue)	*to tell*
sobre	*about*
la abuela	*grandmother*
va a cumplir	*she's going to be*
después	*then*
venir	*to come*

In his first letter to a correspondent Ricardo wrote about himself and his family. Can you fill in the gaps with the missing words?

> Querida Pat:
>
> ¡Hola! Como esta es mi primera carta, quiero contarte algo sobre mí y mi familia. Me **(a)** _____ Ricardo Gutiérrez, **(b)** _____ veintiún años, **(c)** _____ soltero, y **(d)** _____ con mi madre, mis tres hermanos y mi abuela. Mis **(e)** _____ están divorciados.
>
> Yo soy el **(f)** _____ de los cuatro hermanos. El segundo se **(g)** _____ Javier y **(h)** _____ diecinueve años, después viene Carmen, **(i)** _____ tiene dieciséis, y la **(j)** _____ es mi hermana Isabel, que va a cumplir catorce.

2 Ricardo y su familia *Ricardo and his family*

How would you tell someone else about Ricardo? Begin like this: 'Se llama Ricardo Gutiérrez ...'

3 Me llamo Luisa ... *My name is Luisa*

Look at this family tree. How would Luisa write about herself and her family?

Luisa, 45 — Pedro, 47

Teresa, 23 — Raquel, 20 — Felipe, 17

4 Estoy casado *I'm married*

10.04

el/la ingeniero/a	engineer
mi mujer	my wife
el/la abogado/a	lawyer
¿con quién?	with whom?

You'll hear two people, Rodrigo and Rosa, giving information about themselves and their families. Listen and answer these questions:

a ¿Cuántos años tiene Rodrigo?

b ¿Cuántos hijos tiene?

c ¿Cuántos años tiene el mayor? ¿Y la menor?

d ¿Cuántos años tiene su mujer?

e ¿Qué edad tiene Rosa?

f ¿Cuál es su estado civil?

g ¿Con quién vive?

5 Ahora tú *And now you*

¿Cómo te llamas? ¿Cuántos años tienes? ¿Estás casado(a) o soltero(a)? ¿Cómo se llama tu marido/mujer? ¿Cuántos años tiene? ¿Tienes hijos/hermanos? ¿Cómo se llaman? ¿Cuántos años tienen?

6 Un nuevo piso *A new flat*

No te imaginas lo contenta ...!	You can't imagine how happy ...!
la luz	light
exterior	facing the street
dar a	to give onto
además	besides
¡qué lástima!	what a pity!

Elena has moved into a new flat and, in an email, she describes it to her friend Roberto. Read this extract from her email and then answer the questions which follow.

Hola Roberto:

¡No te imaginas lo contenta que estoy! Tengo un nuevo piso. Es estupendo, mucho mejor que el anterior y más barato. Tiene dos dormitorios y un salón bastante grande, con mucha luz. Es exterior y da a una pequeña plaza. El barrio es muy tranquilo y la calle donde vivo no tiene mucho tráfico. Además, tiene calefacción y garaje, pero no tiene terraza. ¡Una lástima! Pero está muy cerca del metro. Tienes que venir. Es muy fácil llegar aquí ...

---

a ¿Cuántos dormitorios tiene el piso de Elena?

b ¿Qué tal es?

c ¿Cómo es el barrio?

d ¿Qué servicios tiene?

The email above is a good model to describe the place where you live in Activity 8 below. Go back through it again and note the use of **ser**, **estar** and **tener** and the expression **Tienes que venir** (*You have to come*). To say I have to do something, use **tengo que ...: Tengo que trabajar** (*I have to work*).

7 ¿Cuál es el mejor? *Which is the best?*

el precio	*price*
el tamaño	*size*
la comodidad	*comfort*
la tranquilidad	*peace*
la situación	*location*

You've been posted to a Spanish-speaking country and are looking for a place to live. You've made notes about two flats you've seen, rating them from 0 to 5, with 5 being the most convenient for you. Write sentences comparing the two flats, using the words in brackets. The first one has been done for you.

	calle Lorca	avenida Salvador
precio	1	3
tamaño	5	3
situación	2	5
comodidad	4	4
seguridad	2	0
tranquilidad	3	3

a (barato) El piso de la avenida Salvador es más barato que el (piso) de la calle Lorca.	**d (cómodo)**
b (grande)	**e (seguro)**
c (céntrico)	**f (tranquilo)**

8 Ahora tú *And now you*

Can you describe the place where you live and your neighbourhood? Use the email in Activity 6 as a model.

 Test yourself

1 Fill in the blanks with the appropriate form of 'ser', 'estar' or 'tener'.

Me llamo Carmen, **(a)** _____ treinta años, **(b)** _____ casada y **(c)** _____ tres hijos. El más pequeño **(d)** _____ Benjamín, que **(e)** _____ cinco años. Nuestra casa **(f)** _____ en un barrio muy tranquilo. **(g)** _____ un barrio muy bueno. La casa no **(h)** _____ grande, pero **(i)** _____ bastante cómoda. (Yo) **(j)** _____ muy contenta con nuestra casa.

2 How would you say the following in Spanish?
  a Mónica's house is bigger than my house.
  b This hotel is better than the other.
  c Pablo is younger than his brother.
  d London is more expensive than Los Angeles.
  e María is the prettiest and the most intelligent.
  f Barcelona is as interesting as Madrid.

Test 1 assesses your knowledge of three very important verbs: ser, estar and tener. If you are still uncertain about the first two, go to section 26 of the Grammar summary for more information and examples of their use. For a revision of comparisons, which is the focus of Test 2, check section 6 of the Grammar summary.

SELF CHECK

I CAN. . .
. . . talk about myself and my family
. . . describe places
. . . make comparisons.

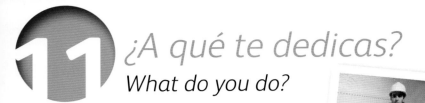

11 ¿A qué te dedicas?

What do you do?

In this unit you will learn how to:
- ▶ *say what you do for a living*
- ▶ *say what hours and days you work*
- ▶ *say how long you have been doing something (1).*

CEFR: *Can say what he/she does (A2);*
Can give a simple description of working conditions (A2); Can find specific information in advertisements (A2); Can write about job or study experience (A2).

The world of work

El paro (*unemployment*) is a serious problem in Spain, especially for young people who, even if they are **licenciados** (*graduates*) and speak a number of languages, do not find **un trabajo** (*a job/work*) easily in their own country.

When they do find one, **el horario** (*the working hours*) are long. According to surveys, Spaniards spend more of their lives working than their European counterparts. It is not unusual for office workers to be at their desks **a las ocho y media** (*at half past eight*) and not leave until **las siete o las ocho** (*seven or eight o'clock*). Shop workers have even longer hours, **hasta las nueve** (*until nine o'clock*). For those who are **autónomos** (*self-employed*) or who work in **la empresa familiar** (*the family business*), there is no such thing as **un horario fijo** (*fixed working hours*).

What are these people saying about their work?
a   Trabajo muchas horas, de ocho a ocho.
b   No tengo trabajo, estoy en paro.

Conversations

el/la estudiante	*student*
desde hace dos años	*for two years*
el colegio	*school*
la actriz/el actor	*actress/actor*

11.01

A group of people attending a conference talk about each other's occupations.

1.1 **Listen to Elena and Álvaro first. Can you say what they do? Two key phrases here are:**

¿A qué te dedicas? and **¿Qué haces?** *What do you do (for a living)?*

Elena	¿A qué te dedicas, Álvaro?
Álvaro	Soy estudiante.
Elena	¿Qué estudias?
Álvaro	Estudio historia. Y tú, ¿qué haces?
Elena	Soy enfermera. Trabajo en un hospital.
Álvaro	¿Cuánto tiempo hace que trabajas allí?
Elena	Trabajo allí desde hace dos años.

Note the special use of **hacer** (*to make, to do*) with an expression of time and a verb in the present tense to say how long you have been doing something: **Trabajo allí desde hace dos años** (*I've been working there for two years*).

1.2 **Now listen to Cristóbal, Cristina and Ángeles tell Rafael what they do. Who is:**
   1 a journalist?
   2 a teacher?
   3 an out-of-work actress?

Rafael	¿Qué haces tú, Cristóbal?
Cristóbal	Soy profesor. Doy clases de inglés en un colegio.
Rafael	Y tú, Cristina, ¿a qué te dedicas?
Cristina	Yo soy periodista, pero estoy jubilada.
Rafael	¿Y tú, Ángeles?
Ángeles	Soy actriz, pero estoy sin trabajo.

1.3 **Now read the dialogues and identify the phrases which mean the following:**

1 What are you studying?
2 I work in a hospital.
3 How long have you been working there?
4 I teach English.
5 I'm retired.
6 I'm out of work.

2 ¿QUÉ HORARIO TIENES? *WHAT ARE YOUR WORKING HOURS?*

el horario (de trabajo)	*working hours, timetable*
de ... a	*from ... to*
las vacaciones	*holiday*
al año	*a/per year*
el horario fijo	*fixed working hours*

11.02

*Hernán, **un técnico en informática** (a computer expert), and Sol, **una traductora** (a translator), talk about their working hours.*

2.1 **Listen and answer the following questions:**

1 What hours does Hernán work?
2 How many weeks' holiday does he have?
3 Where does Sol work?

Sol	¿Qué horario de trabajo tienes?
Hernán	Trabajo de ocho y media a una, y de dos y media a seis y media de la tarde, de lunes a viernes. Los sábados no trabajo.
Sol	¿Cuántas semanas de vacaciones tienes al año?
Hernán	Tengo tres semanas. Y tu horario, ¿cuál es?
Sol	No tengo horario fijo. Soy traductora y trabajo en casa. Pero trabajo muchas horas.

2.2 Find in the conversation the Spanish for:

1 What hours do you work?
2 I don´t have fixed working hours.

2.3 Use the following information about Isabel, a librarian, and Hugo, a shop assistant, to write a similar dialogue.

Isabel, bibliotecaria:	9:00–17:00, lunes a viernes 10:00–14:00, sábados un mes de vacaciones
Hugo, dependiente:	9:00–14:00/16:00–19:00, lunes a sábado

Traditional work hours in Spain and Latin America, especially in smaller places, include a two to three-hour break for lunch, allowing people to go home and escape from the midday heat, especially in summer. Most businesses remain closed during this period, re-opening about 16.30 or even 17.00 and closing around 19.30 or 20.00.

How do you say it?

SAYING WHAT YOU DO FOR A LIVING

¿A qué te dedicas/se dedica Vd.?	What do you do for a living?
¿Qué haces/hace Vd.?	What do you do?
Soy ingeniero(a)/secretario(a)/ estudiante.	I'm an engineer/a secretary/ student.
Trabajo en una fábrica/para una empresa.	I work in a factory/for a company.
Estudio lenguas/español/arte.	I'm studying languages/Spanish/art.
Estoy sin trabajo/en paro.	I'm out of work/unemployed.
Estoy jubilado(a).	I'm retired.

SAYING WHAT HOURS AND DAYS YOU WORK AND WHAT HOLIDAYS YOU HAVE

a   The hours and days you work:

¿Qué horario (de trabajo) tienes/tiene Vd.?	*What are your working hours/is your timetable?*
¿Cuál es tu/su horario?	*What's your timetable?*
Trabajo de 9:00 a 5:00, de lunes a viernes.	*I work from 9.00 to 5.00, from Monday to Friday.*

| **No trabajo los sábados/Los sábados no trabajo.** | *I don't work on Saturdays.* |
| **Tengo clases de 9:00 a 1:00.** | *I have classes from 9.00 to 1.00.* |

b Your holidays:

| **¿Cuántas semanas de vacaciones tienes/tiene Vd.?** | *How many weeks' holiday do you have?* |
| **Tengo tres semanas/un mes.** | *I have three weeks/a month.* |

SAYING HOW LONG YOU HAVE BEEN DOING SOMETHING

| **¿Cuánto tiempo hace que trabaja(s)/vive(s) aquí?** | *How long have you been working/ living here?* |
| **Trabajo/Vivo aquí desde hace un año.** Or **Hace un año que trabajo/vivo aquí.** | *I've been working/living here for a year.* |

Language discovery

1 OMISSION OF *A*, WITH PROFESSIONS AND OCCUPATIONS

To say what your job is, you need the verb **ser** (*to be*), followed directly by the occupation or profession. The Spanish for *a*, as in *a plumber*, is not used in this context.

Soy fontanero/plomero (L.Am.).	*I'm a plumber.*
Soy pintor/a.	*I'm a painter.*
Soy fotógrafo/a.	*I'm a photographer.*

Note that the omission of **a** does not apply if you use a descriptive word before or after the profession or occupation: **Es un buen profesor** (*He's a good teacher*), **Es una estudiante muy inteligente** (*She's a very intelligent student*). This same rule applies to verbs other than **ser**: **Necesito un médico** (*I need a doctor*).

2 'HACE' WITH A TIME PHRASE AND THE PRESENT TENSE

To ask someone how long he or she has been doing something, use the following construction: **¿Cuánto tiempo hace que** + present tense?

| **¿Cuánto tiempo hace que estudias/estudia Vd. español?** | *How long have you been studying Spanish?* |

To reply use either of the following constructions: **Hace** + *time phrase* + **que** + present tense, *or* present tense + **desde hace** + time phrase.

Hace seis meses que estudio español. Or **Estudio español desde hace seis meses.**	*I've been studying Spanish for six months.*

These constructions, which help to establish a link between the present and the past, can refer not just to an action, as above, but also to a state.

¿Cuánto tiempo hace que estás/está Vd. en España?	*How long have you been in Spain?*
Hace diez años que estoy en España. Or **Estoy en España desde hace diez años.**	*I've been in Spain for ten years.*

In short replies, use phrases like the following:

hace una semana/un mes/año	*for a week/month/year*
desde hace mucho tiempo	*for a very long time*

3 *MORE PREPOSITIONS:* **A, DE, DESDE, EN, PARA, SIN**

¿A qué te dedicas?	*What do you do for a living?*
dedicarse a	literally, *to devote oneself to*
al año/mes/día, a la semana	*per year/month/day, per week*
de 8:00 a 1:00	*from 8.00 to 1.00*
dar clases de inglés	*to teach English*
una semana de vacaciones	*a week's holiday*
desde hace un siglo	*for a century*
trabajo en una tienda/en casa	*I work in a shop/at home*
trabajo para una empresa	*I work for a company*
estar sin trabajo	*to be without a job or work*

Pronunciation

11.03

h, as in **h**ace, is silent.
ch, as in o**ch**o, is pronounced like the 'ch' in *chair*.

Practise with:

Hace ocho años que Charo trabaja en Chile. Héctor trabaja desde las ocho de la mañana hasta las nueve de la noche.

Practice

1 Palabra por palabra *Word for word*

escribo (from **escribir**)	*I write*
hago (from **hacer**)	*I make*
conduzco (from **conducir**)	*I drive*
reparto (from **repartir**)	*I deliver*

Can you match each occupation with the most likely activity?

a	Soy médico/a.	**1**	Doy clases en un colegio.
b	Soy azafata.	**2**	Tengo una industria.
c	Soy conductor/a.	**3**	Escribo artículos para una revista.
d	Soy profesor/a.	**4**	Trabajo en un hospital.
e	Soy dependiente/a.	**5**	Hago muebles.
f	Soy cartero/a.	**6**	Conduzco camiones.
g	Soy periodista.	**7**	Reparto cartas.
h	Soy abogado/a.	**8**	Vendo ropa en una tienda.
i	Soy carpintero/a.	**9**	Trabajo en una línea aérea.
j	Soy empresario/a.	**10**	Trabajo en un tribunal.

Here's a chance to increase your vocabulary even further. Draw a list of other occupations and professions and look them up in your dictionary.

2 ¿A qué se dedica? *What does he/she do for a living?*

What might the following people say with regard to their work? Match the drawings with the sentences below.

1 Soy muy rico y no necesito trabajar.
2 Tengo ochenta años y estoy jubilada.
3 Soy ama de casa.
4 No tengo trabajo.

3 ¿Qué hace Alfonso? *What does Alfonso do?*

11.04

el turno (de la mañana)	*(morning) shift*
¿es igual?	*is it the same?*
porque	*because*
durante	*during*

Alfonso talks about his occupation. Listen and answer the questions below.

   a ¿Qué hace Alfonso?
   b ¿Cuánto tiempo hace que trabaja allí?
   c ¿Cuáles son los horarios de trabajo?
   d ¿Qué turno prefiere?
   e ¿Cuántos días de vacaciones tiene?

4 Busco trabajo *I'm looking for work*

ESO (Enseñanza Secundaria Obligatoria)	*compulsory secondary education*
el título	*degree*
particular	*private*
cuidar	*to look after*
licenciado/a	*graduate*
cualquier	*any*
segundo de bachillerato	*second year of secondary education*

Look at these advertisements placed by people offering their services. Who wants to do the following work? Give their names.

   a receptionist or secretary
   b company psychologist
   c childminder
   d waiter
   e teacher and translator
   f shop assistant

Profesor de ESO, con título de inglés a nivel Proficiency, da clases particulares y traduce artículos. Eugenio, Tel. 91 543 02 91, Madrid.

Busco trabajo cuidando niños por las mañanas. Llamar a partir de las 21 horas. María Ángeles, Tel. 91 942 30 56, Madrid.

Tengo 20 años y busco trabajo sólo por las mañanas o por las tardes como recepcionista, secretaria o puesto similar. Mónica, Tel. 93 208 45 83, Barcelona.

Licenciada en psicología en la especialidad industrial, busca trabajo como psicóloga preferentemente en una empresa, en cualquier ciudad de España. Victoria, Tel. 986 85 27 93, Pontevedra.

Tengo 17 años y estudio segundo de bachillerato. Quisiera trabajar por las mañanas. Tengo experiencia como dependienta. Adela, Tel. 93 782 16 74, Barcelona.

Camarero, 23 años, quiere trabajar en hotel o restaurante. Juan Carlos, Tel. 94 672 95 54, Vizcaya.

Note how some of the people who placed the advertisements used verbs in the first person singular (**yo**) while others used the third person (**él** or **ella**). Here are two examples: **Busco trabajo** (*I'm looking for work*) (1st person); **Licenciada ... busca trabajo** (*Graduate is looking for work*) (3rd person).

5 Ahora tú *And now you*

Can you write an advertisement offering your services or expertise? Use as a model the advertisements in Activity 4. Here are some key phrases:

Busco trabajo en/como ...	*I'm looking for work in/as ...*
(Estudiante) busca trabajo en/como ...	*(Student) seeks employment in/as ...*

Quiero/Quisiera trabajar	I want/would like to work
en/como ...	in/as ...
(Persona de habla inglesa)	*(English-speaking person) wants/*
quiere/quisiera trabajar	*would like to work in/as ...*
en/como ...	

6 ¿Cuánto tiempo hace ...? *How long have you ...?*

Your friend Paul has just introduced you to Carmen, who is studying English in your country and is living in your area. How would you ask her how long she has been doing each of the following, and how would she reply? Use the phrases below.

	actividad	*período de tiempo*
	estar aquí	dos meses y medio
a	estar aquí	dos meses y medio
b	estudiar inglés	dos meses
c	vivir en este barrio	tres semanas
d	conocer a Paul	un año y medio

7 Ahora tú *And now you*

Answer the questions below using real or imaginary information.

a ¿A qué te dedicas?, ¿Dónde trabajas?, ¿Cuánto tiempo hace que trabajas allí?, ¿Cuál es tu horario de trabajo?, ¿Cuántas vacaciones tienes al año?

b ¿Qué estudias?, ¿Dónde?, ¿Cuánto tiempo hace que estudias español?, ¿Qué horario de clase tienes?

El empleo en España *Employment in Spain*

The following passage gives an insight into employment in Spain. As you read the text, focus attention on the questions below. Try to get the gist of what the text says rather than translate it word for word. There are no answers in the Key to the activities for this text, as it is an exercise in developing understanding of a longer piece of writing rather than a test in itself.

a Where do most Spanish people work?

b Where do most women work?

c In what areas do most immigrants work?

el empleo	*employment*
los trabajadores (extranjeros)	*(foreign) workers*
los hombres	*men*
las mujeres	*women*

Del total de españoles con trabajo, la mayor parte trabaja en el sector servicios. El segundo lugar lo ocupa el sector industrial. El tercero lo ocupa el sector agrícola, y el cuarto lugar la construcción. Las mujeres trabajan preferentemente en el sector servicios, y en menor número en la agricultura y la industria. En la construcción, la mayoría de los trabajadores son hombres.

En España hay un gran número de trabajadores extranjeros, especialmente árabes, africanos, hispanoamericanos y también de Europa del Este, de países tales como Rumanía, Bulgaria. Estos inmigrantes trabajan preferentemente en los servicios, la agricultura, la construcción y en labores domésticas.

Unemployment in Spain has risen sharply in the last few years and is one of the highest in the European Union. The construction industry has been one of the worst affected and a large number of immigrants working in this sector have joined the dole queue. Under a special programme, the government is offering them economic incentives to return to their home countries.

Test yourself

1 **Match each question with an appropriate answer.**

a ¿A qué te dedicas?	1 De nueve a una, de lunes a viernes.
b ¿Qué hace tu marido?	2 Un año y medio.
c ¿Qué horario tienes?	3 Español y francés.
d ¿Cuántas vacaciones tienes?	4 Soy arquitecta.
e ¿Cuánto tiempo hace que vives aquí?	5 Tres semanas al año.
f ¿Qué estudias?	6 Es traductor.

2 **Each of the sentences below contains one mistake. Can you correct them?**

  a ¿A qué te dedica usted?

  b Trabajo a un colegio.

  c Hace dos años viven en Bilbao.

  d Soy periodista, pero ahora soy sin trabajo.

  e Sábados trabajo sólo por la mañana.

  f ¿Qué es tu horario?

Test 1 assesses your understanding of general information related to someone's occupation. If you got the answers right, go back through the questions again, adapt them to your own situation and answer them accordingly. Test 2 assesses your ability to handle some key grammatical points. Did you spot the mistakes in each of the sentences? Don't be discouraged if you failed in some of them. If necessary, go back through the How do you say it? and Language Discovery sections again before you start Unit 12.

SELF CHECK

	I CAN. . .
○	. . . say what I do for a living
○	. . . say what hours and days I work
○	. . . say how long I have been doing something (1).

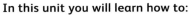

12

Me levanto a las siete

I get up at seven

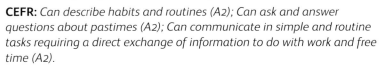

In this unit you will learn how to:

▶ *talk about things you do regularly*
▶ *say how often you do certain things.*

CEFR: *Can describe habits and routines (A2); Can ask and answer questions about pastimes (A2); Can communicate in simple and routine tasks requiring a direct exchange of information to do with work and free time (A2).*

Daily life

With long working hours, a Spaniard **se levanta temprano** (*gets up early*) and **se acuesta tarde** (*goes to bed late*), usually about midnight, for life is not all work and no play. A two-hour lunch break allows this to be the main meal of the day. **Almorzar en casa** (*to have lunch at home*) is an option for many, or else they will have **el menu del día** close to work with colleagues.

After work, time is made for an evening class, **una visita al gimnasio o a la piscina** (*a trip to the gym or the swimming pool*) and/or **unas copas con los amigos** (*drinks with friends*) before **la cena** (*the evening meal*). After this may come **el cine** (*the cinema*), **el teatro** (*the theatre*), or **un concierto** (*a concert*) before bed.

a   Where does María have lunch? Almuerzo con mis colegas en un bar cerca del trabajo.
b   What does she do after work? Siempre voy al gimnasio y los miércoles también voy a una clase de inglés.

Conversations

casi	*almost*
nunca	*never*
a veces	*sometimes*
antes	*before*
el trabajo	*work*
sobre	*about*
u	*or* (before 'o')

12.01

Joaquín, an office clerk, un administrativo, *tells Amaya about his daily routine.*

1.1 **Listen to the dialogue and, as you do, complete the sentences below. Key verbs here are:**

levantarse	*to get up*
empezar (e>ie)	*to start*
tardar	*to take (time)*
ir	*to go*
almorzar (o>ue)	*to have lunch*
salir	*to leave*
volver (o>ue)	*to come back*
acostarse (o>ue)	*to go to bed*

Levantarse *to get up* belongs to a special category of verbs whose dictionary form ends in **-se**, literally *oneself*. **Se** also stands for the third person, as in **Joaquín se levanta** ... *Joaquín gets (himself) up.* **Me** and **te** are used for **yo** and **tú** respectively. See also paragraph 4 of the Language Discovery section.

1 **Joaquín se levanta a las** _____ .

2 **Empieza a trabajar a las** _____ .

3 **Tarda casi** _____ **en llegar a** _____ .

4 **Va al trabajo en** _____ **y a veces en** _____ .

5 **Almuerza en** _____ **cerca de** _____ .

6 Sale del trabajo a las _____ y vuelve a casa sobre las _____ .

7 Nunca se acuesta antes de las _____ u _____ .

Amaya	¿A qué hora te levantas?
Joaquín	Normalmente me levanto a las siete. Empiezo a trabajar a las nueve, pero tardo casi una hora en llegar a la oficina.
Amaya	¿Cómo vas al trabajo?
Joaquín	Voy en autobús, y a veces en el coche.
Amaya	¿Y dónde almuerzas?
Joaquín	Almuerzo en un restaurante cerca de la oficina.
Amaya	¿A qué hora sales del trabajo?
Joaquín	Salgo a las cinco y vuelvo a casa sobre las seis.
Amaya	¿Te acuestas muy tarde?
Joaquín	Nunca me acuesto antes de las once u once y media.

1.2 Now read the dialogue and list the forms corresponding to each of the verbs in 1.1 above, for example 'levantarse' – 'me levanto', 'te levantas'.

1.3 How would you express the following in Spanish? Read the dialogue again if necessary before you reply.

1 I get up at a quarter past seven.

2 I start work at half past nine.

3 I go to work by train.

4 I have lunch in the office.

5 I never leave the office before half past five.

2 ¿QUÉ HACES LOS FINES DE SEMANA? *WHAT DO YOU DO AT WEEKENDS?*

suelo ... (from **soler**)	*I usually ...*
el periódico	*newspaper*
el correo (electrónico)	*email*
siempre	*always*
la novia/el novio	*girl/boyfriend*
los chicos	*children*
alguno/a	*some, a*

Joaquín and Amaya tell each other what they do at the weekends.

2.1 **Which of the activities below are mentioned by them? Listen and tick them as they come up. Note that Joaquín uses mostly the 'yo' (I) form of the verb, whose present-tense ending is normally '-o' while Amaya uses the 'nosotros/as' (we) form, ending in '-mos'.**

Joaquín ...

a se levanta tarde ☐
b escucha música ☐
c lee novelas ☐
d ve televisión ☐
e visita a sus padres ☐
f lee su correo ☐
g va al gimnasio ☐
h almuerza fuera ☐

Amaya y Ramiro...

i hacen la limpieza ☐
j hacen la compra ☐
k van a la piscina ☐
l preparan el almuerzo ☐
m echan una siesta ☐
n salen con los chicos ☐
ñ van al cine ☐
o invitan a sus padres ☐

Amaya	¿Qué haces los fines de semana?
Joaquín	Pues, suelo levantarme tarde, escucho música, leo el periódico, veo la televisión, leo mi correo ... Los sábados por la tarde voy siempre al gimnasio y por la noche suelo salir con mi novia. A veces cenamos fuera o vamos al cine o a bailar. Y vosotros, ¿qué hacéis?
Amaya	Los sábados por la mañana Ramiro y yo hacemos la limpieza y la compra, luego preparamos el almuerzo y por la tarde salimos con los chicos. Por la noche vemos alguna película en la televisión. Los domingos generalmente vamos a casa de mis padres.

2.2 **Read the dialogue several times and then, without looking at the text, try listing as many of the activities as you can remember, using the 'yo' or the 'nosotros/as' form, as appropriate. Which of them do you normally do?**

Think of other activities some people do on a regular basis and express them with the present tense or with **soler**, using the **yo** form of the verb, for example **trabajar en el ordenador** (*to work on the computer*), **conectarse a internet** (*to surf the Net*), **cocinar** (*to cook*), **hacer footing** (*to do jogging*).

How do you say it?

a Asking people what time they do certain things

¿A qué hora te levantas/se levanta Vd.?	*What time do you get up?*
¿A qué hora te acuestas/se acuesta Vd.?	*What time do you go to bed?*
¿A qué hora empiezas/empieza Vd. a trabajar?	*What time do you start work?*
¿A qué hora sales/sale Vd.?	*What time do you leave?*

b Saying what time you do certain things

Me levanto/me acuesto a las 9:00.	*I get up/go to bed at 9.00.*
Empiezo a trabajar/Salgo del trabajo a las 8:00.	*I start/leave work at 8.00.*

c Asking people what they normally do

¿Qué haces/hace Vd. (normalmente) los sábados/fines de semana/en las vacaciones?	*What do you (normally) do on Saturdays/at the weekends/on your holidays?*

d Saying what you do and how often

Voy siempre/normalmente al gimnasio.	*I always/normally go to the gym.*
A veces cenamos fuera.	*Sometimes we have dinner out.*
Nunca me acuesto antes de las 11:00.	*I never go to bed before 11.00.*
Suelo salir con mi novia.	*I usually go out with my girlfriend.*

 Language discovery

1 TALKING ABOUT THINGS YOU DO REGULARLY: THE PRESENT TENSE

a To talk about things you do regularly, you use the present tense. Below is the present tense of three regular verbs: **hablar** (*to speak*), **comer** (*to eat*), **escribir** (*to write*).

	-ar verbs	-er verbs	-ir verbs
yo	habl**o**	com**o**	escrib**o**
tú	habl**as**	com**es**	escrib**es**
él, ella, Vd.	habl**a**	com**e**	escrib**e**
nosotros/as	habl**amos**	com**emos**	escrib**imos**
vosotros/as	habl**áis**	com**éis**	escrib**ís**
ellos/ellas/Vds.	habl**an**	com**en**	escrib**en**

A veces hablo por teléfono con mis amigos.
Sometimes I speak to my friends on the phone.

Siempre comemos en casa.
We always eat at home.

Nunca escribo cartas.
I never write letters.

Draw up a list of other regular verbs used in this or previous units and write some of their present-tense forms. You might want to practise with the singular forms first, then with the plurals. Try varying the order in which you do it.

b You can also talk about actions you do regularly by using the present tense of **soler (o>ue)** – *to usually (do something)* – followed by an *infinitive* (the dictionary form of the verb).

Suelo conocer gente por internet.
I usually meet people through the Internet.

Suelen desayunar muy temprano.
They usually have breakfast very early.

Solemos ir al cine.
We usually go to the cinema.

2 STEM-CHANGING VERBS

In Units 3 and 5 you learned that some Spanish verbs, known as stem-changing verbs, undergo a vowel change in the stem (the verb minus the **-ar**, **-er**, **-ir**), in all forms of the present tense, except the **nosotros** and **vosotros** forms, but that their endings remain the same as for regular verbs. Examples of these were **querer** (*to want*) (Unit 5), in which the **-e** of the stem changes into **-ie** (e.g. **quiero** *I want*), and **poder** (*to be able to, can*) (Unit 3), in which the **-o** changes into **-ue** (e.g. *puedo* **I can**). In this unit you find **empezar (e>ie)** (*to begin*), **almorzar (o>ue)** (*to have lunch*), **volver (o>ue)** (*to come back*), **acostarse (o>ue)** (*to go to bed*), **soler (o>ue)** (*to usually (do something)*), but there are many others. A few verbs change in a different way, for example **jugar** (*to play*), in which the **-u** of the stem changes into **ue**, as in **juego** (*I play*). Here are the full forms for **empezar**, **volver** and **jugar**:

e > ie	o > ue	u > ue
emp**ie**zo	v**ue**lvo	j**ue**go
emp**ie**zas	v**ue**lves	j**ue**gas
emp**ie**za	v**ue**lve	j**ue**ga
empezamos	volvemos	jugamos
empezáis	volvéis	jugáis
emp**ie**zan	v**ue**lven	j**ue**gan

Empiezo muy temprano/ pronto por la mañana. — *I start very early in the morning.*

Vuelven a casa a almorzar. — *They come back home for lunch.*

Los sábados juego al fúbol. — *On Saturdays I play football.*

3 IRREGULAR VERBS

a In the present tense, some verbs are irregular only in the first person singular. **Salir** (*to leave*), **ver** (*to see*), **hacer** (*to do, make*) belong in this category.

Salgo del trabajo a las seis. — *I leave/finish work at six.*

Por la noche veo televisión. — *In the evening I watch television.*

Los lunes hago yoga. — *On Mondays I do yoga.*

b Ir (*to go*) is completely irregular.

Singular		Plural	
v**oy**	*I go*	v**amos**	*we go*
v**as**	*you go* (inf)	v**ais**	*you go* (inf)
v**a**	*you go* (formal)	v**an**	*you go* (formal)
	he, she, it goes		*they go*

(See also **irse** (*to leave*), in 4c below.)

A few very common verbs are either completely irregular or are irregular only in the **yo** form. The following have come up in previous units: **ser**, **estar**, **saber**, **tener**, **hacer**. Can you remember their forms? See also Irregular verbs at the end of the book.

4 ME, TE, SE, NOS, OS, SE: *REFLEXIVE PRONOUNS*

a Definition

Levantarse (*to get up*), like a number of other verbs, carries the particle **se**, literally *oneself*, attached to it, and forms like *I get up, you get up*, carry the Spanish equivalent of words like *myself, yourself*, etc.: **me** (for **yo**), **te** (for **tú**), **se** (for **él**, **ella**, **Vd.**), **nos** (for **nosotros/as**), **os** (for **vosotros/as**) and **se** (for **ellos**, **ellas**, **Vds.**). These words, which are known as reflexive pronouns, refer back to the subject of the sentence, so in a number of verbs a difference in meaning may be established through their use.

Yo levanto (algo).	*I raise/lift (something).*
Yo me levanto.	*I get up.* (Literally, *I myself get up.*)

(See also Unit 8, paragraph 2 of Language Discovery.)

b Usage

Usage does not always correspond to that of English. There are many verbs which function as reflexive in Spanish, but which are used without a reflexive pronoun in English, among them **acostarse** (*to go to bed*), **irse** (*to leave*), **llamarse** (*to be called*), **sentarse** (*to sit down*). But note **divertirse** (*to enjoy oneself*), **dedicarse a** (*to devote oneself to*), in which the reflexive is made explicit in English.

c Forms

The endings of these verbs are the same as for regular verbs, and only the addition of **me**, **te**, **se**, etc., makes them different. Here's an example:

levantarse (to get up)	
yo	**me levanto**
tú	**te levantas**
él, ella, Vd.	**se levanta**
nosotros/as	**nos levantamos**
vosotros/as	**os levantáis**
ellos, ellas, Vds.	**se levantan**

Me levanto a las 7:00 y me acuesto a las 11:30.
I get up at 7.00 and I go to bed at 11.30.

¿A qué hora te vas al trabajo/ a la universidad?
What time do you leave for work/ the university?

Me voy a las 8:00.
I leave at 8.00.

d Position

Reflexive pronouns normally precede the verb, but when a main verb is followed by another form of the verb such as an infinitive, the pronoun can either precede the main verb or be attached to the infinitive:

No quiere acostarse.

Or

No se quiere acostar.
He/she doesn't want to go to bed.

Pronunciation

12.03

y, as in **yo** is pronounced like the 'y' in *yes*, but in some regions, notably Argentina and Uruguay, it is stronger and nearly like the 's' in *pleasure*. In many areas, too, 'y' is pronounced like the 'll' in **calle**. **Y** (*and*) is pronounced like the 'e' in *be*.

Practise with:

yo, yoga, yogur, desayuno, mayo
Yo desayuno en un bar de la calle Dos de mayo.
Yolanda hace yoga.

 Practice

1 Palabra por palabra *Word for word*

Below are some key verbs related to daily activities. Look them up and classify them into the following categories:

a Personal hygiene	b Personal appearance	c Getting dressed
1 ponerse la ropa	4 peinarse	7 afeitarse
2 bañarse	5 vestirse	8 lavarse
3 maquillarse	6 ducharse	9 lavarse los dientes

Note that **vestirse** is a stem-changing verb, with **e** changing into **i**, e.g. **me visto. Ponerse** is irregular in the first person singular of the present tense, **me pongo**.

 ## 2 La rutina de Ramiro *Ramiro's routine*

Ramiro is a very methodical man. Every morning he follows exactly the same routine. How would Ramiro tell someone what he does? Use the pictures to write a description. One of them has been done for you.

a Me levanto a las seis.

3 Mi fin de semana *My weekend*

12.04

las tostadas	*toast*
el cine	*cinema*
el teatro	*theatre*
el concierto	*concert*
la exposición	*exhibition*
el campo	*country*
pasar	*to spend (time)*
algo ligero	*something light*

Listen to Ana saying what she normally does at the weekends, and answer the questions below:

   a What does Ana do after she gets up on Saturdays?

   b What does she do after lunch?

   c What does she do on Saturday night?

   d What does she normally do on Sunday mornings?

4 ¿A qué hora ...? *At what time ...?*

How would you ask your new friend Antonio the following? Use an appropriate question word from the following:

¿dónde?	¿a qué hora ...?	¿qué?,	¿cómo?

   a What time do you get up?

   b How do you go to work?

   c What time do you start work?

   d Where do you have lunch?

   e What time do you leave work?

   f What do you do in the evening?

5 Ahora tú *And now you*

Write a brief passage describing some of the things you do on a normal day or at the weekend, including times where appropriate. Use as models the dialogues and the Activities in the Practice section, including the listening comprehension transcript for Activity 3.

6 Un día en la vida de Plácido Domingo *A day in the life of Plácido Domingo*

la función	*performance*
el compromiso	*engagement*
me quedo (from **quedarse**)	*I stay*
repasar	*to rehearse, to review*
una comida ligera	*a light meal*
un poquito	*a little bit*
la ternera	*veal*
duerme (from **dormir**)	*you sleep*
hasta	*here, up to*

Plácido Domingo, the famous Spanish tenor, was born in Madrid in 1941. His parents, both **zarzuela** (*Spanish light opera*) performers, moved to Mexico when he was eight and it was here where his talent for music and singing was discovered, and his career as an opera singer first started. He has sung over a hundred different roles and taken part in hundreds of performances. He is also a composer and a conductor.

Plácido Domingo talks to a journalist about some of his habits. As you read the interview, try answering the following questions. The vocabulary will help you to understand.

a What is his day like before a performance?

b What sort of meal does he have before a performance?

c How many hours does he normally sleep at night? And when he has a performance?

d Where does he normally spend his holidays?

– ¿Cómo es un día de Plácido Domingo antes de una función?

– Completamente tranquilo, no acepto ningún compromiso, no hago absolutamente nada. Me quedo en casa, repaso, estudio, leo ...

– ¿Alguna dieta especial?

– Como una comida muy ligera, un poquito de pollo o un poco de ternera y algo de sopa.

– ¿Cuántas horas duerme por la noche?

– En días normales duermo ocho horas. El día de la función duermo hasta once horas.

– ¿Dónde pasa sus vacaciones Plácido Domingo?

– Depende, en la playa la mayoría de las veces.

The ending **-mente** in **completamente** (*completely*), **absolutamente** (*absolutely*), corresponds to English *-ly*. To form words of this kind, use the feminine form of the adjective and add **-mente**: **rápidamente** (*quickly*). If the word ends in a consonant just add **-mente** to it: **fácilmente** (*easily*).

Los españoles leen poco

alrededor de	*around*
la mitad	*half*
leer	*to read*
el periódico deportivo	*sports paper*
la revista (del corazón)	*(true romance) magazine*
el más vendido	*the one that sells most*
por igual	*equally*

The following article looks at reading habits among Spanish people. Think of reading habits in your own country before you read the text.

What percentage of Spaniards never read? What are the most popular newspapers and magazines? Do reading habits differ between men and women? Read and find out.

En España, con alrededor de cuarenta y seis millones de habitantes, casi la mitad de los españoles mayores de 18 años no lee nunca, y el 63 por ciento no compra libros. Lo que más se lee son los periódicos deportivos y las revistas del corazón, la más popular de ellas ¡Hola!. De los periódicos serios, el más vendido es El País, con 450.000 ejemplares al día.

Sólo doce millones de españoles leen periódicos, dieciocho millones leen revistas, treinta millones de personas ven televisión y sólo dos millones van al cine.

El hombre lee el doble de periódicos que la mujer; la mujer lee más revistas semanales. El hombre prefiere escuchar radio, pero hombres y mujeres ven por igual la televisión.

1 Antonio describes his daily routine. Fill in the gaps in the sentences with the present tense form of the following verbs.

comer, desayunar, leer, levantarse, trabajar, ver, volver, ducharse, llegar, salir

Normalmente **(a)** _____ a las siete de la mañana, luego **(b)** _____ .
Después de ducharme **(c)** _____ , normalmente un café con leche y unas
tostadas. A las ocho y media **(d)** _____ para la oficina y **(e)** _____ allí
sobre las nueve. Al mediodía **(f)** _____ con unos colegas en un restaurante
cerca de la oficina. Por la tarde **(g)** _____ desde las tres hasta las siete. A
las siete **(h)** _____ a casa, **(i)** _____ el periódico o **(j)** _____ la
televisión un rato.

2 Complete the sentences with an appropriate word from the list:

(1) me   (2) te   (3) se   (4) nos   (5) os

a Federico _____ acuesta siempre muy tarde.
b ¿A qué _____ dedican Paloma y José?
c Normalmente (yo) _____ voy a la oficina a las ocho de la mañana.
d Los sábados por la mañana Alfonso y yo _____ levantamos a las
nueve. ¿A qué hora _____ levantáis vosotros?
e ¿(Tú) _____ levantas a las diez? ¡Qué tarde!

**Did you get most of your answers right? If you did, it means you
are now familiar with the constructions needed for describing one's
daily routine and are ready to move on. If you are still uncertain,
you may need a little more practice. Go back through the relevant
points in the unit and write a few sentences showing their use.**

SELF CHECK

I CAN. . .
○ . . . talk about things I do regularly
○ . . . say how often I do certain things.

Me gusta
I like it

In this unit you will learn how to:
- ▶ *express intentions*
- ▶ *say what you want to do*
- ▶ *express liking and dislike.*

CEFR: *Can discuss what to do in the evening and at the weekend (A2); Can say what he/she likes or dislikes (A2); Can find specific information in advertisements (A2); Can write simple sentences about themselves (A2).*

Sport and leisure

Spaniards enjoy **el deporte** (*sport*), both to participate in and as spectators, so the question **¿Te gusta el deporte?** (*Do you like sport?*) is almost sure to get an answer in the affirmative. **El fútbol** (*football*) is undoubtedly the most popular sport followed by **el ciclismo** (*cycling*) and **el baloncesto** (*basketball*). If you ask **¿Qué haces en tu tiempo libre?** (*What do you do in your free time?*), the most common response is **salir** (*go out*). This can be just meeting up with friends or, in the summer, going with them **de excursión al campo** (*on a trip into the country*).

Annual leave is usually three weeks taken in the summer. A common response to the question **¿Qué vas a hacer este verano?** (*What are you going to do this summer?*) is **Voy a la playa a tomar el sol** (*I'm going to the beach to sunbathe*).

Ester tells you what she likes doing in her free time. Which one does not involve going out?
Me gusta ir de copas, hacer deporte, ir al cine, ver la tele.

Conversations

1 ¿QUÉ VAS A HACER ESTA NOCHE? *WHAT ARE YOU GOING TO DO TONIGHT?*

voy a + infinitive	*I'm going to* + infinitive
gustar	*to like*
encantar	*to love (something/doing something)*
querer + infinitive	*to want* + infinitive
venir (e>ie)	*to come*
conmigo	*with me*
estar cansado/a	*to be tired*

13.01

*Miguel, Nieves and Eduardo talk about their plans for tonight, **esta noche**, and about some of the things they like.*

1.1 **What is each person going to do? First, look at the key words and phrases below, then listen to the dialogue several times and match the names with the drawings, inserting the appropriate numbers in the boxes next to each name.**

Nieves ☐　　　　**Miguel** ☐　　　　**Eduardo** ☐

Miguel	¿Qué vas a hacer esta noche, Nieves?
Nieves	Voy a ir al cine con David.
Miguel	Te gusta el cine, ¿no?
Nieves	Sí, me gusta mucho. ¿Quieres venir conmigo?
Miguel	No, gracias, voy a salir con Raquel. Vamos a ir a una discoteca. A Raquel le encanta bailar y a mí también.
Nieves	Y tú Eduardo, ¿vas a salir?
Eduardo	No, estoy muy cansado. Voy a ver el tenis en la televisión.

Two key points in this dialogue are: **ir a** + *infinitive*, as in **Voy a ver el tenis** (*I'm going to watch the tennis*), which, just as in English, is used to express intentions; the other is **gustar** (*to like*), as in **Me gusta el cine** – literally, *To me is pleasing the cinema* or *The cinema pleases me*.

1.2 Now read the dialogue and say how the following is expressed:

    1 I'm going (to go) to the cinema.
    2 Are you going out?
    3 Do you like the cinema?
    4 I like it very much.
    5 Raquel loves dancing.

2 ME GUSTA IR DE CAMPING *I LIKE TO GO CAMPING*

próximo/a	*next*
no me gusta nada	*I don't like it at all*
tampoco	*neither/not … either*
pensar (e>ie)	*to think*
este verano	*this summer*

13.02

Nieves and Eduardo talk about the things they like to do on their holidays.

2.1 First, look at some of the things people like to do on their holidays. Can you match the pictures to the sentences below?

Me gusta …

    1 ir de camping/acampar.
    2 viajar al extranjero.
    3 montar en bicicleta.
    4 dormir hasta muy tarde.
    5 nadar.
    6 tomar el sol.

a.

b.

c.

d.

e.

f.

2.2 **Which of the activities above does Eduardo like to do on his holidays? Which does Nieves like to do? Listen and find out.**

Nieves	¿Qué haces en tus vacaciones, Eduardo?
Eduardo	Me gusta ir de camping, montar en bicicleta, viajar al extranjero ... En mis próximas vacaciones quiero ir a Nueva York.
Nieves	Me gusta mucho Nueva York, pero viajar en avión no me gusta nada.
Eduardo	A mí tampoco. Y tú, ¿qué piensas hacer este verano?
Nieves	David y yo vamos a pasar diez días en Ibiza. Nos encanta la playa, tomar el sol, nadar y dormir hasta muy tarde.

2.3 **Now read the dialogue and answer the following questions:**
    1 Where does Eduardo want to go on his next holiday?
    2 How does Nieves feel about that place?
    3 What is it they both dislike?
    4 What are Nieves and David's plans for this summer?

Compare **¿Qué piensas hacer?** (literally, *What do you think to do?*) with English *What are you thinking of doing?* (or, more likely, *What are you planning to do?*). While Spanish uses **pensar** + *infinitive*, English uses *to think* in a construction with *-ing*.

How do you say it?

EXPRESSING INTENTIONS

¿Qué va(s) a hacer?	*What are you going to do?* (formal/inf)
¿Qué piensa(s) hacer?	*What are you planning to do?*
Voy a salir/ver el tenis.	*I'm going (to go) out/watch tennis.*

| **Vamos a pasar/estar una semana allí.** | *We're going to spend a week there/ be there for a week.* |

| **Quiero/queremos viajar/ir a los Estados Unidos.** | *I want/we want to travel/go to the United States.* |

| **¿Qué quiere(s) hacer?** | *What do you want to do?* (formal/inf) |
| **¿Quiere(s) venir conmigo?** | *Do you want to come with me?* |

¿Te gusta/gustan?	*Do you like it/them?* (inf)
¿Le gusta/gustan?	*Do you* (formal) *Does he/she/ it like it/them?*
Me gusta/gustan (mucho).	*I like it/them (very much).*
Me gusta el teatro/chatear.	*I like theatre/to chat (Internet).*
No me gusta/gustan (nada).	*I don't like it/them (at all).*
Me encanta/encantan.	*I love it/them.*

 Language discovery

1 EXPRESSING INTENTIONS

To express intentions you can use:

a Present tense of **ir** (*to go*) + **a** + *infinitive* (the form of the verb ending in **-ar, -er, -ir**). For the present tense of **ir**, see Unit 12.

¿Qué vas/vais a hacer?	*What are you going to do?*
Voy a hacer la compra.	*I'm going to do the shopping.*
Vamos a acostarnos.	*We're going (to go) to bed.*

b **Pensar (e>ie)** (*to think, be planning to*) + *infinitive*

| **¿Qué piensa hacer Vd.?** | *What are you planning to do (thinking of doing)?* |
| **Pienso salir.** | *I'm planning to go out (thinking of going out).* |

2 SAYING WHAT YOU WANT TO DO

To say what you want or do not want to do and to ask someone what he/she wants to do, use **querer (e>ie)** (*to want*).

Quiero estudiar español.   *I want to study Spanish.*

Queremos vivir en América del Sur.   *We want to live in South America.*

Use the constructions in 1 and 2 above by writing a few sentences saying what you are going to do, what you are planning to do, and what you want to do in the coming year.

Then imagine these plans include someone else and change the verbs into the nosotros/as form.

3 EXPRESSING LIKING AND DISLIKE

Gustar (*to like*), **encantar**, **fascinar** (*to like very much, to love*)

a   To say you like or do not like something use **gustar**, which literally means 'is pleasing'. The person who does the liking – the person who is being pleased – goes before **gustar**. So you literally say 'to me, to you, etc. is pleasing': **Me gusta el sol** (I like the sun; literally, *To me is pleasing the sun* or *The sun pleases me*), **Me gusta nadar** (I like swimming; literally, *To me is pleasing to swim* or *To swim pleases me*), or simply **Me gusta** (*I like it*; literally, *To me it is pleasing*). If what you like is plural, use **gustan**: **Me gustan** (*I like them* literally, *To me they are pleasing*), and to say that you do not like something, simply place **no** before **me**, **te**, **le**, **nos**, etc.: **No nos gustan** (*We don't like them*).

You'll find a list of the words for *to me*, *to you*, etc. (technically, indirect object pronouns) in Unit 8 and in section 9.1 of the Grammar summary.

b   To express stronger liking, use **encantar**, or **fascinar** for even stronger liking: **Me encanta/fascina la comida española** (*I love Spanish food*), **Le encantan/fascinan las teleseries** (*He/she loves TV series*).

c   For emphasis or to express contrast between your likes and someone else's, use **a** followed by one of the following words: **mí** (for **yo**), **ti** (for **tú**), **usted**, **él**, **ella**, **nosotros/as**, **vosotros/as**, **ellos**, **ellas**: A mí me gusta el jazz (*I like jazz*), ¿A ti te gusta? (*Do you like it?*), A él/ella no le gusta nada (*He/she doesn't like it at all*).

d **A** must also be used before a person's name when you want to make clear who does the liking: **A Isabel le gustan los perros, pero a Carlos no** (*Isabel likes dogs but Carlos doesn't*).

e You also need to use **a** in short questions and replies: **A mi madre le encantan los gatos** (*My mother loves cats*), **¿Y a ti?** (*And what about you?*), **A mí también** (*So do I*), **A él no, y a ella tampoco** (*He doesn't, and she doesn't either*).

Here is a suggestion for practising the above: imagine yourself preparing to be interviewed for a flat share in a Spanish-speaking country. Write as many sentences as you can mentioning the things you like or dislike, and the kind of things you like/dislike or love to do.

Pronunciation

13.03

d: after **l** and **n**, and at the beginning of a word (e.g. **deporte**), when preceded by a pause, **d** is pronounced with the tongue pressing against the upper teeth. In other positions **d** is pronounced nearly like the 'th' in *that*: **ver̲d̲e**, **A̲d̲ela**. There are, however, regional differences: in Andalusia and certain parts of Latin America, for example, in informal language, **d** in final position, as in **Madri̲d̲** and between vowels, as in **pesca̲d̲o**, is pronounced very softly or not at all.

Practise with:
A David le gusta andar y hacer deportes todos los días, sobre todo nadar.
Adela va a pasar diez días en Andalucía.
Eduardo está cansado y va a quedarse en casa para ver un dvd.

 Practice

1 Un email *An email*

Angela, who is studying Spanish, is sending an email to her friend Mario. Can you help her with some of the verbs? Put the infinitives in brackets in the appropriate form, using pronouns where necessary.

Hola Mario:

¿Tienes algún plan para este fin de semana? Carmen y yo **(ir)** a pasar el fin de semana en Cuenca. **(Pensar)** salir el viernes por la noche y volver el domingo por la tarde. ¿**(Querer)** venir con nosotras? **(Ir)** en el coche. Cuenca es una ciudad muy bonita. A mí **(encantar)** y a Carmen también **(gustar)** mucho.

Un abrazo

Ángela

 2   Ahora tú *And now you*

Send an email to your Spanish friend saying what you are planning to do at the weekend and invite him/her to join you.

 3   De vacaciones *On holiday*

alojarse	*to stay at*
¿(a)dónde?	*where (to)?*

Your friend Rocío is going on holiday. How would you ask her about her travel plans? Use question words from the following:

¿(a)dónde?   ¿cuándo?   ¿cuánto tiempo?   ¿qué?   ¿con quién?

a   Ask where she's going to go this summer.
b   ... who she's going with.
c   ... how long she's going to stay.
d   ... where she's going to stay.
e   ... what she likes to do on her holidays.
f   ... whether she likes swimming.
g   ... when she's coming back.

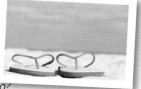

 4   ¿Qué te gusta hacer? *What do you like to do?*

andar	*to walk*
asistir a cursos	*to attend courses*

A group of people were asked what they like to do in their spare time, 'el tiempo libre'. Look at their answers, which are placed in order of preference below, and then write down your own preferences using each of the following phrases:

Me encanta ...   Me gusta ...   (No) me gusta nada ...   Detesto ...

¿Qué te gusta hacer en tu tiempo libre?

1 ver TV/cable/dvd
2 hacer deportes
3 escuchar música
4 realizar tareas domésticas
5 salir con amigos/ir a fiestas
6 leer

7 viajar
8 andar
9 ir al cine
10 trabajar/estudiar
11 ir al teatro/a conciertos
12 asistir a cursos

5 Me encanta cocinar *I like cooking*

cocinar	*to cook*
arreglar	*to tidy up*
la lectura	*reading*
la poesía	*poetry*

13.04

Lola talked to a magazine about her likes and interests. Complete the text with the correct form of the verbs in brackets, then listen to the recording.

A mí **(gustar)** estar con mi familia, mis amigos y mis dos perros. **(Encantar)** cocinar y arreglar la casa, pero **(detestar)** planchar. **(Fascinar)** la lectura, especialmente la novela y la poesía, y también **(gustar)** la fotografía y la pintura. Los fines de semana **(gustar)** desayunar en la cama, levantarme tarde y salir de compras con Pedro, mi marido. En las vacaciones, a Pedro y a mí **(gustar)** ir a la playa. A él y a mí **(encantar)** nadar y tomar el sol. A Pedro también **(gustar)** el campo, pero a mí no **(gustar)** nada.

Try using the constructions and vocabulary you have learned in this unit so far by writing a similar account to the one you have just heard. Use as many expressions as you can from **gustar**, **encantar**, **fascinar**, **detestar**. Remember that **detestar** follows the normal pattern *verb + infinitive*.

6 Pasatiempos *Pastimes*

hacer footing	*to jog, to go jogging*
chatear	*to chat (on Net)*
el ordenador	*computer* (Spain)
la computadora/el computador	*computer* (LAm)
el videojuego	*video game*
la bici (short for **bicicleta**)	*bike*
bajar(se)	*to download*

Four people looking for correspondents wrote to a magazine and listed their hobbies. Look up the new words in your dictionary and then answer the questions below.

Elvira Gutiérrez,
25 años, secretaria

Calle Juárez, 6, Jalisco,
México

Pasatiempos: Me gusta
bailar, ver películas de terror,
leer revistas, salir con amigos,
jugar al baloncesto.

David Escobar,
37 años, psicólogo

Calle Lorca, 12, 4º, 3ª,
Burgos, España

Pasatiempos: Me interesa
conocer gente por Internet,
escribir cuentos, ir al teatro y
conciertos, escuchar música
clásica, hacer atletismo, ver
programas deportivos en la tele.

Cristina López,
18 años, estudiante

Paseo del Mar, 452,
Valparaíso, Chile

Pasatiempos: Me encanta tocar
la guitarra y cantar, dibujar, ver
tele, cocinar, ir a discotecas,
enviar mails a mis amigos,
chatear en el computador,
jugar con videojuegos y salir
en mi bici.

Daniel Miranda,
28 años, futbolista

Calle de la Luz, 86, 5º, B,
Málaga, España

Pasatiempos: Me gusta jugar al
fútbol, hacer footing, pescar, ver
películas de acción y de guerra,
viajar al extranjero, jugar en el
ordenador, bajarme música de
Internet.

Which of the people above likes to do each of the following?

a draw
b watch horror films
c play basketball
d write short stories
e watch war films
f travel abroad
g sing
h watch sports programmes

7 Ahora tú *And now you*

Write about your own interests using the advertisements above as a model. Note the use of 'me interesa' I'm interested in, from 'interesar' to be interested in, a verb which functions like 'gustar'.

Tiempo libre *Leisure time*

la telerrealidad	*Big Brother type of programme (reality TV)*
los programas del corazón	*entertainment TV programmes which tend to focus on people's private lives*
los culebrones	*soap operas (usually from Latin America)*

What would you say is the main leisure activity in your country? What do you think Spanish and Latin American people like to do? Read and find out.

A los españoles y latinoamericanos les encanta ver televisión. Cada español ve unas tres horas y treinta minutos de televisión al día. Los programas más populares son los 'del corazón' y la telerrealidad, y también las películas y teleseries o 'culebrones' y, por supuesto, los deportivos. Entre los deportes, lejos el más popular es el fútbol, aunque en los últimos años se aprecia un mayor interés por otros deportes, especialmente el tenis.

 Test yourself

1 **In an email to a Spanish-speaking acquaintance Pat wrote about the things she and her family like to do in their spare time. Can you help Pat by putting the verbs in bold into the right form?**

A mí **(a) encantar** los deportes, pero a mi marido no **(b) gustar** nada. A mis hijos **(c) fascinar** nadar. A nosotros **(d) encantar** salir fuera de la ciudad los fines de semana. Y a ti, ¿qué **(e) gustar** hacer en tu tiempo libre?

2 **Each of the following sentences contains one mistake. Can you correct them?**
   a ¿Qué vais hacer el sábado por la noche?
   b ¿Quieres venir con mí?
   c Soy un poco cansado. Quiero acostarme pronto.
   d A Rafael encanta el fútbol.
   e A nosotros el fútbol no gusta nada.

Test 1 assesses the correct usage of verbs used for expressing liking and dislike. The construction in which they occur is different from that of ordinary verbs, so if you got them right, congratulations! Test 2 focuses on a range of points. If you are still uncertain about some of them, go back to the relevant sections of Unit 13 before you proceed to the next one.

SELF CHECK

I CAN. . .
. . . express intentions
. . . say what I want to do
. . . express liking and dislike.

¿Dígame?

Hello?

In this unit you will learn how to:
▶ *ask to speak to someone on the phone*
▶ *take and leave messages*
▶ *make appointments on the phone*
▶ *say what you or others are doing.*

CEFR: *Can catch the main point in short, clear, simple messages (A2); Can pass on messages (A2); Can understand and extract the essential information from short, recorded passages (A2).*

On the telephone

The blue **cabina telefónica** (*telephone box*) is not as ubiquitous as it once was as most people have **un móvil** (*a mobile phone*) **para hacer una llamada** (*to make a call*). When you phone someone in Spain, once you have dialled **el número de teléfono**, you will hear a single ring tone.

The most usual way a Spaniard answers the phone is to say **¿Dígame?** (*hello*, literally *tell me*), which is your cue to start talking and ask for the person you wish to speak to: **¿Está el señor Barriga?** (*Is Mr Barriga there?*), **¿Está la señora Castro?**, or more informally **¿Está Ana?** If you have not identified yourself, you may be asked **¿De parte de quién?** or **¿Quién habla?** (*Who's calling?*). If it is the person you want to speak to who has answered the phone, he or she may well say **Al habla** (*Speaking*).

The phone rings in your hotel room.
a   **What are you going to say when you lift up the receiver?**
b   **If, at the other end of the line, someone is asking to speak to you, what will you say?**

Conversations

¿de parte de quién?	*who's calling?*
no puede ponerse	*he/she can't answer/come to the phone*
¿quiere dejarle algún recado?	*would you like to leave him/her a message?*
dígale que ...	*tell him/her that ... (formal)*
le daré su recado	*I'll give him/her your message*
luego	*later*

1 ¿QUIERE DEJARLE ALGÚN RECADO? *WOULD YOU LIKE TO LEAVE HIM/HER A MESSAGE?*

 14.01

Carlos, from London, is trying to reach señor Bravo at a Spanish firm.

1.1   Why can't señor Bravo answer the phone? Listen and choose the right activity from the drawings below.

You will find a number of useful expressions for use on the phone in this dialogue, among them **¿dígame?** or **¿diga?** *(hello?)*, **¿Está (Luis/Silvia)?** *(Is (Luis/Silvia) in?)*, **No puede ponerse** *(He/she can't come to the phone)*, **dejar un recado** *(to leave a message)*.

Secretaria	Agrohispana, ¿dígame?
Carlos	Buenos días. ¿Está el señor Bravo, por favor?
Secretaria	¿De parte de quién?
Carlos	De Carlos Miranda.
Secretaria	Un momentito, por favor ... ¿Señor Miranda?, el señor Bravo no puede ponerse en este momento. Está hablando por otra línea. ¿Quiere dejarle algún recado?

Carlos	Por favor, dígale que voy a llamar más tarde. Necesito hablar con él.
Secretaria	Muy bien, le daré su recado.

1.2 **Now read the dialogue and try learning those expressions which are proper to the use of the phone. Listen to the dialogue again a few times and then put the sentences in the following dialogue in the right order.**
  - No, no está en este momento.
  - De José Luis.
  - Sí, ¿diga?
  - No, luego la llamo.
  - ¿Está María?
  - ¿Quieres dejarle algún recado?
  - ¿De parte de quién?

2 EN SEGUIDA LE PONGO I'LL PUT YOU THROUGH RIGHT AWAY

se ha equivocado	*you've got the wrong number*
no cuelgue	*don't hang up*
en seguida le pongo	*I'll put you through right away*
¡oiga!	*hello?*
está comunicando	*it's engaged*
no se retire	*hold the line!*
ahora mismo se pone	*he/she'll be with you right away*

14.02

Luis phones his friend Gloria at work.

2.1 **Listen to the conversation several times and, as you do so, make a note of the expressions used to say each of the following:**
  1 I'd like to speak to …
  2 This is not her extension.
  3 It's (extension) 368.
  4 Can you put me through to …?

Voz 1	Ibertur, ¿dígame?
Luis	Quisiera hablar con Gloria Araya, por favor.
Voz 1	Se ha equivocado. Su extensión no es esta. Es la tres, sesenta y ocho.
	No cuelgue, por favor. En seguida le pongo.

178

Luis	Gracias.
Voz 1	¡Oiga!, está comunicando. No se retire.
Voz 2	Sí, ¿diga?
Luis	¿Me puede poner con Gloria Araya, por favor?
Voz 2	Sí, ahora mismo se pone.

2.2 **Now match the Spanish and English.**

1 Se ha equivocado.
2 No cuelgue.
3 En seguida le pongo.
4 Ahora mismo se pone.

a I´ll put you through right away.
b You have the wrong number.
c She´ll be with you right away.
d Don´t hang up.

2.3 **Listen to the dialogue again and read it a few times. Then try playing each one of the parts.**

Expressions such as **no cuelgue** (*don't hang up*), **no se retire** (*hold the line*) (both of which are commands, covered in Units 23 and 24), like some other expressions used on the phone, are set phrases, and you can learn them as such, without the need to go into their grammar at this stage.

3 HORA CON EL DOCTOR *AN APPOINTMENT WITH THE DOCTOR*

no hay hora disponible   *there's no appointment available*
me va bien   *it suits me*

14.03

Mónica is trying to make an appointment with her doctor.

3.1 **Listen and answer the following questions.**

1 When does she want her appointment for?
2 Which day is she offered instead?
3 What times is she offered?
4 Which time suits her?

A key word here is **la hora** (*appointment*). **Pedir hora** is *to ask for an appointment*.

Recepcionista	Consulta, ¿dígame?
Mónica	Quisiera pedir hora con el doctor para mañana.
Recepcionista	Lo siento, pero no hay hora disponible hasta el jueves, a las nueve y media, o por la tarde a las cuatro y cuarto.

Mónica	A las nueve y media me va bien.
Recepcionista	¿Su nombre, por favor?
Mónica	Mónica Urrutia.

3.2 How would you express the following in Spanish? Now read the dialogue and then try saying the following in Spanish.

1 I'd like to ask for an appointment with the dentist (**el/la dentista**) for Monday.
2 There's no appointment available until Wednesday at 10.20 or in the afternoon at 2.45.
3 A quarter to three suits me well.

The general word for *appointment* in Spanish is **la cita**, which also means *date*: **Tengo una cita con el/la gerente a las 9:30** (*I have an appointment with the manager at 9.30*). The word **la hora** is used for appointments with doctors, dentists, hairdressers, etc.: **Tengo hora con el/la doctor/a a las 5:15** (*I have an appointment with the doctor at 5.15*). To request an appointment you can say: **Quisiera pedir (una) cita para mañana/las 11:00** (*I'd like to make/ask for an appointment for tomorrow/11.00*) or **Quería pedir hora con .../para el lunes** (*I'd like to make/ask for an appointment with .../for Monday*). And when you arrive for your appointment you may be asked **¿Tiene usted cita/hora?** (*Do you have an appointment?*).

How do you say it?

ASKING TO SPEAK TO SOMEONE ON THE PHONE AND REPLYING

¿Dígame?/¿Diga?/¿Sí?	*Hello?* (especially Spain)
¿Está María/la señora Díaz?	*Is María/Mrs Díaz in?*
Quisiera hablar con Juan/ el señor Ríos.	*I'd like to speak to Juan/ Mr Ríos.*
¿Me puede poner con Carmen?	*Can you put me through to Carmen?*
¡Al habla!/Soy yo.	*Speaking.*
¿De parte de quién?	*Who's speaking?*
De Cristóbal.	*Cristobal.*
¿Quién lo(le)/la llama?	*Who's calling him/her?*
Soy Dolores.	*I'm Dolores.*

José/la señorita Peña no está.	*José/Miss Peña is not in.*
En seguida le pongo.	*I'll put you through right away.*
No puede ponerse.	*He/she can't come to the phone.*
Ahora (mismo) se pone.	*He/she will be with you right away.*
Se ha equivocado (de número).	*You've got the wrong number.*

TAKING AND LEAVING MESSAGES

| **¿Quiere dejar(le) algún recado?** | *Would you like to leave (him/her) a message?* |
| **Por favor dígale/dile que ...** (form/inf) | *Please tell him/her that ...* |

Don't be daunted by the number of new expressions you have encountered in this unit. Many of these telephone expressions are fixed and it is mostly names and gender (**la** instead of **lo** for example) that will vary. Try learning these by making up brief dialogues of your own.

MAKING APPOINTMENTS ON THE PHONE

| **Quisiera pedir hora con el doctor (para ...)** | *I'd like to ask for an appointment with the doctor (for ...)* |
| **Quería pedir/solicitar una cita/ entrevista con la señora Salas.** | *I'd like to ask for/request an appointment/interview with Mrs Salas.* |

SAYING WHAT YOU OR OTHERS ARE DOING

| **Está hablando por otra línea.** | *He/she is speaking on another line.* |
| **Estoy/Está atendiendo a un cliente.** | *I am/He/she is looking after a client.* |

The following passage tells you how to make certain types of calls in Spain:

Para llamar por teléfono fuera de España tienes que marcar, *to dial*, el 00 y luego el prefijo, *code*, del país al que quieres llamar, el prefijo de la ciudad, y después el número al que quieres llamar. Por ejemplo, para llamar a Londres marcas 00-44 (Reino Unido) + 20 (Londres) + número que deseas. Para hacer una llamada personal, *a personal call*, o una llamada de cobro revertido, *a transferred charge call*, tienes que llamar a la operadora o al operador, *operator*, y decir: "Quiero hacer una llamada...", '*I want to make a ... call*'.

Language discovery

1 SAYING WHAT YOU ARE DOING

To express ideas such as 'He is speaking', 'She is working', which refer to actions taking place at the moment of speaking, Spanish uses **estar** (*to be*), followed by the equivalent of *-ing*, as in 'speaking', 'working', which is known as gerund. This is formed by adding **-ando** to the stem of **-ar** verbs, and **-iendo** to that of **-er** and **-ir** verbs: **hablar – hablando, hacer – haciendo, escribir – escribiendo.**

¿Qué está haciendo tu hermano?	*What is your brother doing?*
Está hablando con un amigo.	*He's speaking to a friend.*
¿Qué estás haciendo?	*What are you doing?*
Estoy escribiendo un mail.	*I'm writing an email.*

Note the use of the same construction in:

Está comunicando.	*It's engaged.* (literally, *It's communicating*)

With verbs like **hacer** (*to do*), **hablar** (*to speak*), **llamar** (*to call*), and a few others, you often hear the present tense instead of the construction with **-ando** or **-iendo** above: **¿Qué haces?** (*What are you doing?*), **¿Con quién hablas?** (*Who are you talking to?*), **¿Quién llama?** (*Who's calling?*).

2 PONER *(TO PUT THROUGH)*, PONERSE AL TELÉFONO *(TO COME TO THE PHONE)*

In Unit 7 you learned to use **poner** in the context of shopping. As the English verb *to put*, **poner** has a number of other meanings, for example *to put through*:

¿Me puede poner con Enrique?	*Can you put me through to Enrique?*
¿Me pones con tu madre, por favor?	*Will you put me through to your mother, please?*
En seguida le/te pongo.	*I'll put you through right away.* (formal/inf)

Ponerse (al teléfono) (*to come to the phone* – literally, *to put yourself to the phone*), is another useful expression to learn in this context. The phrase **al teléfono** is normally left out.

Ahora se pone.	*He/she will be with you right now.*

3 LATIN AMERICAN USAGE ON THE PHONE

Latin American usage on the phone is not much different from that of Peninsular Spanish, but there are a few expressions which are different or more proper to the area.

Hello?	**¿Aló?** (especially South America), **¿bueno?** (Mexico), **¿hola?** (Argentina, Uruguay)
Speaking	**Con él/ella (habla) / con él mismo/ella misma / habla Marta**
You've got the wrong number	**Está equivocado/a** or simply **equivocado**
It's engaged	**Está ocupado.**

 Practice

1 Una conversación telefónica *A telephone conversation*

Ricardo phoned his friend Leonor but she wasn't at home. How would you fill the gaps in this conversation between Ricardo and the speaker at the other end of the line?

– ¿Dígame?

– ¿ _____?

– No, Leonor está en la universidad. ¿ _____?

– Soy Ricardo.

– ¿ _____?

– Sí, por favor. Dígale que me llame al número 95 580 21 33, que necesito hablar urgentemente con ella.

– Muy bien.

2 ¿Qué está haciendo? *What's he doing?*

14.04

Listen to Raquel phoning her friend Lorenzo at home.

la entrada   *ticket*

    a What is Lorenzo doing? Choose the right picture below.

    b What message does Raquel leave for him?

3 **¿Me puede poner con la señora Smith?** *Can you put me through to Mrs Smith?*

A Spanish-speaking person phones your place of work and asks to speak to one of your colleagues. Follow the guidelines in English and fill in your part of the conversation.

    – *Hello?*

    – *¿Me puede poner con la señora Smith, por favor?*

    – *Mrs Smith can't come to the phone at the moment. She's having lunch with a client. Who's calling?*

    – Soy Andrés Calle, de Málaga.

    – *Would you like to leave her a message?*

    – Por favor, dígale que la voy a llamar dentro de una hora.

    – *Very well, Mr Calle. I'll give her your message.*

    – Perdone, el señor Roberts, ¿está en su despacho hoy?

    – *Yes, Mr Roberts is in. Please hold the line! He'll be with you right away.*

There are two sentences here in which English uses the will form: *I'll give her your message* and *He'll be with you right away*. You don't need to know the Spanish for *will* at this stage, as the first expression is a fixed one (Conversation 1) while the second one uses the present tense (Conversation 2).

4 Un momento, por favor *One moment, please*

While waiting to be served at a travel agency you hear the receptionist talk to different people on the phone. Complete her sentences with the proper form of the verbs in brackets.

a Hola Ana, soy Camila. Mira, ¿me (**poner**) con Miguel, por favor? La gerente (**necesitar**) hablar con él.

b ¿El señor Ortíz? Lo siento, el señor Ortíz está (**atender**) a una clienta en este momento. ¿(**Querer**) usted dejarle algún recado?

c ¿La señora Martínez? Muy bien, un momentito, por favor. Ahora (**ponerse**).

d Por favor, no (**retirarse**). En seguida (yo) le (**poner**) con ella.

e Un momento, por favor. No (**colgar**).

f ¿Quiere usted esperar un momento, por favor? La extensión del señor González está (**comunicar**).

5 Una entrevista *An interview*

llamar por	to call about
el anuncio	advertisement
el puesto	post, job
solicitar	to request, ask for

14.05

Sandra, a graphic designer, has seen the job advertisements, 'los anuncios', below and she telephones to ask for an interview. How does she express the following? Listen and find out.

Diseñadora Gráfica

Súper despierta y con la mejor disposición.

Necesita
Agencia de Publicidad
Llamar por entrevista al
teléfono: 246 08 17

DISEÑADOR GRÁFICO

Ambiente Macintosh, 3 años

Conocimientos:
Page Maker 7.0,
Freehand, Photoshop,
Disponibilidad inmediata.

Solicitar entrevista:
Lunes 14 ☽ 555.00.68
Depto. Publicidad

a I'm phoning about the advertisement for the post of graphic designer.
b I'd like to ask for an interview.
c Yes, half past nine suits me well.

? Test yourself

1 **You are left in charge of the phone at Anglohispana, a company that does business with Spain. How would you say the following in Spanish?**
   a You've got the wrong number.
   b I'd like to speak to Mr Julián. Can you put me through to him?
   c Who's calling?
   d I'll put you through right away.
   e He'll be with you right away.
   f Do you want to leave a message?

2 **What do the following sentences mean?**
   a Gloria no puede ponerse en este momento. Está duchándose.
   b La señora Martínez está hablando por otra línea.
   c Un momentito, por favor. No cuelgue.
   d ¡Oiga! La extensión del señor Mella está comunicando.
   e No hay hora disponible hasta mañana por la tarde.
   f ¿Tiene usted cita?

Most of the sentences in Tests 1 and 2 correspond to fixed expressions for use on the phone. Check the Key to 'Test yourself' at the end of the book to see whether you got them right. If you didn't, go back to the dialogues and to the How do you say it? section for further revision.

SELF CHECK

I CAN...
... ask to speak to someone on the phone
... take and leave messages
... make appointments on the phone
... say what I am or others are doing.

¿Cuándo naciste?
When were you born?

In this unit you will learn how to:

▶ *ask and give biographical information*
▶ *say how long ago something happened*
▶ *say how long you have been doing something (2).*

CEFR: *Can ask and answer questions about past activities (A2); Can describe past activities and personal experiences (A2); Can describe educational background and recent jobs (B1); Can write accounts of experiences (A2); Can write short, simple biographies (A2).*

Who lived here?

There is a small area in Madrid between **La Puerta del Sol**, which marks not only the centre of Madrid but with its **kilómetro cero** (*okm*) kerbstone, is the point from which all distances are measured, and **El Paseo del Prado** which has poetry and quotations written into the pavement. Plaques on the walls tell us **Aquí nació ...** (*Here ... was born*), **Aquí vivió...** (*Here ... lived*), **Aquí murió ...** (*Here ... died*).

On the main thoroughfare close by, a more elaborate commemorative plaque on the brick wall of a plain building tells us that the first part of *El Ingenioso Hidalgo Don Quijote de la Mancha* written by Miguel de Cervantes Saavedra was printed here **en mayo de 1605** (*in May 1605*).

 What is interesting about Cervantes's date of death?
Miguel de Cervantes nació en Alcalá de Henares el 29 de septiembre de 1547. Murió en Madrid el 23 de abril de 1616. William Shakespeare también murió el 23 de abril de 1616.

Conversations

conocer (here)	*to meet (for the first time)*
hace (here)	*ago*
casarse	*to get married*
el año pasado	*last year*

15.01

Raúl and Gloria work in a hotel in Madrid. In the first dialogue Gloria asks Raúl about some important events in his life.

1.1 Here's the English for Gloria's questions. What are Raúl's answers? Listen and find out.

1 When did you arrive in Madrid?
2 How long ago did you meet Clara?
3 When did you (two) get married?

Gloria	¿Cuándo llegaste a Madrid?
Raúl	Llegué en diciembre de 1997.
Gloria	¿Cuánto tiempo hace que conociste a Clara?
Raúl	La conocí hace un año y medio.
Gloria	¿Y cuándo os casasteis?
Raúl	Nos casamos en octubre del año pasado.

1.2 What phrases are used in the conversation to say:

1 You arrived
2 How long ago ...?
3 We got married ...

This unit brings in the past tense, with the Spanish equivalent of phrases such as *I arrived* (**Llegué**), *I met her* (**La conocí**), *We got married* (**Nos casamos**). Note also the Spanish for *ago* – **hace** – to refer to the past.

1.3 Read the dialogue now and then play, first, Gloria's part then Raúl's, until you feel confident with the new language.

¿Cuánto tiempo llevas ...?	*How long have you been ...?*
¿Dónde trabajaste?	*Where did you work?*
¿Viviste mucho tiempo en ...?	*Did you live a long time in ...?*

15.02

Raúl asks Gloria about her life before she came to work in Madrid.

2.1 **How long has Gloria been working in the hotel, and where did she live and work before? Listen and find out.**

Raúl	¿Cuánto tiempo llevas trabajando aquí?
Gloria	Llevo tres años en este hotel.
Raúl	¿Dónde trabajaste antes?
Gloria	Trabajé dos años en Sevilla, en un hotel más pequeño.
Raúl	¿Viviste mucho tiempo en Sevilla?
Gloria	Sí, viví allí casi cinco años. Estudié en Sevilla.

2.2 **What phrase is used in the conversation to say *How long have you been working here?***

Did you notice the phrase used by Gloria to say how long she has been working in the hotel? She said: **Llevo tres años**, present tense of **llevar** + *a time phrase*. The 'been working' is not expressed here because it is in the question and so it is understood: **¿Cuánto tiempo llevas trabajando aquí?** (*How long have you been working here?*)

2.3 **Read the dialogue now, study the vocabulary and related grammar notes and then give the Spanish for:**
   1 I've been five years in Spain.
   2 I worked in Salamanca for two years.
   3 I studied Spanish there.

3 ¿DÓNDE NACISTE? *WHERE WERE YOU BORN?*

| **¿cuándo?** | *when* |
| **nacer** | *to be born* |

15.03

Raúl is getting a little more personal and he asks Gloria some more questions about her life.

3.1 Where and when was Gloria born? Listen and find out.

Raúl	¿Dónde naciste?
Gloria	Nací en Santander.
Raúl	¿Cuándo naciste?
Gloria	Nací el 15 de marzo de 1983. ¿Y tú?
Raúl	Yo nací el 4 de abril del setenta y nueve, y Clara nació en octubre de 1981. Soy un año y medio mayor que ella.

To be born is **nacer**: **Nací** (*I was born*) **el 3 de septiembre de 1979 (el tres de septiembre de mil novecientos setenta y nueve).** Spanish uses cardinal numbers for the day, **el tres**, instead of ordinal ones as does English, *third*. The year is either expressed in full as above or giving only the last two numbers, **el tres de septiembre del setenta y nueve.**

3.2 What is the Spanish for the following in the conversation?
   1 Where were you born?
   2 When were you born?

3.3 Now read the dialogue, study the vocabulary and complete the following sentences with information about yourself.
   a Nací en …
   b Nací el …

How do you say it?

ASKING AND GIVING BIOGRAPHICAL INFORMATION

¿Dónde/cuándo naciste/nació Vd.?	*Where/when were you born?*
Nací en Toledo/1965/el 20 de enero de 1980.	*I was born in Toledo/1965/on 20th January 1980.*
Él/ella nació en el (año) 2001.	*He/she was born in (the year) 2001.*
¿Dónde estudiaste/estudió Vd.?	*Where did you study?*
Estudié en …	*I studied in …*
¿Dónde trabajaste/trabajó Vd. (antes)?	*Where did you work (before)?*
Trabajé en …/como …	*I worked in …/as …*

¿Cuánto tiempo hace que lo or **le/la conociste/conoció Vd.?**	*How long ago did you meet him/her?*
Lo or **le/la conocí hace un año/el año pasado.**	*I met him/her a year ago/last year.*

ASKING AND SAYING HOW LONG SOMEONE HAS BEEN DOING SOMETHING

¿Cuánto tiempo llevas/lleva Vd. trabajando/viviendo aquí?	*How long have you been working/living here?*
Llevo un año (trabajando/viviendo) aquí.	*I've been (working/living) here for a year.*

 Language discovery

1 MESES Y FECHAS *MONTHS AND DATES*

Months, like the days of the week, are not written with capital letters in Spanish.

enero	*January*	**julio**	*July*
febrero	*February*	**agosto**	*August*
marzo	*March*	**septiembre**	*September*
abril	*April*	**octubre**	*October*
mayo	*May*	**noviembre**	*November*
junio	*June*	**diciembre**	*December*

▶ To say 'in', as in *in January*, use **en**: **en enero.**
▶ To say 'on', as in *on 20th March*, use **el**: **el 20 de marzo.**
▶ Before the year, use **de**: **el 18 de julio de 2007.**

2 SAYING WHAT YOU DID OR WHAT HAPPENED: THE PRETERITE TENSE

To say what you did at some specific point in the past, as in *She finished last year*, you need the simple past, which is known as *preterite tense*: **Terminó el año pasado.** There are two sets of endings for the preterite tense, one for **-ar** verbs and another one for verbs in **-er** and **-ir**. The first person plural **nosotros/as** of **-ar** and **-ir** verbs is the same as for the present tense. Here are the preterite forms of three regular verbs: **trabajar** (*to work*), **conocer** (*to know, meet*), **vivir** (*to live*).

yo	trabaj**é**	conoc**í**	viv**í**
tú	trabaj**aste**	conoc**iste**	viv**iste**
él/ella/Vd.	trabaj**ó**	conoc**ió**	viv**ió**
nosotros/as	trabaj**amos**	cono**cimos**	viv**imos**
vosotros/as	trabaj**asteis**	conoc**isteis**	viv**isteis**
ellos/ellas/Vds.	trabaj**aron**	conoc**ieron**	viv**ieron**

Trabajé dos años en Jamaica. *I worked for two years in Jamaica.*
Conocí a Julia en el año 2000. *I met Julia in the year 2000.*
Vivimos juntos varios años. *We lived for several years together.*

Did you notice the written accents on the first and third person singular? It is important to use them as sometimes these help to establish differences in meaning between verbs, for example **trabajé** (*I worked*), **trabaje** (*work!*) (command), **trabajó** (*he/she/you (formal) worked*), **trabajo** (*I work*).

3 SPELLING-CHANGING VERBS

A few verbs change their spelling – the consonant before the verb ending – in the first person singular of the preterite tense.

a Verbs ending in **-gar** change **g** to **gu** before **e**: **Llegué** (from **llegar**) **ayer** (*I arrived yesterday*).

b Those in **-car** change **c** to **que**: **Lo busqué** (from **buscar**) (*I looked for it*).

c Verbs ending in **-zar**, for example **empezar** (*to begin, start*), change **z** to **c** before **e**: **Empecé anoche** (*I started last night*).

For irregular preterite forms see Unit 16.

4 TIME PHRASES ASSOCIATED WITH THE PRETERITE

The following words and expressions are normally associated with the preterite. Try learning them by using them in sentences with regular verbs:

anoche	*last night*
ayer	*yesterday*
anteayer/antes de ayer (**antier** in some Latin American countries)	*the day before yesterday*
el lunes/mes/año/verano/ invierno pasado	*last Monday/month/year/ summer/winter*
la semana/Navidad/primavera pasada	*last week/Christmas/spring*
en 1945, en el sesenta y tres, en los (años) ochenta	*in 1945, in (the year) sixty-three, in the eighties*
hace un año/mucho tiempo	*a year/long time ago.*

5 ¿CUÁNTO TIEMPO LLEVAS ...? *HOW LONG HAVE YOU BEEN ...?*

In Unit 11 you learned to use the construction **hace ...** + **que** + *present tense verb* to say how long you have been doing something: **Hace un mes que trabajo aquí** (*I've been working here for a month*). An alternative way of expressing the same is by using a construction with **llevar** followed by a time phrase and the **-ando** or **-iendo** form of the verb (known as *gerund*) corresponding to the *-ing* form in English (see Unit 14).

¿Cuánto tiempo llevas trabajando aquí/estudiando español?	*How long have you been working here/studying Spanish?*
Llevo un año trabajando aquí/ estudiando español.	*I've been working here/studying Spanish for a year.*

If the context is clear, especially with verbs such as **vivir**, **trabajar**, **estudiar**, the **-ando** or **-iendo** form of the verb may be left out.

Lleva seis meses en la empresa/ en esta universidad.	*He/she's been in the company/in this university for six months.*
Llevamos mucho tiempo en esta casa.	*We've been a long time in this house.*

Practise this construction with **llevar** by saying how long you have been at a certain place or have been doing certain things. Use the following as a model: **Llevo un año en esta empresa**, **Llevo mucho tiempo trabajando en (place)**, **Llevo dos años en esta casa/este piso**, **Llevo tres meses estudiando/aprendiendo español.**

6 ¿CUÁNTO TIEMPO HACE? *HOW LONG AGO?*

To ask or say how long ago something happened use **hace** with a verb in the preterite tense.

¿Cuánto tiempo hace que llegaste a España?	*How long ago did you arrive in Spain?*
Llegué hace dos años. Or **Hace dos años que llegué.**	*I arrived two years ago.*

7 PERSONAL 'A'

Note the use of **a** before a name or a word referring to a person in sentences like the following. This is a feature of Spanish that has no equivalent in English:

Conocí a Luis hace dos años.   *I met Luis two years ago.*

Invité a todos mis amigos.   *I invited all my friends.*

But:

¿Conoces el Perú?   *Do you know Peru?/Have you ever been to Peru?*

Practice

1 La historia de mi vida *The story of my life*

entrar (here)	*to start*
a la edad de	*at the age of*
la carrera	*career*
como	*as*

Isabel, a journalist, tells her life story. Can you match the pictures with the sentences?

  a Me casé con Antonio en 2004.

  b Entré en la universidad a la edad de 18 años.

  c Nací en Aranjuez el 7 de mayo de 1976.

  d Terminé la carrera a los 23.

  e Empecé el colegio a los 6 años.

  f Empecé a trabajar como periodista en enero de 2000.

2 Con relación a su anuncio ... *With regard to your advertisement ...*

hice (from **hacer**)	*I did*
el puesto/cargo	*post*
trasladarse	*to move*
ocupar	*to hold (job)*
ingresar	*to join*
desempeñar	*to hold (job)*
la carrera	*career*
perder	*to lose*
la plantilla	*workforce*

Sebastián, an unemployed hotel receptionist, wrote the following letter in reply to a job advertisement. Complete the letter by changing the infinitives in brackets into the right form of the preterite tense. New vocabulary is given above.

> Muy señor mío:
>
> Me llamo Sebastián García Robles e hice estudios de hostelería en el Instituto Mediterráneo de Málaga, los que **(terminar)** en 1994. Entre 1995 y 2001 **(trabajar)** como recepcionista en el Hotel Andaluz de Marbella. En junio de 2002 **(trasladarse)** a Alicante e **(ingresar)** en el grupo hotelero Iberotur. **(Desempeñar)** el puesto de recepcionista en el Hotel Don Jaime, cargo que **(ocupar)** hasta diciembre de 2005, fecha en que **(perder)** mi empleo por reducción de plantilla ...

En cartas formales o comerciales, como la anterior, se utiliza la expresión **Muy señor/a mío/a** (*Dear Sir/Madam*). También puedes utilizar la expresión **Distinguido/a señor/a** o **Estimado/a señor/a** (*Dear Sir/ Madam*). La fórmula más común para terminar una carta formal es **Atentamente** o **Muy atentamente** (*Yours sincerely*).

Note the use of a colon (**dos puntos**) instead of a comma (**una coma**) after the salutation, as in **Muy señor mío:**

3 Una entrevista *An interview*

You have been asked to conduct a formal interview in Spanish. How would you say the following? Use the 'usted' form of the verb.

   a Where were you born?
   b When were you born?
   c What did you study?
   d When did you finish your studies (**los estudios**)?
   e Where do you work now?
   f How long have you been working there? (use 'llevar')
   g Where did you work before?

4 ¿Cuánto tiempo llevas ...? *How long have you been ...?*

How would you ask Soledad how long she has been doing each of the following, and how would she reply?

 4.1 First, match the drawings numbered 1–4 with the phrases a–d.

a vivir en Londres: dos años
b estudiar inglés: un año y medio
c hacer atletismo: tres años
d trabajar como enfermera: un año

4.2 Now ask and answer for her using the construction with 'llevar'. Use the 'tú' form of the verb.

5 ¿Cuánto tiempo hace ...? *How long ago ...?*

 emigrar   *to emigrate*
 secretariado bilingüe   *bilingual secretarial course*

15.04

María, Rafael, Fátima, and José, all left their countries to go and live somewhere else. Listen to their stories and answer the questions which follow.

 a When was each person born?
 b How long ago did María marry Antonio?
 c How long ago did Rafael emigrate to Argentina?
 d Where were his children born?
 e How long ago did Fátima's parents arrive in Spain?
 f How long has she been working as a bilingual secretary?
 g How long ago did José arrive in Spain?
 h Where did he work first and where is he working now?

6 ¿Quién es? *Who is it?*

dejar	*to leave*
triunfar	*to succeed*
tales como	*such as*
realizar	*to carry out*
cuyo/a	*whose*
actuar	*to act*
la obra musical	*musical*
obtener (like **tener**)	*to obtain*
el premio	*prize*

Here is part of the life story of a famous Spanish actor. Can you guess who he is? First, complete the text by filling in the blanks with the preterite tense of the verbs in brackets.

> **(Nacer)** _____ en Málaga en 1961. **(Filmar)** _____ cinco películas con el director español Pedro Almodóvar. **(Dejar)** _____ España y **(triunfar)** _____ en Hollywood con películas tales como Philadelphia, La casa de los espíritus y Los reyes del mambo. **(Casarse)** _____ con la actriz Melanie Griffith, y en 1996 (ellos) **(tener)** _____ su primer hijo. **(Ser)** _____ el narrador en Evita, del director de cine Alan Parker. En 1999 **(realizar)** _____ su primer trabajo como director en la película Locos en Alabama, cuyo tema es el racismo. En esta película **(actuar)** _____ con su esposa Melanie Griffith. En el año 2003 **(obtener)** _____ un gran triunfo en Broadway con la obra musical Nine, por la cual fue nominado al premio Tony.

7 Mi biografía *My biography*

As part of a magazine project, you have been asked to write about the life of Rosa Ramírez, a famous photographer. Use the following information given by her to write your text, making all necessary changes to verbs and other grammatical words. Begin like this: 'Se llama Rosa Ramírez, nació ...'

> Me llamo Rosa Ramírez, nací en León el 6 de mayo de 1975, pero llegué a Madrid hace varios años. Soy fotógrafa, estoy casada y tengo dos hijos. Estudié fotografía en Madrid y terminé los estudios en 1997. En 1999 conocí a Julio, mi marido, y nos casamos un año después. Fernando, nuestro primer hijo, nació en octubre del año 2002 y dos años más tarde nació nuestra hija Francisca. Mi marido es guitarrista y lleva dos años tocando con un grupo de música rock.

8 Ahora tú *And now you*

You have been asked to provide information about your own life. Use the above and the previous activities as a model to write about yourself.

 Test yourself

Put the verbs in brackets into the appropriate form.

a Me llamo Julia, soy argentina, **(nacer)** en Buenos Aires en 1975.

b (Yo) **(llegar)** a España en 1990.

c A los veintiún años, en 1997, (yo) **(casarse)** con José, un español.

d José y yo **(conocerse)** en unas vacaciones en Marruecos y (nosotros) **(casarse)** un año después.

e Ahora soy profesora de francés y **(llevar)** un año y medio **(dar)** clases en una escuela de lenguas.

f José es antropólogo y **(llevar)** tres años **(trabajar)** en un museo. Le encanta su trabajo.

g Ahora vivimos en Barcelona, pero antes **(vivir)** un año en Valencia.

h En Valencia **(nacer)** Ana, nuestra primera hija, que tiene ocho años.

i El año pasado, José, nuestra hija y yo **(pasar)** unos días en Buenos Aires.

j A José **(gustar)** mucho la ciudad.

Check your answers in the Key to Test yourself if you are uncertain about how you performed. It's very important that you know how to handle the form of the past, as it is extremely common and useful. Go back to the unit again if you need further revision.

SELF CHECK

	I CAN...
●	. . . ask and give biographical information
●	. . . say how long ago something happened
●	. . . say how long I have been doing something (2).

16 Me gustó muchísimo
I liked it very much

In this unit you will learn how to:

▶ *talk about a past holiday or journey*
▶ *say what you thought of something or someone*
▶ *talk about the weather.*

CEFR: *Can ask and answer questions about past activities (A2); Can write a clear, detailed text on a holiday or journey (A2); Can understand basic types of standard routine letters on familiar topics (B1).*

The rain in Spain

Joan Miró (a contemporary of Picasso), when asked to provide a logo for Spain's tourist board, painted a red-hot sun, **pero no siempre hace sol en España** (*but it isn't always sunny in Spain*). The country stretches from the Atlantic in the north to the Mediterranean in the south, and is the second most mountainous country in Europe, so has a variety of climates.

Llueve (*it rains*) much more in the north than in the rest of Spain making it **la España verde** (*green Spain*). In the mountains, **nieva en invierno** (*it snows in winter*). Not for nothing is **la Sierra Nevada** in the south called the Snowy Mountains. In central Spain, **hace mucho frío en invierno y mucho calor en verano** (*it's very cold in winter and very hot in summer*).

What does Pepe say the weather was like when he was on holiday? Hizo sol y bastante calor. Solamente llovió un día.

Conversations

1 ¿DÓNDE FUISTE? *WHERE DID YOU GO?*

pasar	*to spend (time)*
parecer	*to seem*

🎧 16.01

Elisa, Julio, Laura and Manuel talk about their holidays.

1.1 **Among the following sentences there are three actions which are not mentioned in the dialogue. Listen to the conversation and try to spot them.**

1 I didn't do anything special.

2 I went home.

3 My boyfriend came home from Marbella.

4 I went to Mexico.

5 I was in Mexico for two years.

6 I was in Mexico two years ago.

Elisa	¿Qué hicisteis en las vacaciones?
Julio	Yo no hice nada especial. Me quedé en casa.
Laura	Pues, yo pasé mis vacaciones en Marbella. Estuve en casa de mi novio. Y tú Elisa, ¿dónde fuiste?
Elisa	Fui a México con Tomás. Estuvimos dos semanas allí.
Julio	¿Qué os pareció México? ¿Os gustó?
Elisa	Sí, nos encantó. Nos pareció un país interesantísimo. Fueron unas vacaciones estupendas.
Manuel	Yo estuve en México hace dos años y me gustó muchísimo.

1.2 **Now read the dialogue and find the past tense forms (the preterite, Unit 15) of the following verbs:**

estar	**pasar**	**gustar**	**hacer**	**ir**
ser	**encantar**	**quedarse**	**parecer.**	

You may have noticed that some of the verbs do not follow the pattern that you learned in Unit 15. These correspond to irregular verbs, of which there are few but they are important. The following verbs from the list in 1.2 are irregular in the preterite tense: **estar**, **hacer**, **ir**, **ser**.

1.3 Read the dialogue again and say in which way the meaning of the following two words is intensified: **interesante, mucho.**

2 ¿QUÉ TAL EL TIEMPO? *WHAT WAS THE WEATHER LIKE?*

agradable	*pleasant*
aunque	*although*
tuvimos (from **tener**) **suerte**	*we were lucky*

16.02

*Elisa tells Julio about the weather, **el tiempo**, in Mexico City. Note the use of **hacer**, (to do, make) to refer to the weather.*

2.1 What does Elisa say about the weather and why does she think they were lucky? Listen and find out.

> Julio   ¿Qué tal el tiempo en la Ciudad de México?
>
> Elisa   Me pareció muy agradable. No hace mucho calor, aunque en julio llueve a menudo. Pero tuvimos suerte, sólo llovió una vez.
>
> Julio   Aquí hizo muchísimo calor.

2.2 Read the dialogue now and find the Spanish for the following phrases:
  1 it's not very hot
  2 it often rains
  3 it rained only once
  4 it was very hot.

A number of weather expressions in Spanish use **hacer** (*to do, make*) and translate to be in English, for example **Hace frío** (*It's cold*) (see 'Language discovery' section, paragraph 3). Note also the phrase **Tuvimos suerte**, from **tener suerte** (*to have luck* or *to be lucky*).

How do you say it?

TALKING ABOUT A PAST HOLIDAY OR JOURNEY

a To ask people what they did you can say

¿Qué hiciste/hizo Vd. en tus/ sus vacaciones?	*What did you do on your holidays?*
¿Qué hicisteis el verano pasado?	*What did you do last summer?*

b To say what you did you can say

Me quedé/nos quedamos en casa.	*I/we stayed at home.*
No hice/hicimos nada.	*I/we didn't do anything.*
Fui/fuimos a China.	*I/we went to China.*
Pasé/pasamos unos días en Florida.	*I/we spent a few days in Florida.*

SAYING WHAT YOU THOUGHT OF SOMETHING OR SOMEONE

¿Qué te/le pareció la ciudad/ la gente?	*What did you think of the city/ the people?*
Me pareció muy caro(a)/ agradable.	*It seemed very expensive/ pleasant (to me)*
¿Qué os/les pareció?	*What did you think of it?*
Nos pareció muy bonita.	*It seemed very pretty (to us)*

TALKING ABOUT THE WEATHER

Hace (mucho) calor/frío.	*It's (very) hot/cold.*
Hizo (muchísimo) calor/frío.	*It was (very) hot/cold.*

 Language discovery

1 SAYING WHAT YOU DID: IRREGULAR PRETERITE FORMS

The number of irregular verbs in the preterite tense is small but some of these are very common, so try to learn them as they come up. Many of them have very similar forms, and that should help you to memorize them.

estar (*to be*)

estuve, estuviste, estuvo, estuvimos, estuvisteis, estuvieron

tener (*to have*)

tuve, tuviste, tuvo, tuvimos, tuvisteis, tuvieron

andar (*to walk*)

anduve, anduviste, anduvo, anduvimos, anduvisteis, anduvieron

poder (*to be able to, can*)

pude, pudiste, pudo, pudimos, pudisteis, pudieron

ser (*to be*), **ir** (*to go*)

fui, fuiste, fue, fuimos, fuisteis, fueron

ver (*to see*)

vi, viste, vio, vimos, visteis, vieron

hacer (*to do, make*)

hice, hiciste, hizo, hicimos, hicisteis, hicieron

decir (*to say, tell*)

dije, dijiste, dijo, dijimos, dijisteis, dijeron

venir (*to come*)

vine, viniste, vino, vinimos, vinisteis, vinieron

Anduvimos por el río.	*We walked along the river.*
Miguel no pudo venir.	*Miguel couldn't come.*
Fue un viaje interesante.	*It was an interesting journey.*
Vi sitios maravillosos.	*I saw marvellous places.*
¿Qué te dijeron?	*What did they tell you?*
Ella vino sola.	*She came on her own.*

The preterite form of **hay** (*there is/are*) (from **haber**) is **hubo** (*there was/ were*). For other irregular preterite forms see Irregular verbs.

Try learning the verbs above by writing your own examples. Note that **ser** and **ir** have exactly the same forms in the preterite, so it is the context that will help to establish meaning: **Fui a las Islas Canarias** (I went to the Canary Islands), **Fui feliz** (*I was happy*).

2 PARECER *TO SEEM*

Parecer (*to seem*) functions in the same way as **gustar** and **encantar** (see Unit 13) – that is, with the third person of the verb, singular or plural, preceded by one of the following pronouns: **me**, **te**, **le**, **nos**, **os**, **les**: **¿Qué te pareció La Habana?** (*What did you think of Havana?* – literally, *What to you seemed Havana?*), **Me pareció interesante** (*It seemed interesting* –

literally, *To me it seemed interesting*), **Los cubanos nos parecieron simpáticos** (*Cubans seemed nice* – literally, *Cubans to us seemed nice*).

3 TALKING ABOUT THE WEATHER

a Using 'hacer'

Hace calor/frío/viento.	*It's warm/cold/windy.*
Hace bueno.	*The weather is good.*
Hace buen/mal tiempo.	*The weather is good/bad.*
Ayer hizo sol/frío.	*Yesterday it was sunny/cold.*

b Using 'estar' and 'haber'

Está/estuvo nuboso/cubierto.	*It is/was cloudy/overcast.*
Está lloviendo/nevando.	*It's raining/snowing.*
Hay/hubo niebla.	*It is/was foggy.*
Hay/hubo tormenta.	*There is/was a storm.*

c **Llover (o>ue)** (*to rain*), **nevar (e>ie)** (*to snow*)

Llueve/llovió mucho.	*It rains/rained a lot.*
No nieva/nevó.	*It doesn't/didn't snow.*

4 USING -ÍSIMO/-ÍSIMA

a **-ísimo** or **-ísima** can be added to adjectives to intensify their meaning. If the word you want to emphasize ends in a consonant, just add **-ísimo** (m) or **-ísima** (f), and **-s** for plural: **fácil** (*easy*), **facilísimo/a(s)** (*very easy*). If it ends in a vowel, remove this and add **-ísimo/a(s)**: **caro/a(s)** (*expensive*), **carísimo/a(s)** (*very expensive*). Some adverbs, for example **mucho, poco**, can also take **-ísimo**, in which case this is invariable: **me gustó muchísimo** (*I liked it very much*).

b Words ending in **-co** or **-ca** and **-go** or **-ga** become **-quísimo/a** and **-guísimo/a** respectively, in order to keep the sound of the **-c** or **-g**: **rico** (*rich*), **riquísimo/a(s)** (*very rich*), **largo** (*long*), **larguísimo/a(s)** (*very long*), **poco** (*little*), **poquísimo/a(s)** (*very little/few*).

A number of adjectives do not accept **-ísimo/-ísima** so you should not use it unless you are sure. The alternative of course is to use words such as **muy** (*very*), **bastante** (*quite, rather*), **demasiado** (*too*): **muy/bastante/demasiado difícil** (*very/quite/too difficult*).

 Practice

 1 Un email *An email*

yo (estoy) estupendamente	*I feel great*
algo ligero	*something light*
el/la socio/a	*partner*
recoger	*to pick up*
juntos/as	*together*
pasarlo bien	*to have a good time*

Antonia was sent by her company to Mexico. Here's an email she sent to a colleague back home. Can you put the verbs in brackets in the appropriate form of the preterite tense?

> Hola Carmen:
>
> ¿Qué tal estás? Yo, estupendamente. Llegué a la Ciudad de México hace tres días. El avión **(salir)** a la hora y el vuelo **(ser)** estupendo. El primer día (yo) no **(hacer)** nada especial, **(cenar)** algo ligero y **(acostarse)**. Anteayer **(tener)** una reunión con nuestros socios y por la tarde **(estar)** en el Museo de Antropología, que me **(gustar)** muchísimo. Ayer al mediodía **(ir)** a un mercado e **(hacer)** algunas compras. Por la noche, unos amigos mexicanos **(venir)** a recogerme al hotel y **(ir)** juntos a cenar. (Yo) lo **(pasar)** muy bien. Los mexicanos que (yo) **(conocer)** me **(parecer)** simpatiquísimos ...

Gustar and **parecer** are both regular verbs but you may remember that the construction in which they occur is different from that of the rest of the verbs. If you need to revise this, go back to Unit 13.

 2 ¿Qué hizo? *What did he do?*

Can you say what Alejandro did when he went on holiday to the Caribbean, 'el Caribe'? Match the drawings with the verbs and put these in the appropriate form of the preterite tense.

    a (salir) a bailar
    b (ir) a pescar
    c (nadar) muchísimo
    d (conocer) a una chica guapísima
    e (hacer) vela
    f (tomar) el sol

 la/el chico/a — *girl/boy*

guapo/a — *pretty, good-looking*

3 ¿Qué hicieron? *What did they do?*

 las pirámides — *the pyramids*

la Esfinge — *the Sphynx*

 Here are some of the things María Teresa and Agustín did while on holiday in Egypt, Egipto. Choose an appropriate verb from the list to complete each sentence, using the preterite tense:

| ver | hacer | ir | tener | parecer | estar | andar |

This exercise focuses on the **nosotros** form. Once you have completed sentences a–f and made sure you got the verbs right, imagine you are telling someone else about María Teresa and Agustín's holiday. Start like this: **Agustín y María Teresa … de vacaciones …** You will need the plural form for **ellos**.

a Agustín y yo … de vacaciones a Egipto.

b … una semana en el Cairo y otra semana en Luxor.

c En el Cairo … las pirámides y la Esfinge.

d También … por los mercados, que nos … interesantísimos.

e … un viaje maravilloso por el río Nilo.

f … muchísima suerte con el tiempo. No hizo demasiado calor.

4 Fui a los Estados Unidos *I went to the United States*

A Spanish-speaking friend has just returned from a holiday in the United States. How would you ask him/her the following?

   a Where did you go?
   b How long were you there?
   c Did you stay with friends?
   d What did you do there?
   e What did you think of the place?
   f Was it very hot?

5 Ahora tú *And now you*

Use the previous activities as a model to write a brief account of a real or imaginary holiday or a journey that you made. Don't forget to say what the weather was like and what you thought of the place.

6 ¿Qué tal el tiempo? *What's the weather like?*

6.1 You and a Spanish-speaking colleague will be travelling through Spain on business, so you want to know what the weather is like in the places you'll visit. First match each weather symbol with an appropriate phrase.

   a hace viento
   b está nuboso
   c está nevando
   d hace sol
   e hay tormenta
   f está lloviendo
   g está cubierto
   h hay niebla

6.2 Now look at the weather map and answer your colleague's questions.

   a ¿Qué tal el tiempo en Málaga?
   b ¿Y en Baleares?
   c Y en Bilbao, ¿qué tal?
   d ¿Y en Zaragoza?

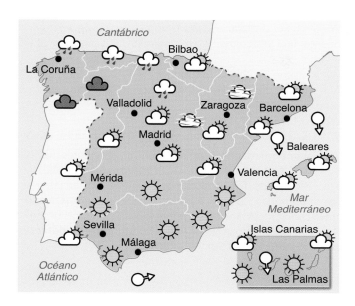

7 Misión hispanoamericana *Spanish American Mission*

el sol	*sun*
la temperatura	*temperature*
los grados	*degrees*
la lluvia	*rain*
fuerte	*strong*
las perspectivas	*prospects*

16.03

Your next assignment will be in Argentina. On your cable TV you hear a weather report for Buenos Aires, the capital city. Look at the key words above and then listen to the report several times and answer the following questions.

a Which one of the following expressions describes the weather in Buenos Aires yesterday? : it was cloudy, it was a sunny day, it was very hot.

b What will the weather be like today?

c At what time of day is Buenos Aires likely to have rain and strong wind tomorrow?

d What will the weather be like after midday?

e What will be the minimum and maximum temperatures tomorrow?

The word **hispanoamericano**, Spanish American, designates the Spanish-speaking countries of Latin America, which excludes Brazil, where the language is Portuguese. The area colonized by Spain is often referred to as **Hispanoamérica** (*Spanish America*). The term **sudamericano** or **suramericano** (*South American*), refers to the inhabitants of the countries south of Panama, a region known in Spanish as **Sudamérica** or **Suramérica** or **América del Sur**.

Test yourself

1 **Change the verbs in brackets into the appropriate form of the preterite tense.**

   a El mes pasado, Laura y yo **(ir)** de vacaciones a Italia y **(estar)** unos días en Florencia.

   b Florencia nos **(gustar)** mucho. Nos **(parecer)** una ciudad interesantísima.

   c **(Hacer)** muchísimo calor, pero sólo **(llover)** una vez.

   d **(Ser)** unas vacaciones estupendas y no **(ser)** fácil volver a la oficina a trabajar.

   e Ayer Laura y yo **(ver)** las fotos de nuestras vacaciones. (Las fotos) Nos **(gustar)** mucho.

2 **How would you express the following in Spanish? Use the preterite tense of the verbs in brackets.**

   a He couldn't come to the party. **(poder)**

   b He had to work. **(tener que)**

   c What did you do yesterday night? *(informal)* **(hacer)**

   d I went to the cinema with Raúl. We saw a very good film. **(ir, ver)**

   e Teresa came on Monday. She was here with her boyfriend. **(venir, estar)**

These tests assess your ability to use the past tense, using mainly irregular verbs. The verbs listed are very common. If you feel you need to revise their forms go back to the grammar in this unit or look up the preterite forms in the list of irregular verbs.

SELF CHECK

I CAN...
○ ... talk about a past holiday or journey
○ ... say what I thought of something or someone
○ ... talk about the weather.

17 Eran muy simpáticos

They were very nice

In this unit you will learn how to:

▶ *ask for and give reasons*
▶ *ask and say what someone was like*
▶ *ask and say what a place or something was like.*

CEFR: *Can describe experiences and give reasons for opinions (B1); Can describe people and places (B1); Can write a clear, detailed text describing his home (B1); Can identify speaker viewpoints and attitudes (B2).*

Tell me what it was like

A television drama of the early years of the twenty-first century was **Cuéntame** (*Tell Me*). Set as it was during the years of the Franco regime (1939–1975), and centred on a family living in a provincial town, the series almost didn't make it to the small screen and was not expected to be a success. Yet it proved to be extremely popular, especially among younger viewers avid to know **cómo eran aquellos tiempos** (*what those times were like*).

Among other things, they learned that **la gente era más pobre** (*people were poorer*) **porque los sueldos eran muy bajos** (*because salaries were very low*). **Muchas familias no tenían coche ni televisor** (*Many families didn't have a car or a television*). Everybody lived in a much stricter society but that did not stop them from enjoying themselves.

What does Ricardo tell you about his father?
Mi padre no tenía muchos amigos porque sus padres, mis abuelos, eran muy estrictos con él.

Conversations

1 ¿POR QUÉ? *WHY?*

además	*besides*
el sueldo	*salary*
bajo/a	*low*
dedicado/a a	*devoted to*

17.01

Rocío, Blanca and Daniel describe people they knew.

1.1 **Below are some of the words used by them to describe people. They include masculine and feminine forms. How many of them can you recognize? Check their meanings first, then listen to the dialogues and tick them as you hear them.**

Note the key expressions:

era	*he/she/it was, you were* (formal, sing)
eran	*they were, you were* (formal, pl)
¿por qué?	*why?*
porque	*because*

agresivo/a	☐	generoso/a	☐	irresponsable	☐
antipático/a	☐	guapo/a	☐	machista	☐
divertido/a	☐	horrible	☐	tímido/a	☐
estricto/a	☐	insoportable	☐	reservado/a	☐
feo/a	☐	inteligente	☐	trabajador/a	☐

1 Rocío

Daniel	¿Por qué dejaste tu trabajo, Rocío?
Rocío	Porque mi jefe era insoportable. Tenía un carácter muy agresivo. Mis compañeros de trabajo eran muy simpáticos, pero mi jefe no, todo lo contrario, él era muy antipático. ¡Era feo, era horrible! Además, mi sueldo era muy bajo.

2 Blanca

Rocío	¿Por qué te divorciaste de Santiago, Blanca?
Blanca	Mira, Santiago era muy guapo, era inteligente y divertido y tenía un gran sentido del humor, pero era muy irresponsable y demasiado machista.

3 Daniel

Blanca	¿Cómo era tu madre, Daniel?
Daniel	Mi madre era una persona reservada, un poco tímida, trabajadora, generosa, dedicada a su familia y bastante estricta con sus hijos.

1.2 Now read the dialogues and answer these questions:

1 Which of the words in exercise 1.1 describe Rocío's former boss?
2 Which fit Santiago and which Daniel's mother?
3 What expressions are used in the dialogues to say *my colleagues, on the contrary, a great sense of humour*?

Forms like **era/n** as in **Era horrible** (*He was horrible*) and **tenía/n** as in **Tenía un gran sentido del humor** (*He had a great sense of humour*) correspond to the imperfect tense, a tense which is often used to describe people (or places and things) known in the past.

2 ¿QUÉ TAL ERA EL HOTEL? *WHAT WAS THE HOTEL LIKE?*

vista(s) al mar	*seaview*
el aparcamiento	*car park*

17.02

After leaving her job and her boss, Rocío took a holiday with her family. In this dialogue Rocío describes the hotel where she stayed.

2.1 **Which of the two hotels below is the one where they stayed? Listen and find out and, as you do, note the following verb forms:**

era (from **ser**)   *it was* (description)

estaba (from **estar**)   *it was* (location)

tenía (from **tener**)   *it had*

había (from **haber**)   *there was/were*

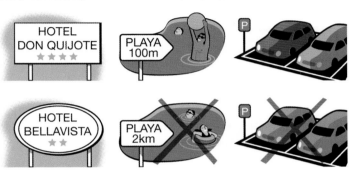

| Daniel | ¿Qué tal era el hotel donde estuviste? |
| Rocío | Era estupendo. Era un hotel de cuatro estrellas, estaba a cien metros de la playa, tenía piscina, un buen restaurante, vistas al mar y aparcamiento. Las habitaciones eran muy cómodas y había aire acondicionado y televisión por cable. |

2.2 **Go back to the conversation and find the Spanish for:**
  1 What was the hotel like?
  2 It was a hundred metres from the beach.
  3 The rooms were very comfortable.

2.3 **A friend of yours may be travelling to the same hotel. Read the dialogue and explain what the hotel was like.**

In this dialogue the description involves a place, a hotel, and the facilities it had. As in Dialogue 1, **era/n** is used to say what the hotel was like, while a new form, **había**, is used for referring to the facilities, **Había aire acondicionado ...** (*There was air conditioning ...*).

How do you say it?

¿Por qué dejó su trabajo/se divorció?
Why did she/he leave her/his job/ get divorced?

Porque su jefe/marido/mujer era insoportable.
Because her/his boss/her husband/ his wife was unbearable.

ASKING AND SAYING WHAT SOMEONE WAS LIKE

¿Cómo era tu madre/abuelo?
What was your mother/ grandfather like?

Era alta(o)/guapa(o).
She/he was tall/good-looking.

Tenía sentido del humor/ paciencia.
She/he had a sense of humour/ patience.

ASKING AND SAYING WHAT A PLACE OR SOMETHING WAS LIKE

¿Qué tal/cómo era el hotel/ el apartamento?
What was the hotel/apartment like?

Era cómodo, tenía servicio de Internet, había garaje.
It was comfortable, it had Internet facilities, there was a garage.

Estaba en el centro de la ciudad.
It was in the centre of the city.

¿Qué tal era tu sueldo?
What was your salary like?

Era bajo/malo/bueno.
It was low/bad/good.

Note **estaba** (from **estar**) (*it was*) to say where a place, a thing, or a person was. **Estaba** is a regular imperfect tense form. Here are some more examples: **Su piso estaba en Mallorca** (His/her flat was in Mallorca), **María estaba en Madrid** (*María was in Madrid*).

 ## Language discovery

1 DESCRIBING PEOPLE, PLACES AND THINGS IN RELATION TO THE PAST: THE IMPERFECT TENSE (1)

Usage

a   To describe people, places or things in relation to the past, you need the *imperfect tense*. Unlike the preterite (Units 15 and 16), the imperfect cannot be used to refer to an action which was completed at a definite point in the past. In **Mi abuela era muy culta** (*My grandmother was* *very cultured*), there is no concern for time, except to show that one is referring to a past experience. Compare this with **Mi abuela murió el año pasado** (*My grandmother died last year*), which signals an event that took place at a specific point in the past, for which you require the preterite tense.

b   The imperfect tense often accompanies the preterite, as a kind of framework or description behind the actions that took place: **Dejé** (preterite**) mi trabajo porque mi sueldo era** (imperfect) **muy bajo** (*I left my job because my salary was very low*). For more examples, see paragraph **b** below. For other uses of the imperfect, see Unit 18 and section 18 of the Grammar summary.

Formation

a   There are two sets of endings for the imperfect tense of *regular verbs*, one for **-ar** verbs and another one for **-er** and **-ir** verbs. The first and third person singular are the same for all three. Here are two examples, one for each set:

	estar (*to be*)	tener (*to have*)
yo	est**aba**	ten**ía**
tú	est**abas**	ten**ías**
él, ella, Vd.	est**aba**	ten**ía**
nosotros/as	est**ábamos**	ten**íamos**
vosotros/as	est**abais**	ten**íais**
ellos/ellas, Vds.	est**aban**	ten**ían**

b   There are only three *irregular verbs* in the imperfect tense: **ser** (*to be*), **ver** (*to see*) and **ir** (*to go*). Below is the imperfect form of **ser**. For **ver** and **ir**, see Unit 18.

ser (*to be*)	
yo	er**a**
tú	er**as**
él, ella, Vd.	er**a**
nosotros/as	ér**amos**
vosotros/as	er**ais**
ellos, ellas, Vds.	er**an**

 Read the passage below which combines the use of the preterite with that of the imperfect tense.

estilo neogótico	neogothic style
imponente	imposing
recordar (o>ue)	to remember
las afueras	outskirts

> Fue la primera ciudad que visitamos en nuestro viaje. No era una ciudad grande, pero era una ciudad atractiva y tenía muchos sitios de interés turístico. Había un museo de arte colonial que nos gustó mucho y la catedral, que era de estilo neogótico, era imponente.
>
> El hotel donde estábamos – no recuerdo cómo se llamaba - estaba en las afueras de la ciudad. Estuvimos dos días allí antes de continuar nuestro viaje. En aquel tiempo Elena y yo éramos muy jóvenes ...

2 TIME PHRASES ASSOCIATED WITH THE IMPERFECT TENSE

The following expressions are often used with the imperfect, although depending on the context they may be found with other forms of the past, for example the preterite: **antes** (*before*), **entonces** (*at that time*), **en esa/aquella época** (*at that time*), **en esos/aquellos años** (*in those years*), **de pequeño(a)/joven** (*when I/he/she was young*).

Practice

el curso	course
el crucero	cruise
mudarse	to move (house)
ruidoso/a	noisy
aburrido/a	boring
la avería	breakdown

1 ¿Por qué? *Why?*

Match each question with an appropriate answer using '¿por qué?' or 'porque'.

¿Por qué?

    a ¿...dejaste el curso?
    b ¿...decidiste estudiar español?
    c ¿...vendió su ordenador/computador(a) (LAm)?
    d ¿...no hicieron el crucero por el Caribe?
    e ¿...se mudaron de casa?
    f ¿...no viniste en el coche/auto, carro (LAm)?

Porque …

1 …el viaje era muy caro.
2 …la calle donde estaba era muy ruidosa.
3 …la profesora era muy aburrida.
4 …mi novio/a habla español.
5 …tenía una avería.
6 …no tenía suficiente memoria.

In the spoken language the only difference between **¿por qué?** and **porque** is the stress on **-qué** in the first and the stress on **por-** in the second, so it is important that you place the stress in the right place.

2 Palabra por palabra *Word for word*

Here are some words used for describing people's characters. How many of them do you know or can you guess? Look them up in your dictionary if necessary and then give the opposite of each word.

a	divertido/a	**h**	simpático/a
b	triste	**i**	fuerte
c	audaz	**j**	desagradable
d	tonto/a	**k**	trabajador/a
e	modesto/a	**l**	irresponsable
f	cortés	**m**	inmaduro/a
g	optimista	**n**	inseguro/a

The focus in this activity is on words related to people's characters, but you might also want to describe someone in terms of their appearance. Think of words you would use to describe someone you know, look them up in your dictionary and then find the opposite of the same words. Note that words ending in **-ista**, like **optimista**, can refer to a male or a female.

3 Sopa de letras *Word search*

Can you spot the opposites of the words listed above in the word square? The completed word square is at the end of the unit.

A	K	X	A	B	U	R	R	I	D	O
R	D	P	N	J	I	O	P	L	M	N
R	E	E	T	B	S	N	G	H	T	P
O	S	S	I	H	G	E	A	T	Y	E
G	C	I	P	A	L	E	G	R	E	R
A	O	M	A	O	M	K	R	U	F	E
N	R	I	T	W	N	A	A	Y	R	Z
T	T	S	I	D	J	S	D	H	H	O
E	E	T	C	E	P	P	A	U	Q	S
U	S	A	O	B	P	P	B	B	R	O
H	T	I	M	I	D	O	L	K	L	O
I	N	T	E	L	I	G	E	N	T	E

4 ¿Cómo era Roberto? *What was Roberto like?*

la capacidad	*capacity*
alegre	*cheerful, happy*
extrovertido/a	*extrovert*
la relación	*relationship*
una carta	*a letter*
nos conocimos	*we met*

17.03

Pepe describes Roberto, someone he once knew. Listen to Pepe's account several times and answer the questions which follow.

    a Where did Pepe and Roberto meet?
    b What was Roberto's profession?
    c How does Pepe describe him?
    d What happened to Roberto?

How would you relate Pepe's account to someone else in Spanish? Listen again before you do it.

5 Ahora tú *And now you*

Write a short description of someone you knew. Try using words from the dialogues and the previous activities, and others suitable for the person you wish to describe.

6 La casa de Marta *Marta's house*

la planta (or el piso)	*floor*
el salón comedor	*sitting room / dining room*

Look at this plan of the house where Marta used to live and then complete the description below with one of the following verbs, using the imperfect tense: *estar, haber, ser, tener.*

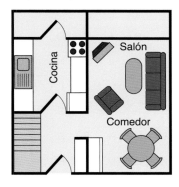

Mi casa no **(a)** _____ ni grande ni pequeña, pero **(b)** _____ muy cómoda. La casa **(c)** _____ dos plantas. En la planta baja **(d)** _____ el salón comedor y la cocina y en la primera planta **(e)** _____ los dos dormitorios y el baño. En uno de los dormitorios **(f)** _____ una cama matrimonial y en el otro **(g)** _____ dos camas. La calle donde **(h)** _____ **(i)** _____ bastante tranquila y cerca de la casa **(j)** _____ tiendas y un supermercado. Mis vecinos **(k)** _____ gente muy simpática y el barrio no **(l)** _____ malo.

Note the use of three negatives in **Mi casa no ... ni grande ni pequeña** (*My house ... neither big nor small*).

7 Ahora tú *And now you*

Use the activity above as a model to describe a place where you used to live. Here are some words you might need:

el garaje   *garage*

el jardín del frente de atrás   *front/back garden*

el patio   *courtyard, patio*

Answer to Activity 3

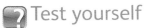 Test yourself

Complete each sentence with the imperfect tense form of *estar*, *haber*, *ser* or *tener*.

a San Alfonso _____ una ciudad muy pequeña.

b La ciudad _____ a pocos kilómetros de la capital.

c La casa de mis abuelos _____ muy cerca de la plaza.

d La casa _____ un patio y un jardín donde _____ muchas flores.

e Mi abuela _____ una persona muy estricta, pero _____ un gran sentido del humor.

f Mi abuelo, que _____ un hombre muy sociable, _____ muchísimos amigos.

g En aquel tiempo no _____ televisión y tampoco _____ un cine en la ciudad.

h Yo _____ buenos amigos en San Alfonso. _____ chicos de mi edad. Mis mejores amigos _____ Paco y Luis.

i Paco y Luis _____ muy simpáticos, pero su hermana no, todo lo contrario, ella _____ un carácter muy especial.

j San Alfonso _____ una escuela, que _____ muy pequeña y _____ cerca de casa. En la escuela _____ tres profesores.

Describing people, places and things with reference to the past is important in every language, and you only need a small number of verbs to do this. If you got the forms right, go on to unit 18 in which you will learn to talk about the things you used to do.

SELF CHECK

	I CAN. . .
○	. . . ask for and give reasons
○	. . . ask and say what someone was like
○	. . . ask and say what a place or something was like.

18 ¿Qué hacías allí?
What were you doing there?

In this unit you will learn how to:
▸ *say where you used to live*
▸ *say what work you used to do*
▸ *talk about things you did regularly in the past.*

CEFR: *Can describe experiences, events and impressions (B1); Can explain what he/she liked or disliked about something (B1); Can write very short, basic descriptions of past activities and personal experiences (B1).*

The *paseo*

The **paseo** (*walk/stroll*) is a time-honoured institution in Spain. Every town and city has its **paseo** (**rambla** in Cataluña), a boulevard with a tree-lined central walkway and plenty of benches to sit on.

With the hectic pace of life these days, most Spaniards only indulge in **el paseo** at weekends and when on holiday, but **antes siempre daban un paseo después del trabajo** (*before, they always went for a stroll after work*). It was a time to meet up with friends and enjoy one another's company.

Paseaban y charlaban (*they strolled and chatted*). **También entraban en un bar** (*they also went into a bar*). On weekdays, the women would be at home preparing the evening meal but at the weekends **toda la familia salía a dar el paseo** (*the whole family went out for their stroll*).

What comparison is Alberto making about his life in the town and in the city?
Cuando vivía en el pueblo, salía todas las noches. Aquí en la ciudad, llego a casa tarde y estoy muy cansado.

Conversations

1 ¿DÓNDE VIVÍAS ANTES? *WHERE DID YOU LIVE BEFORE?*

el/la encargado/a de ventas	*sales manager* (literally, *the one in charge of* ...)
solo/a	*on my/your own, alone*
compartir	*to share*
llevarse bien	*to get on well*

 18.01

At a party Rodolfo meets Elena. Elena tells Rodolfo about her life in Alicante before arriving in Barcelona.

1.1   How long was Elena in Alicante and what was she doing there? Listen and find out.

Rodolfo	¿Dónde vivías antes de llegar a Barcelona?
Elena	Vivía en Alicante. Estuve cinco años allí.
Rodolfo	¿Qué hacías en Alicante?
Elena	Trabajaba en una agencia de viajes. Era la encargada de ventas.
Rodolfo	¿Vivías sola?
Elena	No, compartía un piso con un amigo. Nos llevábamos muy bien.

As Unit 17, this unit focuses on the imperfect tense, but the emphasis here is on actions that occurred over a period of time in the past but without concern for either the beginning or the end of that action, for example **Vivíamos en Sevilla** (*We lived/used to live in Seville*).

1.2   Now read the dialogue and say how the following is expressed:
   1 before arriving
   2 I used to live in ...
   3 I used to work in ...
   4 I was sharing a flat.

2 ME ENCANTABA *I LOVED IT*

pasarlo bien/estupendamente	*to have a good/great time*
ganar	*to earn*
la vida	*life*

 18.02

Rodolfo asks Elena whether she liked living in Alicante.

2.1 **What does Elena say with regard to her friends there? She mentions three things she used to do with her friends. What were they? Listen and find out.**

Rodolfo	¿Te gustaba vivir en Alicante?
Elena	Sí, me encantaba. Tenía muy buenos amigos allí. Los veía prácticamente todos los días, salíamos de copas o a cenar, los fines de semana íbamos a bailar ... Lo pasábamos estupendamente.
Rodolfo	Y el trabajo, ¿qué tal?
Elena	No estaba mal. No ganaba mucho, pero la vida no era tan cara como aquí.

2.2 **What does Elena say about her job in Alicante? And about her salary? How does she express both ideas? Read and find out.**

Gustar and **encantar** here are in the imperfect tense: **te gustaba**, **me encantaba**. Both are in the third person and they take the ending **-aba** for **-ar** verbs. Note also **(yo) no ganaba**. In the imperfect, the ending for the first person (**yo**) is the same as for the third person (**él**, **ella**, **Vd.**).

How do you say it?

ASKING PEOPLE WHERE THEY USED TO LIVE, AND RESPONDING

¿Dónde vivías/vivía Vd.?	*Where did you live/were you living?*
Vivía en Florencia.	*I lived/used to live/was living in Florence.*

ASKING PEOPLE WHAT WORK THEY USED TO DO, AND RESPONDING

¿Dónde trabajabas/trabajaba Vd.?	*Where did you work/were you working?*
¿En qué trabajabas/ trabajaba Vd.?	*What work did you do?*
¿Qué hacías/hacía Vd.?	*What did you do/were you doing?*
Trabajaba en un banco.	*I used to work/was working in a bank*
Era contable/secretario/a.	*I was an accountant/secretary.*

226

TALKING ABOUT THINGS YOU DID REGULARLY IN THE PAST

Salía/salíamos mucho.	*I/we used to go out a lot.*
Iba/íbamos al teatro/a conciertos.	*I/we used to go to the theatre/ concerts.*
Veía/veíamos televisión.	*I/we used to watch television.*

 # Language discovery

1 SAYING WHAT YOU USED TO DO OR WERE DOING: THE IMPERFECT TENSE (2)

In Unit 17 you learned to use the imperfect tense to describe people and places you knew in the past. This unit focuses on the use of the imperfect to refer to:

a a state or an action which continued in the past over an unspecified period.

En aquel tiempo María vivía conmigo.	*At that time María lived/used to live/was living with me.*
Ella trabajaba en radio y televisión.	*She worked/used to work/was working on radio and television.*

Note that if a definite period of time is mentioned, even when the action took place over a long period, the preterite and not the imperfect must be used (see units 15 and 16): **Estuve allí cinco años** (*I was there for five years*).

b habits or repeated events in the past

Siempre salíamos por la noche.	*We always went out at night.*
Me llamaba todos los días.	*He/she used to call me every day.*

2 IRREGULAR VERBS IN THE IMPERFECT TENSE

Other than **ser** (see Unit 17), only **ir** (*to go*) and **ver** (*to see*) are irregular in the imperfect tense. Note that the endings for **ver** are the same as those of regular **-er** and **-ir** verbs (see Unit 17).

	ir	ver
yo	iba	veía
tú	ibas	veías
él/ella/Vd.	iba	veía
nosotros/as	íbamos	veíamos
vosotros/as	ibais	veíais
ellos/ellas/Vds.	iban	veían

| **Él iba al pueblo todos los veranos.** | *He went/used to go to the village every summer.* |
| **Yo la veía a menudo.** | *I saw/used to see her often.* |

Words such as practically, regularly, are called adverbs (see also Glossary of grammatical terms). In English, adverbs often end in *-ly*, and the Spanish equivalent of this is **-mente**. In English you simply add *-ly* to the adjective to form the adverb, for example: *practical – practically*. In Spanish the rule is as follows:

If the adjective ends in **-o**, for example **práctico**, change the **-o** (masculine) to **-a** (feminine) and add **-mente**: **práctica – prácticamente**. If the adjective does not have a feminine form, simply add **-mente**: **fácil – fácilmente**. Note that if the adjective has a written accent, the adverb must keep the accent.

There are many adverbs which do not end in **-mente**, for example **bien** (*well*), **mal** (*badly*), **aquí** (*here*), **allí** (*there*), **antes** (*before*), **ahora** (*now*).

Note that in the phrase **antes de llegar** before arriving, Spanish uses the infinitive, whereas English uses the gerund, the *-ing* form of the verb. The general rule in Spanish is that verbs which follow a preposition (words like **a**, **de**, **para**, **sin**) must be in the infinitive, which often translates in English with the gerund: **después de salir** (*after going out*), **para oír mejor** (*to/in order to hear better (for hearing better)*), **sin recordar nada** (*without remembering anything*), **al empezar** (*on starting*).

 Practice

1 ¿Qué hacía Pablo? What did Pablo use to do?

Pablo remembers his childhood years. How would he tell someone what he used to do? Match the drawings with the phrases below, and put the verbs in the right form of the imperfect tense.

 a **(dormir)** la siesta
 b **(jugar)** con mi pelota
 c **(ir)** a la escuela
 d **(hacer)** los deberes
 e **(levantarse)** a las 8.00
 f **(comer)** con mi madre

Before you move on to Activity 2, write a few sentences mentioning some of the things you used to do when you were a child. Use either verbs from the list or others suitable for what you want to say.

2 Cuando tenía 18 años ... When I was 18 ...

mensual(es)	*monthly* (sing/pl)
dar un paseo	*to go for a walk*
verse	*to see one another*
el amor	*love*

Elvira, from Jaén, tells a friend about her life when she was eighteen. Put the infinitives in the right form of the imperfect tense.

Cuando **(yo)** tenía dieciocho años ...

(Vivir) con mis padres en Jaén.

(Trabajar) como dependienta en un supermercado.

(Ir) al trabajo en bicicleta.

(Empezar) a las 9.00 y **(salir)** a las 7.00.

(Ganar) 40.000 pesetas mensuales, unos 240 euros de ahora.

(Estar) soltera.

(Tener) un novio que **(llamarse)** Manuel.

Manuel y yo **(verse)** por la tarde, **(dar)** largos paseos y **(hablar)** de amor.

3 Ahora tú *And now you*

¿quién?   *who*

la escuela   *school*

¿Dónde vivías cuando eras pequeño/a? ¿Qué hacía tu padre? ¿Y tu madre? ¿Quién te llevaba a la escuela? ¿Te gustaba ir a la escuela? ¿Dónde pasabas tus vacaciones? ¿Qué hacías allí?

4 ¿A QUÉ SE DEDICABAN? *WHAT DID THEY DO FOR A LIVING?*

la Unión Europea	*European Union*
el/la maestro/a	*teacher (primary school)*
el/la programador/a (de ordenadores)	*computer programmer*
la programación	*programming*

18.03

Begoña, Esteban and Víctor talk about their previous and present jobs. Can you say what they used to do and what they do now? Listen and fill in the gaps with the appropriate names and change the infinitives in brackets into the right tense, the present or the imperfect.

_____ a   **(Ser)** intérprete. **(Trabajar)** para la Unión Europea.

_____ b   **(Ser)** maestra. **(Trabajar)** en un colegio.

_____ c   **(Trabajar)** en un restaurante. **(Ser)** camarero.

_____ d   **(Estar)** sin trabajo.

_____ e   **(Ser)** estudiante. **(Estudiar)** lenguas.

_____ f   **(Ser)** programador. **(Trabajar)** en una empresa de programación.

5 ¿Qué hacían Delia y Pepe? *What did Delia and Pepe do?*

5.1 Delia and Pepe had similar duties in the company where they both worked. Can you say what they were? Choose from the phrases in the box below and write an appropriate sentence under each drawing indicating what they used to do, e.g. *asistir a reuniones – Asistían a reuniones.*

---

mandar faxes
servir café a los clientes
contestar el teléfono
trabajar en el ordenador
leer la correspondencia
atender al público

5.2 Here are some other things Delia and Pepe used to do at work. Can you identify them? Look them up if necessary and practise following the example above:

enviar emails

hacer fotocopias

despachar pedidos

escribir informes

llamar por teléfono a clientes

concertar citas

6 Asistíamos a reuniones *We used to attend meetings*

 How would Delia and Pepe tell someone else what they used to do? Begin like this: 'Asistíamos a reuniones ...'

 7 Una entrevista *An interview*

You've been asked to interview a Spanish-speaking person who is applying for a job. How would you ask the following in Spanish? Choose between the imperfect or the preterite tense, as appropriate, using the formal 'Vd.'.

Read each question first and decide whether the action referred to is one which took place over a period of time, without concern for its length or its beginning or end (*imperfect tense*), or whether it involves a specific period of time or a certain point in the past (*preterite tense*).

a What work did you do before?

b How long did you work there?

c How much were you earning?

d Why did you leave your job?

8 Ahora tú... *And now you*
el tiempo libre   *spare time*

¿A qué te dedicabas antes?

¿Trabajabas o estudiabas?

¿Dónde trabajabas/estudiabas?

¿Qué hacías en tu tiempo libre?

You may remember the phrase **¿A qué te dedicas?** (from **dedicarse**) that you learned in Unit 11, used for asking people what they do for a living. In the first sentence above the question concerns the past. Note that the verb is not normally used in the reply.

Test yourself

Choose the right verb form, the preterite or the imperfect.

a (Yo) **(conocí/conocía)** a Elisa en el año 1951, cuando yo **(tuve/tenía)** sólo veinte años.

b En aquel tiempo yo **(estuve/estaba)** en la universidad.

c Elisa **(fue/era)** mi nueva vecina, **(tuvo/tenía)** diecisiete años y **(vivió/vivía)** con su madre, que **(trabajó/trabajaba)** en correos.

d El primer día que la **(vi/veía)**, (yo) **(fui/iba)** a la universidad y ella **(volvió/volvía)** de la compra.

e Días más tarde la **(vi/veía)** otra vez y le **(hablé/hablaba)**.

f Esa **(fue/era)** la primera vez que (yo) **(estuve/estaba)** con Elisa.

g Desde ese momento Elisa y yo **(fuimos/éramos)** inseparables.

h Elisa y yo **(salimos/salíamos)** por las tardes cuando ella **(terminó/terminaba)** su trabajo.

i Los fines de semana (nosotros) **(fuimos/íbamos)** a nadar al río.

j Fue allí en el río, un domingo por la tarde, la primera vez que la **(besé/besaba)**.

How do you think you did in the test? If you are uncertain, check your answers in the Key to 'Test yourself' before you proceed to Unit 19. If you feel you need some further revision go back to the dialogues and to paragraphs 1 and 2 of the Language discovery section.

SELF CHECK

I CAN...
. . . say where I used to live
. . . say what work I used to do
. . . talk about things I did regularly in the past.

19 ¿Qué has hecho?
What have you done?

In this unit you will learn how to:
▶ *talk about past events related to the present*
▶ *complain about a service*
▶ *claim lost property.*

CEFR: *Can ask and answer questions about past activities (B1); Can make a complaint (B1); Can explain a problem which has arisen (B1); Can describe possessions (B1).*

Spaniards on the world stage

Down the centuries, Spaniards have contributed to the world of science and the arts. Cervantes's **El Quijote** met with immediate international success and still tops polls for the world's best novel. Ask any Spaniard **¿Has leído El Quijote?** (*Have you read* El Quijote?) and the answer is likely to be **¡Sí!**, for, although written at the beginning of the seventeenth century, the adventures of Don Quixote are as entertaining and as relevant today as they were then.

We may not be aware that Pedro Duque **ha viajado en el espacio** (*has travelled in space*) as it is more the feats of Spanish sportsmen and women that make the news. Rafael Nadal **ha sido el número uno en tenis** (*has been Number One in tennis*) and **La Selección Nacional de Fútbol de España ha ganado la Copa Mundial** (*Spain's national football team has won the World Cup*).

 If, when you go to bed tonight, you tell yourself: 'Hoy he estudiado un poco de español', what are you saying you have done today?

Conversations

1 HE IDO AL MUSEO *I'VE BEEN TO THE MUSEUM*

he estado	*I have been*
he ido	*I have been* (literally, *gone*)
todavía no	*not yet*
he visto	*I have seen*
me han dicho	*I've been told*
he hecho	*I have done*

19.01

In this unit you will learn the Spanish equivalent of phrases such as I have been to the museum, What have you done?, which are expressed through the perfect tense. In Conversation 1 you will hear María Luisa talk to Patricia, whom she has met on a city tour, about some of the things they have done.

1.1 **Each of the sentences below contains some wrong information. Listen to the conversation and put them right.**
   1 He estado varias veces aquí.
   2 Es la segunda vez que vengo.
   3 He ido a la catedral, pero todavía no he visto el museo.
   4 Por la noche he salido con unas amigas a cenar.

Mª Luisa	¿Es la primera vez que vienes aquí?
Patricia	No, he estado dos veces aquí. ¿Y tú?
Mª Luisa	Es la primera vez que vengo. ¿Has visitado el museo y la catedral?
Patricia	Esta mañana he ido al museo, pero todavía no he visto la catedral. Me han dicho que es maravillosa. Y tú, ¿qué has hecho hoy?
Mª Luisa	Por la mañana no he hecho nada especial. Por la tarde, he salido con unos amigos a comer.

1.2 **Find the Spanish for the following in the conversation:**
   1 Have you visited ...?
   2 I have gone (been) to ...
   3 I haven´t seen ...

1.3 **How would you express the following in Spanish? Refer back to the dialogue and the vocabulary above.**

1 This is the second time I come to Spain.
2 Today I have been (gone) to the market.
3 I haven't seen the ruins (las ruinas) yet.
4 I've been told they are very interesting.

Vez (f) translates *time*, as in *the first time* – **la primera vez**. It is also used in the Spanish for *once*, *twice*, *three times*, etc: **una vez**, **dos veces**, **tres veces**. In the plural **z** changes into **c** and the word adds **-es**.

2 HE OLVIDADO MI PARAGUAS *I'VE FORGOTTEN MY UMBRELLA*

olvidar	*to forget, leave behind*
no hay de qué	*you're welcome!*

19.02

Mª Luisa has left her umbrella in the restaurant where she had lunch with her friends, and she goes back to claim it.

2.1 **How does Mª Luisa describe her umbrella? Listen to the dialogue and note the following key words and phrases:**

he olvidado (from **olvidar**)	*I have forgotten*
el paraguas	*umbrella*
de cuadros	*checked*

Patricia	Perdone, esta tarde he comido aquí con unos amigos y he olvidado mi paraguas. Es un paraguas azul, de cuadros.
Camarero	¿Es este su paraguas?
Patricia	Sí, es ese. Muchísimas gracias.
Camarero	No hay de qué, señora.

2.2 **What expressions are used in the dialogue for:**

1 I've had lunch here
2 Is this your umbrella?
3 Yes, that's it.

Unos amigos translates *some friends*.

The Spanish for *the umbrella* is **el paraguas**, a compound word (**para** + **aguas**, *it stops water*) ending in **-s**. The plural *the umbrellas* is **los paraguas**.

3 Hemos pedido una habitación exterior *We have asked for a room facing onto the street*

hemos pedido	*we have asked for*
nos han dado	*you have given us*
exterior	*outward-facing*
interior	*facing a central patio*
faltar	*not to be enough, to be lacking*

19.03

Marta, who is staying at a hotel with her husband, phones the hotel reception to complain about the room they have been given.

3.1 What is Marta's complaint? Listen and find out.

Recepcionista	Recepción, ¿dígame?
Marta	Hola, llamo de la habitación trescientos diez. Mi marido y yo hemos pedido una habitación exterior y ustedes nos han dado una interior. Además, el aire acondicionado no funciona y faltan toallas.
Recepcionista	Usted perdone, señora. Ahora mismo les doy otra habitación.

3.2 What expressions are used in the dialogue to say:
1 I'm calling from ...
2 it doesn't work
3 I do apologize
4 I'll give you another room right now.

Ustedes nos han dado ... (*You have given us ...* – literally, *You us have given ...*). **Nos**, like other words of this kind – for example **me**, **te** – must come before **haber**, *to have* in English (not to be confused with **tener** *to have* which may indicate possession).

How do you say it?

TALKING ABOUT PAST EVENTS RELATED TO THE PRESENT

¿Has visitado el museo?	*Have you visited the museum? (inf)*
¿Ha visto la catedral?	*Have you seen the cathedral? (formal)*
He/hemos estado/ido allí.	*I/we have been there.*

COMPLAINING ABOUT A SERVICE

El aire acondicionado/la calefacción no funciona.	*The air conditioning/heating doesn't work.*
Falta champú.	*There's not enough/There's no shampoo.*
Faltan toallas.	*There are not enough/There are no towels.*
No hay toalla de manos/baño.	*There's no hand/bath towel.*

CLAIMING LOST PROPERTY

He olvidado mi bolso/la cartera (LAm)	*I've forgotten/left my handbag.*
(Me) he dejado la cartera/ el maletín.	*I've left/forgotten my briefcase.*

 # Language discovery

1 TALKING ABOUT PAST EVENTS RELATED TO THE PRESENT: THE PERFECT TENSE

Usage

a The Spanish *perfect tense*, like the English perfect, is used for past events which have taken place in a period of time that has not yet ended, that is, a past which is somehow related to the present.

He estado dos veces aquí.	*I've been here twice* (until now).
Todavía no han visitado el Palacio Real.	*They still haven't visited the Royal Palace* (so far).
Ya ha salido.	*He/she has already left.*

b Events which have taken place in the recent or the immediate past are usually expressed in Peninsular Spanish with the perfect tense. Here, English may use the preterite tense.

Esta tarde he visto a Eva.	*I've seen/saw Eva this afternoon.*
Hoy hemos ido al teatro.	*Today we've been/went to the theatre.*
Han llegado hace un momento.	*They arrived a moment ago.*
¿Has oído ese ruido?	*Did you hear/Have you heard that noise?*

c There are regional differences in the use of the perfect tense, especially in the Spanish-speaking countries of Latin America where, overall, the tendency is to use the preterite tense in contexts where Peninsular Spanish would show preference for the perfect, for example:

Hoy fui al palacio de gobierno.	*Today I went/have been to the government palace.*
Esa película ya la vi.	*I've already seen that film.*

instead of:

Hoy he ido al palacio de gobierno.

Esa película ya la he visto.

Formation

The perfect tense is formed with the present tense of the auxiliary verb **haber** (*to have*), and *a past participle*, which is that part of the verb which in English usually ends in *-ed*. In Spanish, the endings of past participles are **-ado** for **-ar** verbs and **-ido** for verbs in **-er** and **-ir**. In the perfect tense these past participles are invariable. Here are the perfect tense forms of three regular verbs: **estar** (*to be*), **comer** (*to eat*), **ir** (*to go*).

yo	he	estado	comido	ido
tú	has	estado	comido	ido
él, ella, Vd.	ha	estado	comido	ido
nosotros/as	hemos	estado	comido	ido
vosotros/as	habéis	estado	comido	ido
ellos, ellas, Vds.	han	estado	comido	ido

2 IRREGULAR PAST PARTICIPLES

The following are the most common irregular forms:

abrir – abierto (*opened*)	**escribir – escrito** (*written*)
decir – dicho (*said*)	**freír – frito** (*fried*)

hacer – hecho (*done, made*)	**romper – roto** (*broken*)
morir – muerto (*dead*)	**ver – visto** (*seen*)
poner – puesto (*put*)	**volver – vuelto** (*returned, come back*)

3 TIME PHRASES ASSOCIATED WITH THE PERFECT TENSE

Among time phrases associated with the perfect tense we find:

hoy	*today*
esta mañana/tarde/semana	*this morning/afternoon/week*
esta noche	*tonight*
este mes/año	*this month/year*
alguna vez	*ever*
nunca	*never*
ya	*already*
todavía/aún	*yet*

¿Te ha llamado alguna vez?	*Has he/she ever called you?*
Nunca lo ha hecho.	*He/she has never done it.*
Todavía/aún no han vuelto.	*They haven't come back yet.*

Practise forming sentences in the perfect tense using regular and irregular forms and some of the time phrases listed above. Remember that the past participle remains unchanged for all persons of the verb whether it is a regular or an irregular form.

4 IMPERSONAL SENTENCES WITH THE THIRD PERSON PLURAL

A simple way to form impersonal sentences, that is, sentences in which you do not need to specify the identity of the person who performed the action expressed by the verb, is to use the third person plural of the verb.

Me han dicho que es importante.	*I've been told it's important.*
Aceptaron mi reclamación.	*They accepted my complaint.*

Practice

1 Un recado *A message*

encontrar	*to find*
aplazar	*to put off*

19.04

Your boss does business with Spain and Latin America. On your answerphone this morning you find a message from María Bravo, from Mexico. Listen and make a note of it in English to pass it on to your boss.

2 ¿Qué han hecho? *What have they done?*

mudarse	*to move (house)*
pintar	*to paint*

What have the following people done this summer? Fill in the blanks in these sentences with an appropriate verb from the list, using the perfect tense.

Notice that there are two reflexive verbs (Unit 12) in the list below, **mudarse** and **quedarse**. The reflexive pronouns, **me**, **te**, **se**, **nos**, etc. must precede the form of **haber**.

> mudarse viajar abrir pintar quedarse hacer volver pasar

a Patricia _____ un curso de inglés intensivo.

b Marta y Victoria _____ sus vacaciones en Marruecos.

c Agustín _____ a Londres a visitar a unos amigos.

d Mónica _____ a Chile, después de vivir tres años en Europa.

e Esteban y Rosa María _____ a un nuevo piso.

f Yo no tenía dinero y _____ en casa.

g Pilar y yo _____ nuestro piso.

h José Manuel y Juan Carlos _____ una pequeña tienda de ropa.

3 ¿De qué se queja? *What is she complaining about?*

¡Esto es el colmo!	*This is the last straw!*
¡Es increíble!	*This is incredible!*
contar con (o>ue)	*to have*
disponer de	*to have*

Laura and her husband had booked a hotel room through an agency, but on arrival they were greatly disappointed and complained to the hotel manager. Something went wrong.

3.1 **Listen to the conversation several times, and say which of the two ads below best fits their expectations.**

HOTEL CONDES **

Zona Comercial Carabela,
Puerto de Alcudia,
Tel.: 971 54 54 92

Situado a 100 mt. de la orilla del mar, en un lugar perfecto donde podrá practicar toda clase de deportes acuáticos. Dispone de una gran piscina y solarium, salón de T.V y vídeo, bares en el interior y en la terraza y zona especial para niños entre los jardines. Las habitaciones disponen todas de baño completo y terraza con vistas al mar.

HOTEL EXCELSIOR *

**Vara del Rey, 17,
San Antonio,
Tel.: 971 34 01 85**

Situado en pleno centro de San Antonio a escasos minutos de la playa, hotel de ambiente y explotación familiar, todas sus habitaciones cuentan con baño o ducha. Asimismo dispone de salón social y de televisión, al igual que de bar y restaurante.

3.2 **Listen again a few times and say whether the following statements are true or false (*verdadero o falso*).**

   a El recepcionista les ha dado una habitación con vistas a un aparcamiento.

   b Laura y su marido han estado dos veces en esa ciudad.

   c Es la segunda vez que les pasa algo así.

4 Palabra por palabra *Word for word*

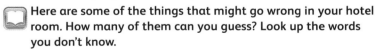

Here are some of the things that might go wrong in your hotel room. How many of them can you guess? Look up the words you don't know.

   a La calefacción, el aire acondicionado, la televisión, el grifo del agua caliente/fría ... no funciona.

   b El wáter, el lavabo, la bañera ... está atascado/a.

   c Falta jabón, champú, papel higiénico.

   d No hay suficientes toallas/mantas.

5 Ahora tú *And now you*

It's your first day in your hotel room and you call reception to complain about some of the facilities in the room. How would you say the following?

a The heating doesn't work.
b The washbasin is blocked.
c There is no soap in the bathroom.
d I need more blankets on my bed.

6 Objetos perdidos *Lost property*

Margarita left something behind in señor Palma's office. What did she leave and how does she describe it? Read and find out.

| los objetos perdidos | *lost property* |
| el despacho | *office* |

Margarita	Perdone, he estado en el despacho del señor Palma esta mañana y he dejado una cartera con unos documentos. Es una cartera negra, de piel. ¿Puede decirme si la han encontrado? Es muy importante.
Recepcionista	Sí, señora. Su cartera está aquí en la recepción.

7 Ahora tú *And now you*

After leaving a bar you realized that you had left something behind. Tell the waiter what you have lost, and ask whether he has found it.

8 ¿Ha llamado usted al director del banco? *Have you phoned the bank manager?*

You have a busy day at the office today. Here is a list of the things you needed to do, with a tick for those you have already done. How would your boss ask whether you have done each of the following? And how would you reply? Follow the examples.

- ¿Ha llamado Vd. al director del banco?
- No, todavía no lo (*or* le) he llamado.
- ¿Ha contestado Vd. el email de Ángela Salas?
- Sí, ya lo he contestado.

Todavía no lo he llamado (*I still haven't called him*): **le** for **lo** is also correct. For masculine nouns referring to things you must use **lo**. For feminine nouns referring to things and for females use **la**: **No la he llamado** (*I haven't called her*).

a	Llamar al director del banco	✗
b	Contestar el email de Ángela Salas	✓
c	Pedir hora con el doctor Prado	✓
d	Escribir a los distribuidores en Nueva York	✓
e	Hacer el pedido de material de oficina	✗
f	Ver a la señora Martínez	✓
g	Abrir la caja con las mercancías	✗

 Test yourself

1 **Choose an appropriate verb from the list to complete the sentences below. The first sentence in each group has been done for you.**

> (1) hablar (2) entrevistar (3) hacer (4) ir (5) responder
> (6) volver (7) escribir (8) asistir

Julio

- **a** Hoy he llegado a la oficina a las 8:30.
- **b** _____ muchas llamadas telefónicas.
- **c** _____ algunos emails.
- **d** _____ con varios clientes.
- **e** _____ a dos reuniones.

Silvia y Rafael

f Hemos despachado varios pedidos.

g _____ muchísimas cartas.

h _____ a tres personas para un nuevo puesto.

i _____ al aeropuerto.

j _____ a casa muy cansados.

2 How would you tell someone else what Julio has done? And Rafael and Silvia? Change the verbs into the appropriate form.

This test assesses your ability to talk about the recent past and, more generally, about the things you or others have done. If you feel you need more practice on this before you move on to the next unit, think of some of the things you have done today and try saying it in Spanish.

SELF CHECK

I CAN. . .
. . . talk about past events related to the present
. . . complain about a service
. . . claim lost property.

20 Te veré mañana
I'll see you tomorrow

In this chapter you will learn how to:
- *confirm travel arrangements*
- *cancel a hotel reservation*
- *talk about the future*
- *express conditions.*

CEFR: *Can describe plans and arrangements (B1); Can explain a problem which has arisen (B1); Can understand standard letters of confirmation (B1); Can understand messages (B1).*

Tomorrow for sure

Mañana (*tomorrow*) has been used to stereotype Spaniards, but that is because they do not like to get too far ahead of themselves and prefer to leave the firming-up of arrangements nearer to the time. If you say **llegaremos el lunes a las diez** (*we'll arrive on Monday at ten*) and your Spanish friend says **estaré allí** (*I'll be there*), you can be sure that will be the case. If he or she says **te llamaré** (*I'll call you*), then you'll get that call.

El pronóstico del tiempo (*the weather forecast*) will tell you **hará sol** (*it'll be sunny*), or **lloverá en Galicia y las temperaturas bajarán en toda la Península** (*it will rain in Galicia and temperatures will drop in the whole Peninsula*).

What has Inés got planned for you both tomorrow?
Mañana comeremos paella en la playa. Te gustará.

Conversations

1 IRÉ AL AEROPUERTO A RECOGERTE *I'LL COME AND PICK YOU UP AT THE AIRPORT*

¡qué sorpresa!	*what a surprise!*
alegrarse/me alegro	*to be/I'm glad*
suponer/supongo	*to/I suppose*
mío/a	*mine* (m/f)
bueno (here)	*OK*
¡hombre! (here)	*hey! well!*

20.01

Ángel is flying to Madrid to visit his friend Ana. In a phone call to her he confirms his travel arrangements.

1.1   When is Ángel leaving and when is he arriving in Madrid? Listen and find out.

Ana	¿Sí, dígame?
Ángel	Hola, Ana. Soy Ángel.
Ana	Ángel, ¡qué sorpresa! ¿Qué tal estás?
Ángel	Muy bien. Mira, te llamaba para confirmar mi viaje. Salgo esta tarde y llego a Madrid mañana a las ocho y media.
Ana	¡Hombre, me alegro! Iré al aeropuerto a recogerte. Supongo que traerás mucho equipaje.
Ángel	Sí, bastante.
Ana	Bueno, le pediré el coche a Rafael. El mío es demasiado pequeño.
Ángel	Gracias, Ana. ¿Qué tal está el tiempo en Madrid?
Ana	Estupendo. Seguro que mañana hará calor.
Ángel	Bueno, Ana. Te veré mañana, entonces. Si el vuelo se retrasa, te llamaré.
Ana	Vale, Ángel. Hasta mañana y buen viaje. Un beso.

1.2   Now read the dialogue and focus attention on those verbs that refer to the future, for example *salgo* (I'm leaving), *llego* (I'm arriving). These are in the present tense, but there are others, such as *iré* (I'll go), *traerás* (you'll bring), which are in the future tense. Try to spot them and then answer the following questions.

   1   What does Ana promise to do?
   2   Whose car is Ana borrowing and why?
   3   What will Ángel do if his flight is delayed?

4 What expression does Ana use to say 'It's sure to be warm tomorrow'.

¡Hombre! This expression, meaning literally *man*, is used frequently in Spanish, especially in Spain, to convey different types of emotions, so its exact meaning will depend on the context, for example *come on!, cheer up!, you bet!*

2 NO PODREMOS VIAJAR *WE WON'T BE ABLE TO TRAVEL*

no podremos (from **poder**)	*we won't be able to*
tendremos que (from **tener**)	*we'll have to*

20.02

Julio is cancelling a hotel reservation he had made for him and his wife.

2.1 **Listen to the dialogue and try to spot the expressions meaning the following:**
1 I was calling about ...
2 a reservation in the name of ...
3 We won't be able to travel.
4 We'll have to cancel it.

Recepcionista	Hotel Foresta, ¿dígame?
Julio	Buenas tardes. Llamaba por una reserva que hice para dos personas a nombre de Julio Pérez, para el 10 de octubre. No podremos viajar en esa fecha y tendremos que anularla. Lo siento.
Recepcionista	Perdone, ¿me puede repetir su nombre, por favor?
Julio	Julio Pérez.
Recepcionista	Sí, sí, aquí está. Muy bien, señor, su reserva está anulada.

Está anulada (*It is cancelled*). In this construction with **estar**, the **-ado** or **-ido** form of the verb (see past participles, Unit 19) must agree in gender (m/f) and number (sing/pl) with the word it refers to: **el pedido está anulado** (*the order is cancelled*), **las habitaciones están reservadas** (*the rooms are booked*).

2.2 **Your holiday plans have changed and you need to cancel a hotel reservation. How would you express the following in Spanish? Read the dialogue before you reply.**
Good evening. I was phoning about a reservation I made in the name of ... for 20th August. I won't be able to travel on that date and I'll have to cancel it. I'm very sorry.

How do you say it?

Salgo/Llego (pasado) mañana/el lunes.
I'm leaving/arriving (the day after) tomorrow/on Monday.

Saldremos/Llegaremos esta noche/el 15.
We'll leave/arrive tonight/on the 15th.

CANCELLING A HOTEL RESERVATION

Llamo/Llamaba para anular una reserva.
I am/was calling to cancel a reservation.

No podré/podremos viajar.
I/we won't be able to travel.

TALKING ABOUT THE FUTURE

Te veré mañana.
I'll see you tomorrow.

Seguro que hará calor.
It's sure to be warm.

EXPRESSING CONDITIONS

Si el vuelo se retrasa, te llamaré.
If the flight is delayed, I'll call you.

Si no viajo hoy, viajaré el domingo.
If I don't travel today, I'll travel on Sunday.

Language discovery

1 TALKING ABOUT THE FUTURE

As in English, in Spanish you can refer to the future in more than one way:

a Using **ir a** + *infinitive* (see Unit 13): **Voy a viajar a Perú** (*I'm going to travel to Peru*).

b Using the present tense, especially with verbs indicating movement, but also with some other verbs: **Llegan dentro de dos días** (*They are arriving in two days' time*), **¿Qué película ponen mañana?** (*What film are they showing tomorrow?*).

c Using the future tense: **Le pediré el coche a Rafael** (*I'll borrow Rafael's car*).

2 THE FUTURE TENSE

Usage

The use of the future tense to refer to future actions and events has become relatively uncommon in everyday spoken language, where the tendency now is to use **ir a** + *infinitive* or the present tense (see 1 above), but it remains common when expressing

a Supposition (including supposition in the present), certainty and predictions

Supongo/Me imagino que vendrás.	*I suppose/imagine you'll come.*
Ahora estará durmiendo.	*He/she must be sleeping now.*
Seguro que nos invitarán.	*I'm sure they'll invite us.*

b Promises and determination

Te prometo que lo haré.	*I promise you I'll do it.*
Se lo diré.	*I'll tell him/her.*

c The idea of '*I wonder ...*'

¿Qué hora será?	*I wonder what time it is.*
¿Dónde estarán?	*I wonder where they are.*

d The future tense remains common in all forms of writing, especially so in more formal styles and in the language of the press.

El presidente será recibido por las autoridades.	*The president will be received by the authorities.*

Some uses of *will* in English do not correspond to the future tense in Spanish but to the present tense: *Will you pass the salt?* (**¿Me pasas la sal?**), *Will you take a seat for a moment?* (**¿Quiere sentarse un momento?**), *She won't listen to me* (**No quiere escucharme**).

Formation

a Regular verbs

The future is formed with the whole of the infinitive, to which the endings are added, the same for **-ar**, **-er** and **-ir** verbs. Here are the future forms of three regular verbs **llamar** (*to call*), **ver** (*to see*), **ir** (*to go*). Note that all forms, except the first person plural **nosotros/as** have a written accent.

yo	llamar**é**	ver**é**	ir**é**
tú	llamar**ás**	ver**ás**	ir**ás**
él, ella, Vd.	llamar**á**	ver**á**	ir**á**
nosotros/as	llamar**emos**	ver**emos**	ir**emos**
vosotros/as	llamar**éis**	ver**éis**	ir**éis**
ellos, ellas, Vds.	llamar**án**	ver**án**	ir**án**

b Irregular verbs

The endings of irregular verbs are the same as those of regular ones. Here is a list of the most common:

decir (*to say, tell*): diré, dirás, dirá, diremos, diréis, dirán.

hacer (*to do, make*): haré, harás, hará, haremos, haréis, harán.

poder (*to be able, can*): podré, podrás, podrá, podremos, podréis, podrán.

poner (*to put*): pondré, pondrás, pondrá, pondremos, pondréis, pondrán.

querer (*to want, love*): querré, querrás, querrá, querremos, querréis, querrán.

saber (*to know*): sabré, sabrás, sabrá, sabremos, sabréis, sabrán.

salir (*to leave, go out*): saldré, saldrás, saldrá, saldremos, saldréis, saldrán.

tener (*to have*): tendré, tendrás, tendrá, tendremos, tendréis, tendrán.

venir (*to come*): vendré, vendrás, vendrá, vendremos, vendréis, vendrán.

The future form of **haber** is **habrá** (*there will be*) (**hay** in the present tense).

Verbs which derive from these irregular verbs form the future in a similar way, for example: **predecir** (*to predict*), **deshacer** (*to undo*), **componer** (*to compose*), etc.

3 SI... *IF...*

To express ideas such as *If I can I'll go, If it rains we'll stay at home*, use the construction **si** + *present tense* + *future tense*: **Si puedo, iré; Si llueve, nos quedaremos en casa**. In the spoken language, the future tense is sometimes replaced by the present tense: **Si puedo, voy; Si llueve, nos quedamos en casa**.

4 MÍO, TUYO, SUYO ... *MINE, YOURS, HIS, HERS, ITS ...*

You are already familiar with words like **mi** (*my*), **tu** (*your* (inf)), **su** (*your* (formal), *his*, *her*, *its*), the short form of possessives (see Unit 3). Words like **mío**, **tuyo**, **suyo**, etc, correspond to the long forms of possessives, and they agree in gender (m or f) and number (sing or pl) with the thing possessed, not with the possessor. The following are all their forms:

singular	plural	
mío/a	**míos/as**	*mine*
tuyo/a	**tuyos/as**	*yours* (inf)
suyo/a	**suyos/as**	*his/hers/its/yours* (formal)
nuestro/a	**nuestros/as**	*ours*
vuestro/a	**vuestros/as**	*yours* (inf)
suyo/a	**suyos/as**	*theirs/yours* (formal)

Long forms are normally preceded by **el**, **la**, **los** or **las**:

Mi impresora no funciona, usaré la tuya.   *My printer doesn't work, I'll use yours.*

El, **la**, **los**, **las** are not needed in sentences which translate in English as *of mine*, *of yours*, etc.: **Son amigos nuestros** (*They are friends of ours*).

El, **la**, **los**, **las** are also omitted after the verb **ser**, unless identification is also implied: **Esta casa es mía** (*This house is mine*) (implying possession only), **Esta casa es la mía (no la otra)** (*This is my house (not the other one)*) (implying possession and identification, with the emphasis on **esta**). The second example could equally be expressed as **Mi casa es esta (no la otra)** (*My house is this one (not the other one)*).

 Practice

1   Un viaje de negocios *A business trip*

me es muy grato   I have pleasure in
esa misma mañana   (*literally*) *that same morning* (emphatic)

Álvaro García is travelling to South America on business. In an email to his business contacts he confirms his journey. Fill in the gaps in the text with one of the following verbs: *quedarse*, *llevar*, *llamar*, *llegar*, *salir*. Use the future tense.

Estimada señora Álvarez:

Con relación a mi próxima visita a Santiago, me es muy grato informarle que **(a)** _____ de Madrid en el vuelo AB 145, el jueves 28 de abril a las 10:45 de la noche y que **(b)** _____ a Santiago el viernes 29 a las 7:00 de la mañana, hora local. **(c)** _____ en el hotel San Carlos en la calle La Concepción, y la **(d)** _____ por teléfono esa misma mañana para confirmar nuestra reunión. **(e)** _____ toda la documentación que usted me ha solicitado.

Atentamente,

Álvaro García

Estimado/a señor/señora (*Dear Sir/Madam*) es más personal que **Muy señor/a mío/mía** (*Dear Sir/Madam*) y se utiliza frecuentemente en correspondencia comercial con el apellido *surname* de la persona (*see email above*). También se utiliza con el nombre de pila *first name*, en correspondencia a personas a las que no se conoce bien, por ejemplo **Estimada Victoria** (*Dear Victoria*).

2 Mensajes en el contestador *Messages on the answerphone*

20.03

Mónica, from Seville, found two recorded messages on her answerphone, one from her friend María and another one from Mark. What did each say? Listen and find out.

3 Si ... *If ...*

apuntarse para cobrar el paro   *to go on the dole*

Paco is speculating about his future at work. Form conditional sentences by matching the phrases on the left with those on the right.

a Si tengo que trabajar horas extras
b Si no me aumentan el sueldo
c Si hago un curso de informática
d Si aprendo inglés
e Si no encuentro trabajo

1 trabajaré como programador
2 podré irme a Estados Unidos
3 me apuntaré para cobrar el paro
4 pediré un aumento de sueldo
5 buscaré otro trabajo

The form **irme** in sentence 2 above comes from **irse** (*to leave (for)*). *I'm leaving* is **Me voy**. In sentence 2 this verb is in the infinitive, so **me** is added to the infinitive: **podré irme ...**

4 Seguro que te las pedirán *I'm sure they'll ask you for them*

Your friend Ángela is uncertain about getting the job she applied for, but you try to reassure her. Look at the first sentence, which has been done for you, and reply to each of Ángela's statements in a similar way.

a Si me piden referencias tendré que dar tu nombre.
Seguro que te las pedirán.

b Si me entrevistan tendré que prepararme muy bien.
Estoy seguro/a de que ...

c Si me ofrecen el puesto lo aceptaré.
Seguramente ...

d Si el sueldo no es muy bueno pediré más dinero.
Estoy seguro/a de que ...

e Si me dan un coche de la empresa elegiré un Mercedes.
Seguro que ...

5 Supongo que sí *I suppose so*

While doing a Spanish course in Salamanca, Peter will be staying with a Spanish family. Everyone in the family is speculating about Peter. Rephrase their questions, using the expressions given to you. The first sentence has been done for you.

a ¿Conoce Salamanca?   Supongo que conocerá Salamanca.
b ¿Viene solo?   Me imagino que ...
c ¿Tiene nuestra dirección?   Supongo que ...
d ¿Sabe cómo llegar aquí?   Me imagino que ...
e ¿Entiende algo de español?   Supongo que ...

6 Está mal aparcado *You've parked in the wrong place*

Fill in the gaps with a possessive, using either short forms like *mi, tu, su*, or long forms such as *mío, tuyo, suyo*, as appropriate. Use *el, la, los* or *las* where necessary.

Remember that **mi**, **tu**, **su** change for number (sing/pl) but not for gender, while **mío**, **tuyo**, **suyo** change for both number and gender, as in **¿La casa es tuya?** (*Is the house yours?*), **¿Estos libros son tuyos?** (*Are these books yours?*).

Test yourself

1 **Ana tells someone what she will do on her next holiday. Complete the following sentences with an appropriate verb from the list, using the future tense.**

hacer	quedarse	ir	llegar	viajar	volver	salir	tener

a Este año _____ de vacaciones a Chile.

b _____ de Madrid el día 23.

c _____ en Hispanoair.

d El vuelo _____ escala en Buenos Aires.

e _____ a Santiago de Chile al día siguiente.

f _____ en casa de unos amigos chilenos.

g _____ a Madrid el 7 de agosto.

h El 8 de agosto _____ que volver a trabajar.

2 **How would you tell someone else what Ana will do? Change the verbs into the appropriate form of the future tense.**

Promises and resolutions are a good context for the future tense, so if after doing this test you feel you still need more practice, think of things you will do in the near future and put those ideas in writing. Check irregular forms in the grammar section again if necessary.

SELF CHECK

	I CAN. . .
⬤	. . . confirm travel arrangements
⬤	. . . cancel a hotel reservation
⬤	. . . talk about the future
⬤	. . . express conditions.

21 *Me encantaría*
I'd love to

In this unit you will learn how to:
▶ *make suggestions*
▶ *say what you would like to do*
▶ *arrange to meet someone*
▶ *invite someone and accept or decline an invitation.*

CEFR: *Can make and respond to suggestions, invitations and apologies (A2); Can arrange to meet someone (A2); Can write personal letters of invitation (B1).*

El puente

Días festivos (*bank holidays*) are taken on the day on which they fall. This means that if this is a Tuesday or a Thursday, a bridge can be made to the weekend, giving four days off in all. **El puente** (*the bridge*) is seized upon by travel agents and hotels to offer all sorts of mini breaks. The best **puente** is that afforded by the two holidays of **El Día de la Constitución** on 6 December and **El Día de la Inmaculada Concepción** on 8 December.

These are times when you can think about what you would like to do: **Me encantaría visitar Granada** (*I would love to visit Granada*); **Podríamos ir a Estambul** (*We could go to Istambul*). Or you could just arrange to meet friends: **¿Qué os parece si vamos al concierto?** (*What about going to the concert?*); **¿Quedamos a las cinco?** (*Shall we meet at five?*).

How might Rosario use 'el puente'?
Podría visitar a mi hermana pero preferiría viajar un poco.
Me encantaría ir a París.

Conversations

1 ¿QUÉ TE APETECE VER? *WHAT WOULD YOU LIKE TO SEE?*

vamos	*let's go*
poner	*to show (a film)*
quedar	*to arrange to meet*
sobre	*about, around (with the time)*
si no iría	*otherwise I'd go*

21.01

Margarita and her friend Santiago make arrangements to go out.

1.1 **Listen to the dialogue several times and answer the questions below. Key expressions here are:**

¿qué te parece si …?	*what about …?*
¿qué te apetece …?	*what would you like/do you feel like …?*
me gustaría …	*I'd like to …*
me encantaría …	*I'd love to …*
tengo que …	*I have to …*
podríamos quedar …	*we could meet …*

1 What does Margarita suggest doing this evening?

2 Where and when do she and Santiago arrange to meet?

3 Why is Antonio not coming with them?

Margarita	¿Qué te parece si vamos al cine esta noche?
Santiago	Sí, sí, vamos. ¿Qué te apetece ver?
Margarita	Me gustaría ver Sin palabras. ¿La has visto?
Santiago	No, pero me gustaría verla. ¿Sabes dónde la ponen?
Margarita	En el cine Plaza. Empieza a las diez. Podríamos quedar delante del cine sobre las nueve y media. ¿Te parece bien?
Santiago	Vale, me parece bien.
Margarita	¿Vienes con nosotros, Antonio?
Antonio	Me encantaría, pero tengo que trabajar, si no iría.

The focus here is on the conditional tense, normally expressed with *would* in English. Like the future tense, it requires the whole infinitive. The endings are the same as those of the imperfect of **-er/-ir** verbs: **vivir** (*to live*), **vivíamos** (*we lived/used to live*), **viviríamos** (*we would live*). Irregular forms are those of the future: **diría**, **haría**, **podría**, etc.

1.2   Find the following phrases in the conversation.

   1   What about going ...? (What if we go ...?)
   2   What would you like to see?
   3   We could meet ...

1.3   Now read the dialogue and then try putting the following sentences in Spanish:

   1   What about going to the theatre tomorrow?
   2   I'd like to see *Historia de dos vidas*.
   3   I've seen the play **(la obra)**, but I'd love to see it again **(otra vez)**.
   4   We could meet right here **(aquí mismo)** about 7.45.

2 ¿QUERÉIS VENIR A CENAR A CASA? *WOULD YOU LIKE TO COME TO MY HOUSE FOR DINNER?*

encantado/a   *I'll be delighted* (said by a man/woman)
quizá, quizás   *perhaps*

21.02

Margarita invites Antonio and Santiago for dinner at her house.

2.1   Who accepts the invitation and who doesn't? What expression does each person use in reply to the invitation? Listen and find out. A key expression here is *tener un compromiso* (to have an engagement).

Margarita	¿Queréis venir a cenar a casa el viernes? He invitado a Sara también.
Antonio	Yo, encantado, gracias.
Santiago	Me encantaría, pero no puedo. Tengo un compromiso. ¿Otro día, quizá?
Margarita	Sí, sí, otro día.

2.2 What phrase is used in the conversation to say *Would you like to come for dinner?*

2.3 Now read the dialogue and use some of the expressions in it to give the Spanish for the following:

    1 Would you like to come to my house on Saturday? I have a party (**una fiesta**) and I have invited other friends. (Use the **vosotros** form.)

    2 I'd love to but I can't. I have an engagement with some friends from the office. Next time (**la próxima vez**) perhaps?

How do you say it?

MAKING SUGGESTIONS

¿Qué te/le parece si (vamos a ...)?	*What about (going to ...)?*
¿Qué tal si (cenamos en ...)?	*What about (having dinner at ...)?*
¿Qué os parece invitar a Mercedes?	*What about inviting Mercedes?*
Podríamos ir a tomar una copa, , ¿qué te parece?	*We could go and have a drink what do you think?*

ASKING PEOPLE WHAT THEY WOULD LIKE TO DO, AND RESPONDING

¿Qué te/le gustaría/apetece (hacer)?	*What would you like (to do)?*
Me gustaría/apetece (salir un rato).	*I'd like (to go out for a while).*

ARRANGING TO MEET SOMEONE

¿A qué hora/Dónde quedamos?	*What time/Where shall we meet?*
Podríamos quedar en (la puerta).	*We could meet at (the entrance).*
¿Quedamos (aquí mismo)?	*Shall we meet (right here)?*

¿Quieres/quiere Vd. venir a (cenar)?	*Would you like to come for (dinner)?*
Encantado/a.	*I'll be delighted.*
Me encantaría, pero no puedo.	*I'd love to, but I can't.*
Tengo un/otro compromiso.	*I have an/another engagement.*
Tengo que (trabajar/estudiar).	*I have to (work /study).*

Language discovery

1 THE CONDITIONAL

Usage

a In the sentence *I would buy it but I don't have money*, 'would buy' is *conditional*. As the name implies, the conditional is used to refer to actions or events which might take place given certain conditions (in the example above, *If I had money ...*). Spanish expresses conditions in a similar way: **Lo compraría, pero no tengo dinero.**

b The conditional is also used with verbs such as **poder** *to be able to, can,* **deber** *to have to, must,* followed by the infinitive:

Podríamos quedar en la esquina.	*We could meet at the corner.*
Deberías decírselo.	*You should tell him/her.*

c It is also used for politeness in sentences like the following:

¿Le/te importaría no fumar?	*Would you mind not smoking?*
¿Le/te gustaría venir a mi fiesta de cumpleaños?	*Would you like to come to my birthday party?*

Formation

Like the future tense (see Unit 20), the conditional is formed with the whole infinitive, to which the endings are added, the same for **-ar**, **-er** and **-ir** verbs. Here is the conditional of three regular verbs, **invitar** (*to invite*), **ser** (*to be*), **ir** (*to go*). Note that the first and third person singular have the same forms and that all forms have a written accent.

yo	invitaría	sería	iría
tú	invitarías	serías	irías
él, ella, Vd.	invitaría	sería	iría
nosotros/as	invitaríamos	seríamos	iríamos
vosotros/as	invitaríais	seríais	iríais
ellos, ellas, Vds.	invitarían	serían	irían

Yo los invitaría a todos.   *I'd invite them all.*

Hoy no puedo, otro día   *Today I can't, another day would*
sería mejor.   *be better.*

Iríamos con vosotros, pero   *We'd go with you but we are busy.*
estamos ocupados.

2 IRREGULAR CONDITIONAL FORMS

Irregular conditional forms are the same as those for the future tense
(see Unit 20), their endings being no different from those of regular verbs.

decir (*to say, tell*): diría, dirías, diría, diríamos, diríais, dirían.

hacer (*to do, make*): haría, harías, haría, haríamos, haríais, harían.

poder (*to be able to, can*): podría, podrías, podría, podríamos, podríais, podrían.

poner (*to put*): pondría, pondrías, pondría, pondríamos, pondríais, pondrían.

querer (*to want, love*): querría, querrías, querría, querríamos, querríais, querrían.

saber (*to know*): sabría, sabrías, sabría, sabríamos, sabríais, sabrían.

salir (*to leave, go out*): saldría, saldrías, saldría, saldríamos, saldríais, saldrían.

tener (*to have*): tendría, tendrías, tendría, tendríamos, tendríais, tendrían.

venir (*to come*): vendría, vendrías, vendría, vendríamos, vendríais, vendrían.

The conditional form of **haber** is **habría** (**hay**, in the present tense) –
there would be.

One possible context in which to practise the conditional is to imagine
the things you might do given certain conditions, for example **Si ganara
mucho dinero (yo) ...** (*If I won a lot of money I would ...*), **Si viajara a
Sudamérica (yo) ...** (*If I travelled to South America I would ...*).

3 APETECER *(TO APPEAL, TO FEEL LIKE, TO FANCY),*
PARECER *(TO SEEM)*

a To say something appeals to you or you feel like something or doing something, use **apetecer**, in a construction similar to that with **gustar** (*to like*) (see Unit 13), in which the person to whom something is appealing goes before **apetecer**: **Me apetece un helado** (*I feel like an ice cream – literally, To me appeals an ice cream*). As with **gustar**, **apetecer** will be preceded by one of the following pronouns: **me**, **te**, **le**, **nos**, **os**, **les** (see Units 8 and 13). Here are some more examples:

¿Te apetece dar un paseo?   *Do you feel like going for a walk?*

Me apetece un café bien caliente.   *I fancy a very hot coffee.*

Apetecer is used especially in Spain but is rather uncommon in Latin America. The alternative, of course is to use **querer** or **gustar**, which are used in all countries: **¿Qué quieres/te gustaría hacer?** (*What do you want/would like to do?*).

b **Parecer** (*to seem*) (see also Unit 16) functions in the same way above, so a suggestion such as **¿Qué te parece si vamos al fútbol?** (*What about going to the football?*) translates literally as *What to you it seems if we go to the football?* Here are some more examples of the use of **parecer** in suggestions:

Practice

¿Qué te/le parece si la llamamos?   *What about calling her/if we call her?*
¿Qué os parece comenzar mañana?   What about starting tomorrow?

1 **¿Qué haría Maite?** *What would Maite do?*

Maite is busy at the office today and she is dreaming about the things she would do if she did not have to work. Change the infinitives into the appropriate form of the conditional tense.

Yo

   a **(Hacer)** la compra.

   b **(Lavar)** la ropa.

   c **(Escribir)** algunos emails.

   d **(Llamar)** a mi novio.

Mi novio y yo

   e **(Salir)** en el coche.

   f **(Ver)** alguna exposición.

   g **(Tener)** tiempo para ir a nadar.

   h **(Poder)** ir a bailar.

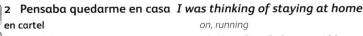

2 Pensaba quedarme en casa *I was thinking of staying at home*

en cartel   *on, running*

la guía del ocio   *what's on* (literally, *leisure guide*)

It's Saturday and you are making plans for the evening, so you phone a Spanish friend and make arrangements to see a play (*una obra de teatro*). Fill in your part of the conversation by following the guidelines below.

  – ¿Dígame?

  – *Say who you are and ask your friend if he/she has any plans for the evening.*

  – No, ninguno. Pensaba quedarme en casa. ¿Por qué?

  – *Suggest going to the theatre together.*

  – ¿Qué te apetece ver?

  – *Say you would like to see La evitable ascensión and ask your friend if he/she has seen it.*

  – No, no la he visto, pero me encantaría verla.

  – *Say it is on at the Olimpia and that it starts at 7.00. Suggest meeting in the cafe opposite the theatre at 6.30. Ask if that is all right with him/her.*

  – Sí, me parece bien.

Pensaba quedarme (*I was thinking of staying*). Note the use of **pensar** followed by the infinitive form of the verb: **quedarme**, from **quedarse** (*to stay*), a reflexive verb (see Unit 12). You are already familiar with **quedar** (*to arrange to meet*), a non-reflexive verb: **He quedado con Carmen** (*I've arranged to meet Carmen*).

3 Unas invitaciones *Some invitations*

el cóctel	*cocktail party*
la bienvenida	*welcome*
nuevo/a	*new*
celebrar	*to celebrate*

21.03

Lucía, señor Flores and Mario, each have an invitation. Where are they being invited? Which of them accepts the invitation, and what excuse is given by those who decline it? Listen and fill in the box below.

Nombre	Invitación	¿Acepta o no?	Excusa
Lucía			
Sr. Flores			
Mario			

4 Una invitación informal *An informal invitation*

This morning you receive an email from a Spanish colleague. Where is he inviting you, and where and at what time does he suggest you meet?

> ¡Hola!
>
> Tengo dos entradas para ver a Joaquín Cortés. ¿Te gustaría venir conmigo? La función es a las 8:00 y podríamos quedar en el bar que está al lado del teatro a las 7:30. Después de la función, si te apetece, me gustaría invitarte a cenar.
>
> ¿Qué te parece? Llámame.
>
> Rafael

The word **la entrada** (*ticket*) is used for theatres and shows in general.
A bus, plane or train ticket is **el billete** (**el boleto** in Latin America).
La función is a *performance* or *show* (theatre, music, dance, etc).
A *showing* (cinema) is **la sesión**.

5 Ahora tú *And now you*

la obra de teatro	*play*
el partido	*game*
la carrera	*race*
el caballo	*horse*

**Write an email to your Spanish friend inviting him/her somewhere.
Choose something that interests you or one of the following and
suggest a place and a time you can meet:**

una función de ballet/ópera
un concierto de rock/jazz/música clásica
una obra de teatro
un partido de fútbol/tenis/rugby
una carrera de coches/caballos

6 Una invitación formal *A formal invitation*

la Cámara de Comercio	*Chamber of Commerce*
tener el agrado de	*to have pleasure in*
la apertura	*opening*
realizarse	*to take place*

**On a visit to a Spanish-speaking country you and your travelling
companion receive a formal invitation. Your colleague does not
understand Spanish so he/she asks you to translate it for him/her.**

> La Cámara de Comercio de Santa Cruz tiene el agrado de invitarle a la
> ceremonia de inauguración de sus nuevas oficinas.
>
> El acto de apertura, en el que participarán las autoridades locales, se realizará
> en la Avenida del Libertador, 52, el martes 25 de mayo a las 19:30.

La puntualidad *Punctuality*

Read this passage dealing with invitations and punctuality among Spanish and Latin American people, and find out how their customs differ from those in your country.

En España y en Latinoamérica, en invitaciones y citas de tipo formal, cuando no hay una relación íntima o de amistad con los anfitriones, la gente es más o menos puntual. Pero, si el que invita es un amigo o pariente, la puntualidad no suele ser la norma. ¿Un amigo te ha invitado a una fiesta para las 9:00 o las 10:00? Pues, si llegas a la hora exacta tu amigo seguramente se sorprenderá, y quizá él mismo no estará preparado para recibirte a esa hora. Media hora o más incluso una hora de retraso se considera normal. En algunos países de habla española se utiliza la expresión hora inglesa cuando se espera puntualidad, por ejemplo Quedamos a las seis, pero a las seis hora inglesa (*literally, English time*), ¿eh? So, six o'clock it is, but six o'clock sharp, OK?

There are a few expressions worth remembering here: **más o menos** (*more or less*), **ser puntual** (*to be punctual*), **llegar a la hora** (*to arrive on time*), **si el/la que invita ...** (*if the one (male/female) who invites ...*).

Test yourself

José and his friends Raquel and Pablo talk about the things they would do if they won a big prize in the lottery. Speak for them by changing the infinitives in brackets into the appropriate form of the conditional tense.

José

a No **(trabajar)** más.

b **(Hacer)** un viaje alrededor del mundo.

c **(Comprar)** una casa para mí y otra para mis padres.

d **(Poner)** el dinero en un banco y **(vivir)** de los intereses.

e **(Casarse)** con mi novia y **(tener)** muchos hijos.

Raquel y Pablo

f (**Poder**) pagar todas nuestras deudas.

g (**Enviar**) a nuestros hijos a los mejores colegios.

h (**Ayudar**) a nuestras familias.

i (**Mudarse**) al mejor barrio de la ciudad.

j (**Saber**) cuidar nuestro dinero.

If after checking your answers you feel you need more practice on the use of the conditional go back to dialogues 1 and 2 and look at the examples in the How do you say it? section. Try also making up sentences like those in Test 1 above saying what you would do in the same circumstances.

22 ¿Le sirvo un poco más?

Shall I give you some more?

In this unit you will learn how to:
▶ *talk about what you had done*
▶ *express compliments*
▶ *offer something and respond to an offer*
▶ *express gratitude and pleasure.*

CEFR: *Can establish social contact and express thanks (A2); Can say what he/she thinks about things (B1); Can convey degrees of emotion and write letters highlighting the personal significance of an event (B2).*

An invitation

Spaniards are justifiably proud of **la cocina española** (*Spanish cuisine*) which draws on a wide variety of fine fresh ingredients and a long tradition. The creativity of chefs has given Spain its fair share of Michelin-rated restaurants, Ferran Adrià's *El Bulli* being the most famous. Indeed, three Spanish restaurants are among the top ten in the world.

Spaniards are attentive hosts whether they entertain you in a restaurant or at home, concerned that you are enjoying your meal. To put their minds at rest, you can say about your plate of food: **Está delicioso** (*It's delicious*) or **Está buenísimo** (*It's very good*). Your host, worried that you are getting enough to eat and drink, will ask: **¿Le sirvo un poco más?** (*Shall I give you some more?*), and will not immediately take: **no, gracias** for an answer, until you say: **no, de verdad** (*no, really*). When it is time to go, your show of appreciation will be reciprocated: **Ha sido un placer** (*It's been a pleasure*); **Gracias por haber venido** (*Thank you for having come*).

 At the end of the meal, your host is pressing you to have a liqueur with your coffee. You would rather not. What can you say?

Conversations

1 ¿QUÉ LE PARECE LA CIUDAD? *WHAT DO YOU THINK OF THE CITY?*

había estado   *I/you/he/she had been*
había venido   *I/you/he/she had come*
precioso/a   *beautiful*

22.01

On a business trip to Mérida in Mexico, Laura, from Spain, meets Victoria. The relationship is formal and this is reflected in the language of the dialogues below.

1.1   Had Laura been to Mérida before? What does she think of the city? Listen and find out.

Victoria	¿Había estado aquí antes?
Laura	Había estado en la Ciudad de México, pero nunca había venido a Mérida.
Victoria	¿Qué le parece la ciudad?
Laura	Me encanta. Es una ciudad preciosa.

1.2   What expression is used in the conversation to say:
  1 Had you been here before?
  2 I had never come to …

1.3   Read the dialogue, study the vocabulary and new expressions, and then translate the following into Spanish.
  1 Had you been to Spain before?
  2 I had been in Barcelona, but I'd never come to Granada.
  3 What do you think of the hotel?
  4 I like it. It's a very good hotel.

You are already familiar with forms such as **he estado** (*I have been*), **ha venido** (*he/she has / you have*) come which correspond to the perfect tense (Unit 19). In this unit you will learn to say what you had done, a form of the verb which is used much the same as in English.

2 ESTÁ BUENÍSIMO *IT'S VERY GOOD*

la especialidad	*speciality*
había comido	*I/you/he/she had eaten*
servir (e>i)	*to serve*
¿de verdad?	*Are you sure? / Really?* (literally, *truly?*)
de verdad	*I'm sure, really*

22.02

Victoria and her husband invite Laura for dinner and she compliments her hosts on the meal.

2.1 **Listen to the conversation and focus attention on the phrases used by Laura to describe the dish, and on how she's been offered some more food or something more to drink. As you listen, try completing the following sentences.**

1 El pescado está _____ .
2 Está _____ .
3 ¿Le sirvo _____ ?
4 ¿Quiere _____ vino?

Laura	El pescado está buenísimo.
Victoria	Es una especialidad mexicana. ¿No lo había comido nunca antes?
Laura	No, nunca, está delicioso.
Victoria	¿Le sirvo un poco más?
Laura	No, gracias.
Victoria	¿De verdad?
Laura	De verdad, gracias.
Jorge	¿Quiere un poco más de vino?
Laura	Sí, gracias, pero sólo un poco.

2.2 **Read the dialogue and study the expressions you might need when being invited for a meal or when playing host to a Spanish-speaking person. Then try saying the following in Spanish:**

1 The paella is very good.
2 The chicken is delicious.
3 Shall I give you some more dessert? (*formal*)
4 Would you like some more coffee? (*formal*)

In an informal relationship the exchanges between host and guest tend not to follow strict rules and many of the social niceties one may hear in formal relationships are usually dispensed with.

amable	*kind*
el placer	*pleasure*
me alegro (from **alegrarse**)	*I'm glad*
haber	*to have* (auxiliary verb)

 22.03

Laura is leaving and she and her hosts exchange some compliments.

3.1 **Choose from the following expressions to complete the sentences in the bubbles below, then listen to the conversation to see whether you were right.**

1 tenerla en nuestra casa

2 de haberla conocido

3 la invitación

4 muy amables

> Muchas gracias por ...
> Han sido ustedes ...

> Ha sido un placer ...
> Me alegro mucho ...

Laura	¡Uy, qué tarde es! Debo irme. Muchas gracias por la invitación. Han sido ustedes muy amables.
Jorge	Ha sido un placer tenerla en nuestra casa. Me alegro mucho de haberla conocido.
Victoria	Gracias por haber venido. ¡Que tenga un buen viaje!
Laura	Adiós, y muchísimas gracias.

3.2 **Read the dialogue and find the expressions meaning the following:**

1 How late it is!
2 I must go.
3 Thank you for coming.
4 Have a nice journey!

Deber (*must, like*), **tener que** (*to have to*), expresses obligation or need: **Debo volver** (*I must go back*), **Tengo que estudiar** (*I have to study*). Another verb with a similar meaning is **haber que** (*to have to*), which is used in an impersonal way: **Hay/Había que hablar español** (*One has/had to speak Spanish*).

En España cuando se quiere invitar a una persona, especialmente a una persona a la que no se conoce bien, generalmente se la invita a un restaurante u otro sitio similar. La mayor parte de la vida social en España y en la mayoría de los países latinoamericanos tiene lugar en sitios públicos, tales como restaurantes, bares o cafés. La invitación a comer o cenar en casa generalmente está reservada para amigos más íntimos o parientes, y en ocasiones más especiales. En algunos países de Latinoamérica, sin embargo, la gente acostumbra invitar a sus amigos y conocidos a casa con más frecuencia.

Si la invitación es para comer o cenar en casa de un amigo, no es obligación llevar algo, pero si quieres hacerlo, puedes llevar una botella de vino o el postre. Pero, si la relación es formal, tendrás que llevar algo, por ejemplo champán o flores o bombones (*chocolates*) para la señora de la casa.

How do you say it?

TALKING ABOUT WHAT YOU HAD DONE

Nunca había estado/venido aquí. *I/you (formal)/he/she had never been/come here.*

No lo habíamos comido antes. *We hadn't eaten it before.*

EXPRESSING COMPLIMENTS ABOUT FOOD

Esto/el pescado está muy bueno/buenísimo/delicioso. *This/the fish is very good/delicious.*

EXPRESSING GRATITUDE AND PLEASURE

Gracias por la invitación/ la comida. *Thanks for the invitation/the meal.*

Ha sido Vd. muy amable. *You've been very kind.* (formal)

Ha sido un placer/gusto. *It's been a pleasure.* (formal)

OFFERING SOMETHING AND RESPONDING TO AN OFFER

¿Te/le sirvo un poco más?   *Shall I give you some more?* (inf/formal)

¿De verdad?/¿De veras?   *Are you sure?/Really?*

De verdad/De veras.   *I'm sure/Really.*

Sí, gracias/por favor.   *Yes, thank you/please.*

 # Language discovery

1 SAYING WHAT YOU HAD DONE: THE PLUPERFECT TENSE

To express ideas such as *I had never visited Argentina, We hadn't seen it,* you need the *pluperfect tense*. This is formed with the imperfect of **haber** (see Unit 17) and a *past participle* (see Unit 19): **Nunca había visitado Argentina, No lo/la habíamos visto**. Below is the pluperfect tense of **estar** (*to be*), **comer** (*to eat*), **venir** (*to come*). Note that, as for the imperfect, the first and third person singular are the same.

yo	había	estado	comido	venido
tú	habías	estado	comido	venido
él, ella, Vd.	había	estado	comido	venido
nosotros/as	habíamos	estado	comido	venido
vosotros/as	habíais	estado	comido	venido
ellos, ellas,Vds.	habían	estado	comido	venido

For irregular past participles see Unit 19.

Había estado ocupado/a.   *I/you/he/she had been busy.*

Todavía no habían comido.   *They hadn't eaten yet.*

¿Por qué no habías venido a verme?   *Why hadn't you come to see me?*

2 OFFERING SOMETHING: *SHALL I ...?, WOULD YOU LIKE ...?*

To offer someone something, as in *Shall I bring you something to drink?*, Spanish uses the present tense in a construction in which the person being offered something comes first: **¿Te traigo algo para beber**? (literally, *To you I bring something to drink?*). Here are some more examples:

¿Le(s) sirvo (un poco) más (de) té?   *Shall I give you some more tea?* (formal, sing/pl)

¿Te/os doy un bocadillo?   *Shall I give you a sandwich?* (inf, sing/pl)

The use of the present tense for *shall* in English is also found in other contexts: *It's hot here. Shall I open the door?* – **Hace calor aquí. ¿Abro la puerta?**, *Shall we go to the cinema tonight?* – **¿Vamos al cine esta noche?**

Alternative ways of offering someone something are through the use of **querer** in the present tense or the conditional.

¿Quiere(s) un poco más de ensalada?	*Do you want some more salad?* (formal/inf)
¿Querría usted algún licor?	*Would you like a liqueur?* (formal)

3 EXCLAMATIONS

To say *how*, as in *How late it is!, How kind you are!, How difficult it is!* use **qué**: **¡Qué tarde es!, ¡Qué amable es usted!, ¡Qué difícil es!** Note the use of a double exclamation mark and a written accent on **qué**.

Practice

 1 Lo que había hecho Francisco *What Francisco had done*

Here are some of the things Francisco had done before he got married. Match the drawings with the phrases below, then use the verbs in brackets to say what he had done.

a (**escribir**) un libro de poemas
b (**terminar**) la carrera de medicina
c (**viajar**) por el mundo
d (**aprender**) a conducir
e (**hacer**) el servicio militar
f (**estudiar**) guitarra clásica

Compulsory military service in Spain, **el servicio militar**, known popularly as **la mili** came to an end in December 2001.

2 ¿Qué había ocurrido? *What had happened?*

Events which were prior to some past event or state, and which are somehow related, are normally expressed with the pluperfect tense, for example *El campo estaba muy verde. Había llovido mucho* (The country was very green. It had rained a lot). Now match the phrases below and form similar sentences.

a La llamé a su casa.	**1** Lo había estudiado en el colegio.
b Lo/le reconocí inmediatamente.	**2** Ya había salido.
c Hablaba español perfectamente.	**3** Habían andado muchas horas.
d Estaban muy cansados.	**4** Habíamos trabajado juntos.

3 Una invitación formal *A formal invitation*

22.04

You are visiting a Spanish-speaking country and during your stay you are invited for lunch. Follow the guidelines and fill in your part of the conversation.

Mujer	¿Había estado aquí antes?
Tú	Say you had never been here before. Add that it is a very nice country.
Mujer	Gracias.
Tú	(The main course consists of mariscos, seafood.) Tell your hosts that the mariscos are very good.
Marido	Es un plato típico de aquí.
Tú	Say they are delicious.
Mujer	¿Le sirvo un poco más?
Tú	Say yes, but just a little.

Marido	¿Le pongo un poco más de vino?
Tú	Say no, thank you.
Marido	¿De verdad?
Tú	Say yes, sure, thank you, you can't drink any more because you have to drive (conducir).

As you play your part, focus not only on the compliments you need to pay to your host but also on the grammar, for example whether to use **ser** or **estar** in *it is a very nice country, the mariscos are very good, they are delicious*.

 4 Ahora tú *And now you*

You are having a formal dinner party with people you don't know well. How would you offer your guests more of the following? Try varying the expressions you use.

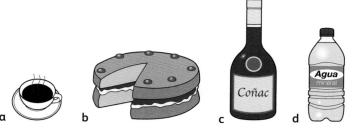

a   b   c   d

 5 ¿Qué dirías tú? *What would you say?*

el regalo   *present*

Each of these sentences contains one mistake. Can you spot it?

a   Muchas gracias para tu regalo. Es precioso.

b   Gracias, señora. Has sido usted muy amable.

c   Me alegro mucho haberte conocido, Antonio.

d   Ha sido un placer conocerlo, señora.

 6 Una carta de agradecimiento *A thank you letter*

On her return to Spain, Laura sent a thank you letter to her host in Mexico. Fill in the gaps in her letter with one of the following words.

agradecer	*to thank*
la estancia	*stay*
de igual forma	*in the same way*

> placer visita marido poder agradecer estancia
>
> Estimada Victoria:
>
> Quisiera **(a)** _____ a usted y a su **(b)** _____ las muchas atenciones que tuvieron conmigo durante mi **(c)** _____ en México. Fue realmente un **(d)** _____ haberlos conocido y espero **(e)** _____ corresponder de igual forma durante su próxima **(f)** _____ a España.
>
> Atentamente
>
> Laura Sánchez

Thank you letters are much less common in Spanish than in English, except in more formal situations such as the one above. In more informal relationships people, especially the young, normally dispense with such formalities.

 ## Test yourself

Below are some expressions used in English in formal social occasions. Can you give the Spanish for them?

a The fish/meat is delicious.

b Shall I give you some more? (*formal*)

c 'Are you sure?' – 'Sure, thank you'.

d Do you want some more wine? (*formal*)

e Yes, thank you, but just a little.

f Thank you very much for the invitation.

g You've been very/most kind. (*addressed to more than one person, formally*)

h I'm very glad to have met you. (*addressed to a woman, formally*)

i Thank you for coming.

j Have a nice journey! (*addressed to one person, formally*)

Check your answers in the Key to 'Test yourself' and go back to the dialogues and to the How do you say it? section if you need to revise the expressions in the test.

SELF CHECK

	I CAN. . .
○	. . . talk about what I had done
○	. . . express compliments
○	. . . offer something and respond to an offer
○	. . . express gratitude and pleasure.

23

Siga todo recto
Go straight on

In this unit you will learn how to:
▶ *ask for directions (2)*
▶ *give directions (2)*
▶ *give instructions.*

CEFR: *Can ask for and give directions referring to a map or plan (A2); Can follow short written directions (A2); Can give and follow simple instructions (A2).*

Wandering the streets

El casco viejo (*the old quarter*) of a Spanish city dates back at least to medieval times and with its **morería** (*Moorish quarter*) and **judería** (*Jewish quarter*) can be a maze of twisting, turning, narrow streets. Old wooden doors open directly onto the cobbled pavements, but windows are not placed at street level. Stone family crests over doorways let us know that a Christian **caballero** (*knight,* or nowadays, *a gentleman*) once lived here. Many medieval towns and old city quarters are **Patrimonio Nacional** (*National Heritage*), and a good number, like Toledo, are **Patrimonio Mundial** (*World Heritage*) sites.

Even with a **plano** (*street map*), it is easy to get lost in **el casco viejo**. You know the key words for directions from Unit 4, but the instructions that go with them like **gire** or **doble** (*turn*), **siga** (*go on/carry on*), **tome** (*take*) help greatly in the understanding of them.

How do you get to La Casa de El Greco?
Siga todo recto y al final de la calle, gire a la izquierda y luego tome la primera a la derecha.

Conversations

1 GIRE A LA DERECHA *TURN RIGHT*

 23.01

In Conversation 1, as in Conversation 2, you'll hear people asking for and giving directions.

1.1 Agustín, who is outside the Telefónica (16 on the map) on avenida Tejada, stops his car to ask for directions. What place is he looking for? Listen and try to follow the directions on the map. Key phrases here are *siga todo recto* (go straight on), ... *al llegar a* (...when you get to), *gire a la derecha/izquierda* (turn right/left).

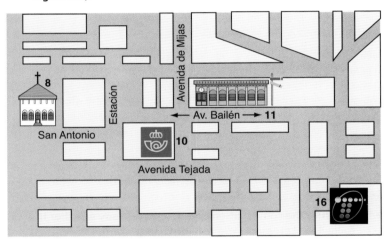

Agustín	Oiga, por favor, ¿podría decirme dónde está Correos?
Señora	Mire, siga todo recto y al llegar a la avenida de Mijas gire a la derecha. Correos está en la calle de Bailén, la segunda a la izquierda.
Agustín	¿Hay que tomar la avenida de Mijas, me ha dicho?
Señora	Sí, tome la cuarta calle a la derecha.
Agustín	Gracias.
Señora	De nada.

1.2 **Find the Spanish for the following in the conversation:**
  1 Could you tell me ...?
  2 the second on the left
  3 the fourth street on the right

1.3 **Read the dialogue now, study the vocabulary and try saying the following in Spanish.**

— Could you tell me where the museum is?

— Go straight on and when you reach Cervantes Street turn left. The museum is on San Alfonso Avenue, the third on the right.

As a visitor in a Spanish-speaking country you are much more likely to be asking for directions than giving them, but even so it is important to understand them so that eventually you may be able to use them. The directions given in Dialogues 1 and 2 correspond to the formal **usted**.

2 SUBA POR ESA ESCALERA *GO UP THOSE STAIRS*

subir	*to go up*
el primer piso	*first floor*
la escalera	*stairs*
el pasillo	*corridor*
hasta	*to/up to*
pasado	*past*

 23.02

Back at his hotel, Agustín asks the hotel receptionist how to get to the restaurant.

2.1 **Listen to the conversation a few times and say whether the following statements are true or false (*verdaderos o falsos*).**
  1 Para ir al restaurante hay que bajar al primer piso.
  2 El restaurante está en el pasillo de la izquierda.
  3 Está enfrente del bar.

Agustín	Perdone, ¿dónde está el restaurante, por favor?
Recepcionista	Suba usted por esa escalera hasta el primer piso y tome el pasillo de la izquierda. El restaurante está pasado el bar.
Agustín	Gracias.

2.2 Now complete the following sentence without looking at the dialogue; then read this and check if you were right:

Suba usted **(1)** _____ esa escalera **(2)** _____ el primer piso y tome el pasillo **(3)** _____ la izquierda.

3 HÁGALO DESPUÉS DE LA SEÑAL *DO IT AFTER THE TONE*

la consulta	*surgery*
lamentar	*to regret*
la señal	*tone*
pedir hora	*to ask for an appointment*

23.03

Agustín phoned a doctor's surgery to make an appointment, but he got a recorded message.

3.1 Listen to the recorded message several times, each time focusing attention on a different point.

1 ¿Cuál es el horario de atención al público del doctor García?

2 ¿A qué número hay que llamar para urgencias?

3 ¿Qué número hay que marcar para anular una cita?

Contestador   Esta es la consulta del doctor Ignacio García. Lamentamos no poder atender a su llamada en este momento. Nuestro horario de atención es de 9:00 a 11:30 de la mañana y por la tarde de 4:00 a 6:00. Para urgencias, llame al 952 642 21 09. Para anular una cita, marque el 952 759 55 32. Para pedir hora con el doctor, indíquenos su nombre y número de teléfono y le confirmaremos su cita. Hágalo después de la señal. Gracias.

3.2 Formal instructions can also be given with the infinitive, for example *dejar* instead of *deje su número de teléfono*, leave your telephone number. Now read the transcript and try to identify the verb forms corresponding to these infinitives, and study the way in which they have been used:

1 marcar

2 llamar

3 indicar

4 hacer

The formal instructions in this recorded message, like the directions in Conversations 1 and 2, use similar forms. Note that in the words **hágalo** and **indíquenos** the pronouns **lo** (*it*) and **nos** (*us*) are added to the end of the verb. See Language discovery section.

How do you say it?

ASKING FOR DIRECTIONS

¿Podría decirme dónde está ... / el museo?	*Could you tell me where it is / the museum is?*
¿Sabe Vd. dónde está ... / el ayuntamiento?	*Do you know where it is... /the town hall is?*

GIVING DIRECTIONS FORMALLY

Siga todo recto/de frente/derecho. (LAm)	*Go straight on.*
Gire/Tuerza/Doble a la izquierda.	*Turn left.*
Tome/Coja la primera calle ...	*Take the first street/turning ...*
Suba/Baje por esa escalera.	*Go up/down those stairs.*
Está pasada la recepción/ pasado el bar.	*It's past the reception /the bar.*

GIVING INSTRUCTIONS FORMALLY

Llame al/ Marque el (número ...)	*Call/Dial (number ...)*

Language discovery

1 GIVING DIRECTIONS AND INSTRUCTIONS: THE IMPERATIVE

Usage

a Directions and instructions are usually given in English through the imperative or command form of the verb: *Turn left, Go straight on, Dial 999.* In Spanish there are two main ways of giving directions and instructions, one is with the *present tense* (see Unit 4), the other with the *imperative*. Compare the following sentences in which the first verb form corresponds to the present tense, the other to the imperative (both for **Vd.**): **Gira/Gire a la izquierda**, **Sigue/Siga de frente**, **Marca/Marque el 999**. Both forms are just as frequent in this context.

b The imperative has a number of other uses, both in English and Spanish. It is used to give orders or commands, *Do it now!*, **¡Hágalo ahora!**, in certain forms of requests, *Come in, please* **Pase, por favor**, and in suggestions, *Speak to her* **Hable con ella**. The present tense is much less common in this context.

Formation

Spanish uses different imperative forms, depending on whether you are addressing someone formally or informally (formal and informal imperative forms), and whether you are talking to one or more than one person (singular and plural forms). Informal imperatives also have different positive and negative forms. This unit focuses on the formal imperative. For the informal imperative, see Unit 24.

a The imperative for **usted** is formed with the stem of the first person singular of the present tense (**yo**) to which the endings are added: **-e** for **-ar** verbs and **-a** for verbs **in -er** and **-ir**. For the **ustedes** form add **-n**. Stem-changing and most irregular verbs follow the same rule. Here are some examples, of which the first three correspond to regular verbs.

Infinitive	Present tense	Imperative (sing/pl)
tom**ar** (*to take*)	tom**o**	tom**e/n**
beb**er** (*to drink*)	beb**o**	beb**a/n**
sub**ir** (*to go up*)	sub**o**	sub**a/n**
segu**ir** (*to go on*)	sig**o**	sig**a/n**
torc**er** (*to turn*)	tuerz**o**	tuerz**a/n**
dec**ir** (*to say, tell*)	dig**o**	dig**a/n**

Tome(n) la primera calle a la derecha. — *Take the first street on the right.*

Suba(n) por aquí. — *Go up this way.*

Siga/(n) hasta el primer semáforo. — *Go on as far as the first traffic light.*

Tuerza(n) a la izquierda. — *Turn left.*

b A few verbs change their spelling in the imperative in order to keep the same consonant sound as the infinitive. Among these we find:

Infinitive	Present tense	Imperative (sing/pl)
bus**car** (*to look for*)	busc**o**	busqu**e/n**
mar**car** (*to dial*)	marc**o**	marqu**e/n**
cog**er** (*to take*)	coj**o**	coj**a/n**
lleg**ar** (*to arrive*)	lleg**o**	llegu**e/n**

Coja(n) la primera a la derecha.   *Take the first on the right.*

Marque(n) el 100.   *Dial 100.*

c Some irregular imperatives have forms which do not follow the pattern of the present tense.

Infinitive	Present tense	Imperative (sing/pl)
d**ar** (to give)	doy	**dé/n**
est**ar** (to be)	estoy	**esté/n**
ir (to go)	voy	**vaya/n**
sab**er** (to know)	sé	**sepa/n**
ser (*to be*)	soy	**sea/n**

Dé(n) la vuelta aquí.   *Turn round here.*

Vaya(n) despacio.   *Go slowly.*

¡Sea(n) prudente(s)!   *Be careful!*

d For negative formal imperatives simply place **no** before the verb: **No beba si va a conducir** (*Don't drink if you are going to drive*), **No diga/ haga nada** (*Don't say/do anything*).

To make the imperative sound less abrupt, as in commands or requests, you are advised to use polite forms such as **por favor** (*please*), **si no le importa** (*if you don't mind*), **si es tan amable** (*if you would be so kind*).

Envíemelo por email, si no le importa.   Send it to me by email, if you don't mind.

2 POSITION OF PRONOUNS WITH IMPERATIVES

Pronouns like **me**, **te**, **lo/a**, **le**, etc., are attached to the end of positive imperatives but precede negative ones: **Démelos, por favor** (*Give them to me, please*), **¡No me los dé!** (*Don't give them to me!*), **¡Hágalo!** (*Do it!*), **¡No lo haga!** (*Don't do it!*).

A written accent is usually necessary to show that the stress remains in the same position when the pronoun is added, as in **haga – hágalo**, **diga – dígame**.

The formal imperative is not entirely new to you, as you already encountered it in earlier units in the following phrases: **perdone** (*excuse me/I'm sorry*), **¿diga/dígame?** (*hello* (on the phone) / *can I help you?*), **deme** (*give me* (in a shop)), **póngame** (*give me* (when buying fruit or vegetables)).

Practice

1 Señales de tráfico *Traffic signs*

 Can you match the following traffic signs with their meanings below?

- **a** Gire a la derecha.
- **b** No toque la bocina.
- **c** Ceda el paso.
- **d** Cruce de peatones. Conduzca con cuidado.
- **e** Zona de escuela. Disminuya la velocidad.
- **f** Cruce ferroviario. Pare, mire y escuche.
- **g** No adelantar.
- **h** No entrar.

1

2

3

4

5

6

7

8

2 Está una calle más arriba *It's one street further up*

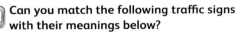

al salir	*when you leave/on leaving*
doble (from **doblar**)	*turn* (to turn)
más arriba	*further up*

23.04

Look at this map showing some hotels in a South American town and then listen to the directions given to a tourist who is trying to find a hotel. In which hotel is the tourist now and which one is he looking for?

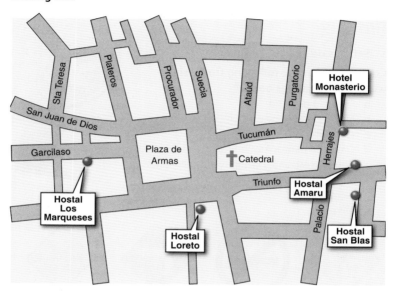

3 Hay una desviación *There's a diversion*

la carretera	road, highway
la desviación	diversion
hacia	towards
hasta	until, as far as
la planta	floor

Read this email with directions sent to Antonia by someone she is visiting, and fill in the gaps with the appropriate formal imperative forms of these verbs: *tomar, subir, seguir, preguntar, girar.*

Some key expressions in the text are:

por la avenida de ...	along ... avenue
al llegar a ...	when you get to ...
en dirección a ...	towards/in the direction of ...

286

hacia	*onwards*
hasta llegar a ...	*until you get to ...*
suba usted hasta ...	*go up to ...*
en la tercera planta	*on the third floor*

> **(a)** _____ usted de frente por la avenida de Suel y al llegar a la carretera nacional 340 **(b)** _____ usted a la izquierda en dirección al aeropuerto. Antes de llegar al aeropuerto hay una desviación hacia Santa Clara. **(c)** _____ usted esa desviación y **(d)** _____ todo recto hasta llegar a una estación de servicio. Nuestra fábrica está pasada la estación de servicio. **(e)** _____ usted hasta nuestras oficinas, que están en la tercera planta, y **(f)** _____ por mí en recepción.

4 ¿Sabe usted dónde hay un banco? *Do you know where there is a bank?*

 A Spanish speaker asks you for directions in your own town. Use the guidelines below to complete your part of the conversation.

– Perdone, ¿sabe usted dónde hay un banco?
– Say yes and tell him/her to go straight on and take the third turning on the left, then take the first turning on the right and go straight on as far as the end of the road. The bank is opposite the station.

5 Ahora tú *And now you*

You are outside the church, *la iglesia*, on calle San Antonio (8 on the previous map that goes with Conversation 1) when someone approaches you to ask for directions to the station (11 on the same map). How would you reply?

 – Perdone, ¿podría decirme dónde está la estación?

Practise playing the part of someone asking for directions to a place in your own town. What questions might they ask? Think then of directions you might give from another point in the town.

6 Tráigamela, por favor *Bring it to me, please*

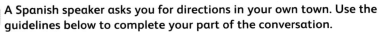

hacer un pedido	*to place an order*
la carpeta	*file*
enseñar	*to show*
el informe	*report*

Read this brief exchange between Elsa and her boss.

Elsa	¿Le traigo la correspondencia de hoy? **(sí)**
Jefe/a	Sí, tráigamela, por favor.
Elsa	¿Abro la ventana? **(no)**
Jefe/a	No, no la abra.

How would Elsa's boss reply to each of the following? Follow the examples, using written accents where appropriate.

    a ¿Envío el fax?**(sí)**
    b ¿Llamo a la secretaria? **(sí)**
    c ¿Hago el pedido? **(no)**
    d ¿Le paso las carpetas? **(sí)**
    e ¿Contesto el mail? **(no)**
    f ¿Le enseño el informe? **(sí)**

There are two main points in this exercise: one is to practise positive and negative imperative or command forms, the other is to give you further practice in the use of pronouns with imperatives in both positive and negative sentences.

 Test yourself

1 **How would you say the following in Spanish? Use the formal form where appropriate.**
    a Could you tell me where the station is?
    b Excuse me, do you know where the square is?
    c Where are the toilets, please?
    d Where's a bank, please?
    e Can you tell us where the Granada hotel is?
    f Do you know if there is a supermarket nearby?

2 **What do the following directions mean?**
    a Siga todo recto por esta avenida y luego tome la cuarta calle a la derecha. Continúe por esa calle hasta llegar a una iglesia. El hotel Cóndor está al lado de la iglesia.
    b Suba por la escalera hasta la tercera planta (*or* el tercer piso) y luego tome el pasillo de la izquierda. La oficina de la señora Castro es la número 310 y está al fondo del pasillo.

c El bar está en la segunda planta, pasado el restaurante. El ascensor está junto a la recepción.

d Esta es la consulta del doctor Palma. Para pedir hora con el doctor marque uno, para cambiar o anular su hora marque dos, para otras consultas* marque tres, para volver al menú principal marque 0.

* The word 'consultas' in 'para otras consultas' means *enquiries*.

Test 1 assesses your ability to ask for directions while Test 2 focuses on understanding directions given to you. As a beginner in Spanish, you are much more likely to be asking for and understanding directions than giving them. Unit 23 is a recycling of Unit 4, so if you think you need to revise this topic you should go back to both.

SELF CHECK

	I CAN. . .
○	. . . ask for directions (2)
○	. . . give directions (2)
○	. . . give instructions.

24 Me duele la cabeza
I have a headache

In this unit you will learn how to:
- ▶ *say how you feel*
- ▶ *describe minor ailments*
- ▶ *make requests*
- ▶ *give advice.*

CEFR: *Can explain how he/she feels (B2); Can explain a problem (B1); Can give and follow simple instructions (A2); Can understand the description of events and feelings in personal letters (B2).*

Minor ailments

La farmacia *(the chemist's)* is, in Spain, just that, and the green Maltese Cross sign outside makes it readily identifiable. Toiletries, which are not of the medicated kind, are to be found in **la perfumería** *(the perfume shop)*. **El farmacéutico** or **la farmacéutica** *(the chemist)* is able to dispense a wide range of **medicamentos** *(medicines)* without prescription so this is the place to go for a minor ailment.

¿Puede recomendarme algo para ...? *(Can you recommend something for ...?)* is a good opening question or: **Quisiera algo para ...** *(I would like something for ...)* followed by your complaint: **la diarrea** *(diarrhoea)*, **las quemaduras del sol** *(sunburn)*, **el resfriado** *(a cold)*. Or you may be want something for **el dolor de cabeza** *(a headache)* or **el dolor de estómago** *(stomach ache)*. The chemist will give you instructions for the medication: **Tome una pastilla tres veces al día con la comida** *(Take one tablet three times a day with food)*.

What is Julio suffering from?:
¿Puede recomendarme algo para el resfriado? También tengo dolor de cabeza.

1 UN DOLOR DE CABEZA *A HEADACHE*

la cabeza	*head*
el vaso	*glass*
tener sed	*to be thirsty*

24.01

Marta is feeling unwell and she describes her symptoms to her friend Luis.

1.1 **Listen to the conversation a few times and, without looking at the text below, try completing these sentences:**

1 Por favor, _____ una aspirina.

2 _____ muchísima sed.

3 Sí, _____ un momento.

Luis	¿Qué te pasa?
Marta	Tengo un dolor de cabeza horrible.
Luis	¿Quieres tomar algo?
Marta	Sí, por favor tráeme una aspirina y un vaso de agua. Tengo muchísima sed.
Luis	Sí, espera un momento. Vuelvo en seguida.

1.2 **Now read the text and find the phrases which mean the following:**

1 What's wrong with you?

2 I'll be right back.

There are more imperatives in this unit, but this time the focus is on familiar ones. **Trae** (from **traer** – *to bring*) and **espera** (from **esperar** – *to wait*) correspond to the **tú** form of the verb. **Trae** adds a written accent when a syllable is added: **tráeme** (*bring me*).

2 TENGO MUCHO CALOR *I'M VERY HOT*

encontrarse (o>ue)	*to feel*
apagar la luz	*to turn off the light*
tratar de	*to try to*
descansar	*to rest*

Luis comes back to Marta after some time.

2.1 **Listen to the conversation and answer these questions:**
  1 How is Marta feeling now?
  2 Why does she ask Luis to open the window?
  3 What does Luis suggest she does?

Luis	¿Te encuentras mejor?
Marta	No, no me encuentro bien. Me duele la cabeza todavía y tengo mucho calor. Por favor, abre la ventana un poco.
Luis	Sí, claro. Mira, ¿por qué no descansas un rato? Trata de dormir. Te hará bien. No te levantes.
Marta	¿Podrías apagar la luz, por favor? Y no me esperes para cenar.
Luis	Muy bien. No comas nada hasta mañana.

2.2 **Now read the dialogue and find phrases which are similar in meaning to the following:**
  a No estoy bien.
  b Tengo dolor de cabeza.
  c ¿Puedes abrir la ventana?
  d Tienes que descansar.

Abre (from **abrir** – *to open*), **mira** (from **mirar** – *to look*), **trata** (from **tratar** – *to try*), **no te levantes** (from **levantarse** – *to get up*), **no me esperes** (from **esperar** – *to wait*), and **no comas** (from **comer** – *to eat*), are all familiar imperative forms. The endings of negative forms are different from those of positive ones.

How do you say it?

SAYING HOW YOU FEEL

No me encuentro bien.	*I don't feel well.*
Tengo sed/calor.	*I'm thirsty/hot.*

DESCRIBING MINOR AILMENTS

Me duele la cabeza/el estómago.   *I have a headache/a stomach ache.*

Tengo dolor de cabeza/   *I have a headache/stomach ache/*
estómago/muelas/garganta.   *toothache/sore throat.*

MAKING REQUESTS

Tráeme una aspirina/un   *Bring me an aspirin/a glass of*
vaso de agua.   *water.*

Abre/cierra la ventana/puerta.   *Open/close the window/door.*

¿Podrías apagar/encender la luz?   *Could you turn off/on the light?*

GIVING ADVICE

Trata de descansar/dormir.   *Try to rest/sleep.*

No te levantes/comas.   *Don't get up/eat.*

 # Language discovery

1 THE INFORMAL IMPERATIVE OR COMMAND: 'TÚ' AND 'VOSOTROS'

In Unit 23 you learned to use the formal imperative or command form, for **usted** and **ustedes**. In this unit you will learn to use the informal imperative, for **tú** and **vosotros**. Unlike the formal imperative, which has similar positive and negative forms, for example **tome** (*take*), **no tome** (*don't take*), the informal one has different positive and negative forms.

Formation

a The **tú** form of the positive imperative or command is like the **tú** form of the present tense, but without the **-s.**

tú esper**as** (*you wait*)   esper**a** (*wait*)

tú com**es** (*you eat*)   com**e** (*eat*)

tú abr**es** (*you open*)   abr**e** (*open*)

b For the **vosotros** form, replace the **-r** of the infinitive with **-d.**

esper**ar**   esper**ad**

com**er**   com**ed**

abr**ir**   abr**id**

c Stem-changing verbs, for example **cerrar (e>ie)** (*to shut, close*), **volver (o>ue)** (*to come back*), make a similar change in the **tú** form of the imperative: **cierra** (*shut, close*), **vuelve** (*come back*). The endings are the same as for regular verbs in **a** above.

d A few verbs have irregular positive imperative or command forms for **tú**. For **vosotros** follow the pattern in **b** above.

decir	**di**	*say*
hacer	**haz**	*do, make*
ir	**ve**	*go*
poner	**pon**	*put*
salir	**sal**	*go/get out*
ser	**sé**	*be*
tener	**ten**	*have*
venir	**ven**	*come*

e Negative imperatives for **tú** and **vosotros** are different from positive ones. The general rule is as follows: verbs ending in **-ar** take **-e** and those in **-er** and **-ir** take **-a.**

esperar	**no esperes – no esperéis**	*don't wait*
comer	**no comas – no comáis**	*don't eat*
abrir	**no abras – no abráis**	*don't open*

f Some verbs form the negative informal imperative in a different way. (See irregular imperatives Unit 23.)

dar (*to give*)	**no des – no deis**	*don't give*
estar (*to be*)	**no estés – no estéis**	*don't be*
ir (*to go*)	**no vayas – no vayáis**	*don't go*
ser (*to be*)	**no seas – no seáis**	*don't be*

g Verbs ending in **-car** and **-gar**, **-ger** and **-gir** change their spelling in the negative imperative form in order to keep the same consonant sound of the infinitive.

buscar (*to look for*)	**no busques – no busquéis**	*don't look for*
llegar (*to arrive*)	**no llegues – no lleguéis**	*don't arrive*

| coger (*to take, catch*) | **no cojas – no cojáis** | *don't take/catch* |
| elegir (*to choose*) | **no elijas – no elijáis** | *don't choose* |

Look at the examples which follow and see how they fit the rules above.

Espera un momento.	*Wait a moment.*
Come sólo un poco.	*Eat just a little.*
Abrid las ventanas.	*Open the windows.*
Ve a por un médico.	*Go and get a doctor.*
Haz lo que digo.	*Do as I say.*
Ponlo aquí.	*Put it here.*
Ten paciencia.	*Have patience.*
No nos esperes.	*Don't wait for us.*
No vayáis en el coche.	*Don't go in the car.*
No lleguéis tarde.	*Don't be late.*

2 POSITION OF PRONOUNS WITH IMPERATIVES

Just as with formal commands, pronouns are attached to the end of positive forms but precede negative ones (see Unit 23): **Hazlo** (*Do it*), **No lo hagas** (*Don't do it*).

3 ME DUELE ... (*IT HURTS ...*), TENGO DOLOR DE ... (*I HAVE A PAIN IN ...*)

a **Doler** (*to hurt*) is used in a construction similar to that with **gustar** (see Unit 13), in which the person who is affected by the pain goes before the verb. So you literally say *to me, to you, etc. it hurts*: e.g. **Me duele la cabeza** (*I have a headache* – literally, *To me hurts the head*). If what hurts is plural, *doler* has to be plural: **Me duelen los pies** (*My feet ache* – literally, *To me hurt the feet*).

Note that in place of the English possessive, *as in my feet, my back, etc.*, Spanish uses a definite article: **los pies, la espalda**. The use of **me**, **te**, **le**, etc. makes the use of a possessive unnecessary.

This construction with **doler** is much more common than that with **tener dolor de ...** below and it can be used with most parts of the body.

Here are some other useful expressions with **doler**: **¿Dónde te/le duele?** (*Where does it hurt?*), **¿Te/le duele mucho?** (*Does it hurt much?*), **Me duele la espalda** (*I have a backache*).

b Tener dolor de ... (*to have a pain in ...*) can replace **doler** in expressions such as **Tengo dolor de cabeza/estómago/muelas/espalda** (*I have a headache/a stomach/tooth/backache*). With other parts of the body most speakers will use **doler**, so, if in doubt, use this.

Other expressions worth learning are those you might need on a visit to a chemist's, **una farmacia**: **Quisiera algo para el dolor de cabeza/estómago** (*I'd like something for a head/stomach ache*), **¿Puede recomendarme algo (para el resfriado/la diarrea/las quemaduras del sol)?** (*Can you recommend something (for a cold/diarrhoea/sunburn)?*).

4 'TENER' FOR *TO BE*

Note the use of **tener** for *to be* in expressions like the following: **Tengo hambre/sed/frío/calor** (*I'm hungry/thirsty/cold/hot*).

Other expressions of this kind are:

tener cuidado	*to be careful*
tener éxito	*to be successful*
tener miedo	*to be afraid*
tener paciencia	*to be patient*
tener razón	*to be right*
tener sueño	*to be sleepy*
tener suerte	*to be lucky*
tener vergüenza	*to be ashamed*

Practice

1 Las dolencias más comunes *The most common ailments*

Look at the chart below which lists the most common complaints in different European countries, including Spain, and compare the figures. How many words can you guess? Which countries seem the most healthy, according to the chart?

Las dolencias más comunes en Europa							
%	España	Bélgica	Alemania	Italia	Países Bajos	Francia	Reino Unido
Fiebre/resfriado	70	69	51	65	51	64	81
Dolor de cabeza	48	43	35	46	35	49	63
Fatiga	31	40	14	29	14	47	45
Reumatismo	33	34	32	49	32	43	38
Ansiedad/insomnio	41	42	25	37	25	41	39
Problemas digestivos	27	32	22	33	22	34	28

Fuente: secodip

2 Una visita al doctor *A visit to the doctor*

me siento (from **sentirse e>ie**) *I feel (myself)*

intranquilo/a *anxious*

estresado/a *under stress*

a ver ... *let's see ...*

estomacal *stomach* (adjective)

recetar *to prescribe*

la pastilla *tablet, pill*

24.03

You will hear two conversations between a patient and a doctor. Listen to the dialogues and answer the following questions.

　1 Which of the complaints in the chart above do you associate with the patients' symptoms?

　2 What does each doctor advise the patient to do or what does he or she prescribe?

3 Describe los síntomas *Describe the symptoms*

el cuerpo　　　　　　　　　　　　　　　　*body*

On a visit to a Spanish-speaking country you go to the doctor because you are feeling unwell. Describe your symptoms by filling in the gaps with one of these verbs:

a No _____ bien.

b _____ la cabeza.

c _____ de estómago.

d _____ un poco de fiebre.

e _____ todo el cuerpo.

f _____ muy cansado/a.

 4 Un día de mucho calor *A very warm day*

The heat seems to have affected you during your stay in a Spanish-speaking country, so you ask a friend for help. Follow the guidelines below and fill in your part of the conversation.

Amigo/a	¿Qué te pasa?
Tú	*Tell your friend that you are not feeling well.*
Amigo/a	¿Qué tienes?
Tú	*Say that you have a terrible headache and you are feverish.*
Amigo/a	¿Quieres tomar algo?
Tú	*Ask your friend to bring you a glass of mineral water. Say you are very thirsty.*
Amigo/a	Muy bien. ¿Quieres algo más?
Tú	*Ask your friend to open the door. Say you are very hot.*
Amigo/a	¿Quieres comer algo?
Tú	*Say no, thank you, you are not hungry.*

 5 Cartas al director *Letters to the editor*

el peso	*weight*
lograr	*to manage*
bajar/subir de peso	*to lose/gain weight*
ponerse a régimen	*to go on a diet*
sentir (e>ie)	*to feel*
acabar en	*to end up in*
poner fin	*to put an end*
ayudar	*to help*

Two readers of a health magazine wrote to the editor seeking help with their problems. What are their problems? Read the letters and find out.

Dolores de cabeza crónicos

Me llamo Ricardo, tengo 28 años y trabajo en un banco desde hace un año. Mi problema es que al final del día siento un dolor de cabeza devastador en la parte superior izquierda de la cabeza que me incapacita para todo. Después siento náuseas, que normalmente acaban en vómitos. He tratado de poner fin a este problema tomando analgésicos, pero no he tenido éxito. ¡Por favor ayúdenme y díganme qué puedo hacer!

Ricardo

Un problema de peso

Me llamo Isabel, tengo 45 años y tengo un problema común a mucha gente: no logro bajar de peso. Soy muy sociable y me encanta salir a comer con mis amigos. A veces me pongo a régimen durante unos días y bajo algunos kilos, pero no soy constante y subo de peso otra vez. Necesito una solución definitiva para terminar con este problema. ¿Qué puedo hacer?

Isabel

Go back to the letters and see how the following has been used: **lograr +** infinitive (*to manage to do something*), **otra vez** (*again*), **tener éxito** (*to succeed/to have success*), **¡Qué puedo hacer!** (*What can I do!*).

6 **¿Qué consejos les darías?** *What advice would you give them?*

| el azúcar | sugar |
| las grasas | fat |

Consider these words of advice. Which would be suitable for Isabel and which for Ricardo? Classify them accordingly using 'I' for Isabel and 'R' for Ricardo.

a No trabajes demasiado.

b No comas en exceso.

c Reduce el consumo de azúcar y grasas.

d Haz gimnasia o yoga para controlar tu estrés.

e Busca otro trabajo.

f Cambia tu dieta.

| la mayoría | majority |
| a través de | through |

En España la mayoría de la gente recibe atención médica a través de la Seguridad Social, *social security*. Otros utilizan la sanidad privada, *private health services*. Los visitantes de otros países de la Unión Europea pueden recibir atención médica a través de la Seguridad Social. En caso de accidente u otra emergencia se puede recibir atención rápida en una Casa de Socorro o en un Puesto de Socorro (*first-aid post*).

 Test yourself

1 **Match each statement on the left with an appropriate request or advice on the right.**

a Tengo sed.	**1** Abre la ventana, por favor.
b Tengo hambre.	**2** Ve al dentista.
c Tengo frío.	**3** Tráeme algo para beber.
d Tengo calor.	**4** Por favor, dame una aspirina.
e Tengo dolor de cabeza.	**5** Ponte un jersey.
f Me duelen las muelas.	**6** Come algo.

2 **Make the following commands negative.**

a Cierra la puerta.

b Enciende la luz.

c Ponlo sobre la mesa.

d Por favor, hazlo.

e Díselo ahora.

f Tomad el autobús.

If you are uncertain about the meaning of some of the expressions in Test 1, go back to the dialogues and to the How do you say it? section. For **doler** see also paragraph 3 of the Language discovery and for **tener** with the meaning of *to be* go to paragraph 4. Test 2 focuses exclusively on commands, which have been covered in paragraphs 1 and 2 of the Language discovery section. Don't get discouraged if you had difficulty with them, as understanding is more important at this stage than actually producing them.

SELF CHECK

I CAN. . .
. . . say how I feel
. . . describe minor ailments
. . . make requests
. . . give advice.

25 *Quería alquilar un piso*

I'd like to rent a flat

In this unit you will learn how to:
▶ *say what sort of place or person you want*
▶ *express hope*
▶ *express uncertainty.*

CEFR: *Can describe ambitions and hope (B1); Can find specific information in advertisements (A2); Can understand the description of wishes in personal letters (B2); Can write simple connected text on a topic of personal interest (B1); Can explain a viewpoint and identify speaker viewpoint and attitudes (B2).*

 Housing

Traditional house types vary across Spain according to region. The stone-walled, pitched roof houses of the north, where the animals inhabited **la planta baja** (*the ground floor*) and the family **el primer piso** (*the first floor*), give way to the flat-roofed, whitewashed houses of the south where **el patio** (*the courtyard*) forms the central feature. City dwellers live in **pisos** (*flats*) and here again there are differences. In the colder climes of the north **las terrazas** (*the balconies*) are glassed in to become **miradores.**

As the cities have grown, **urbanizaciones** (*housing developments*) have mushroomed on their outskirts, and **agencias inmobiliarias** (*estate agencies*) to deal with prospective buyers and tenants who will have an idea of what they are looking for: **Quiero una casa que tenga piscina** (*I want a house that has a swimming pool*), or **Busco un piso que esté amueblado** (*I'm looking for a flat that is furnished*).

 Where does María want her house to be?
Quiero una casa que no esté lejos de las tiendas.

Conversations

1 ¿QUÉ TIPO DE PISO BUSCA? *WHAT KIND OF FLAT ARE YOU LOOKING FOR?*

siéntese/siéntate (from **sentarse e>ie**, formal/inf)	*sit down*
la inmobiliaria	*estate agent*
el local	*premises*
la urbanización	*housing development*
la torre	*villa*
de una planta	*one-storey*
la parcela	*plot*

25.01

Paloma would like to rent a flat and she makes enquiries at an estate agent.

1.1 **What kind of flat is Paloma looking for and how much is she prepared to pay? Listen and reply. Key words here are:**

alquilar	*to rent*
el piso	*flat*
buscar	*to look for*
amueblado	*furnished*

Empleado	Buenos días. ¿Qué desea?
Paloma	Buenos días. Quería alquilar un piso.
Empleado	¿Qué tipo de piso busca usted? Tenemos varios.
Paloma	Pues, busco algo que esté cerca del centro, que tenga tres o cuatro dormitorios, y que no sea demasiado caro. No quiero pagar más de 800 euros mensuales. Y lo prefiero amueblado.
Empleado	Muy bien, veré lo que tenemos. Siéntese, por favor.

1.2 **Now read the dialogue, then look at the advertisement below and say which of the flats listed in it might suit Paloma.**

1.3 *¿Qué tipo de piso o casa buscas tú?* **Adapt Paloma's part and state your own requirements, for example 'cerca de la playa/ en el campo, 2/3 dormitorios/garaje/jardín, que no cueste más de …, amueblado/sin amueblar'.**

This unit focuses on a form of the verb which is used to express ideas which are not yet a reality or which are less certain. In Dialogue 1 **esté** (from **estar**), **tenga** (from **tener**) and **sea** (from **ser**) correspond to this new form which is explained in the Language discovery section.

2 ESPERO QUE ENCUENTRES A ALGUIEN *I HOPE YOU FIND SOMEONE*

25.02

Paloma has rented a flat and is looking for someone to share it with her.

2.1 **What sort of person is Paloma looking for? Listen to a conversation between her and her friend Teresa and say whether the statements below are true or false (*verdaderos o falsos*). Key words here are:**

compartir	*to share*
alguien	*someone*

| la edad | age |
| fumar | to smoke |

1 Paloma busca a alguien que tenga su misma edad.
2 Quiere una persona que trabaje en casa.
3 Prefiere una persona que no fume y que sea vegetariana.
4 Quiere una persona que tenga gatos.

Paloma	Estoy buscando a alguien para compartir el piso. Si sabes de alguna persona, dímelo.
Teresa	¿Qué tipo de persona buscas?
Paloma	Pues, quiero una persona de mi edad, que trabaje fuera de casa, que no fume, que sea vegetariana... y que le gusten los gatos, como a mí.
Teresa	Espero que encuentres a alguien, pero no creo que sea fácil.

2.2 Read the dialogue and find the expressions meaning *I hope you'll find someone, I don't think it'll be easy.*

More new forms of the verb in this dialogue to add to those in Dialogue 1 are **trabaje** (from **trabajar**), **fume** (from **fumar**), **gusten** (from **gustar**), **encuentres** (from **encontrar**). These are formed like the formal imperative (Unit 23).

2.3 Ahora tú *And now you*

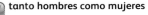

dímelo	let me know (literally, tell me it)
fuera de	away from
el gato	cat
como a mí	like me

Imagine you want to share the place where you live. Adapt Paloma's part and say what sort of person you are looking for. Here are some ideas:

(ser) joven/mayor, estudiante/profesional, tranquilo/a, (tener) sentido del humor, (gustar) los deportes.

| tanto hombres como mujeres | men as well as women |

En España, es común que muchos jóvenes de veinte, veinticinco o incluso (*even*) treinta años vivan con sus padres. La imposibilidad de encontrar un empleo (*job*) limita su independencia. La vivienda (*housing*) es cara en las grandes ciudades como Madrid y Barcelona, y los jóvenes que trabajan a menudo prefieren compartir un piso con amigos, al menos (*at least*) en los primeros años.

How do you say it?

SAYING WHAT SORT OF PLACE YOU WANT

Quiero un piso que tenga dos dormitorios.
I want a flat with (literally which has) two bedrooms.

Busco una casa que no sea demasiado cara.
I'm looking for a house which is not too expensive.

Prefiero que esté cerca de la playa.
I prefer it to be near the beach.

SAYING WHAT SORT OF PERSON YOU WANT

Busco a alguien que no fume.
I'm looking for someone who doesn't smoke.

Quiero una persona que trabaje fuera de casa.
I want a person who works away from home.

Prefiero una persona que hable español.
I prefer a person who speaks Spanish.

EXPRESSING HOPE

Espero que encuentres a alguien.
I hope you find someone.

Esperamos que sea agradable.
We hope he/she/it will be pleasant.

EXPRESSING UNCERTAINTY

No creo que sea fácil/difícil.
I don't think it will be easy/difficult.

No creo que tenga garaje.
I don't think it has a garage.

 Language discovery

1 THE SUBJUNCTIVE

Sentences such as **Busco un apartamento que esté cerca de la oficina** (*I'm looking for an apartment which is near the office*), **No creo que sea difícil** (*I don't think it'll be difficult*), like the rest of the examples above, refer to something which is hypothetical or uncertain, something which may or may not become a reality. To express ideas such as these, Spanish uses a special form of the verb which is known 'technically' as *subjunctive*. The subjunctive is not a tense. It is described as a mood of the verb, itself comprising tenses of its own, just as the tenses you have learned so far are part of the indicative mood. The subjunctive is used very rarely in modern English, but there are remnants of it in sentences such as the following: *I insist that he come* (**Insisto en que venga**), *If I were you* (**Yo en tu lugar** – literally, *I in your place*).

The subjunctive is very common in all forms of Spanish, spoken and written, formal and informal. Of the tenses of the subjunctive, the present subjunctive is the one used most, and the only one covered in this book. Look at the notes below to see how this is used and what its forms are.

2 THE PRESENT SUBJUNCTIVE

Formation

The present subjunctive is formed by removing the **-o** of the first person singular of the present tense (or present indicative), to which the endings are added: **-e** for **-ar** verbs and **-a** for verbs **in -er** and **-ir**, just as for the formal imperative, with stem-changing and most irregular verbs following the same rule (see Unit 23).

Here are the full forms of **hablar** (*to speak*), **comer** (*to eat*), **vivir** (*to live*).

yo	habl**e**	com**a**	viv**a**
tú	habl**es**	com**as**	viv**as**
él, ella, Vd.	habl**e**	com**a**	viv**a**
nosotros/as	habl**emos**	com**amos**	viv**amos**
vosotros/as	habl**éis**	com**áis**	viv**áis**
ellos, ellas, Vds.	habl**en**	com**an**	viv**an**

A few verbs form the present subjunctive in a different way:

Infinitive	Present subjunctive
dar (*to give*)	dé, des, dé, demos, deis, den
estar (*to be*)	esté, estés, esté, estemos, estéis, estén
haber (*to have* – auxiliary verb)	haya, hayas, haya, hayamos, hayáis, hayan
ir (*to go*)	vaya, vayas, vaya, vayamos, vayáis, vayan
saber (*to know*)	sepa, sepas, sepa, sepamos, sepáis, sepan
ser (*to be*)	sea, seas, sea, seamos, seáis, sean

Usage

a The subjunctive normally occurs in a construction with a main verb, for example **quiero** (*I want*), followed by **que** (*that, which, who*) and the *subjunctive verb*.

Quiero un hotel que no sea muy caro.	*I want a hotel which is not too expensive.*
Necesitan una persona que les ayude.	*They need a person who can help them.*

b It is used after verbs and expressions indicating possibility, wishes and requests, and thinking, the latter in negative sentences only.

Puede que lo encuentres.	*You may find it.* (possibility)
Quiero que me llames.	*I want you to call me.* (wish or request)
No creo que vayan.	*I don't think they'll go.* (thinking)

c It occurs after verbs and expressions indicating some kind of emotion and hope.

Me molesta que me interrumpan.	*It bothers me to be interrupted.*
Me alegro de que vengan.	*I'm glad they are coming.*
Espero que sea cierto.	*I hope it's true.*

d It is also used after impersonal expressions such as **es normal** (*it is normal*), **es importante** (*it is important*), **es extraño** (*it is strange*).

Es normal que vivan con los padres.	*It is normal for them to live with their parents.*

| **Es importante que lo hagáis.** | *It's important that you should do it.* |
| **Es extraño que no estén en casa.** | *It's strange that they are not at home.* |

e It is required after **cuando** (*when*), and other time expressions referring to the future, and after **para que** (*so that*) and with similar expressions indicating purpose.

| **Cuando llegue María se lo diré.** | *When María arrives I'll tell her.* |
| **Allí está para que lo veas.** | *There it is so that you can see it.* |

Cuando llegue María se lo diré points to something which is not yet a reality. Compare this with **Cuando llega María prepara la cena** (*When Maria arrives she prepares dinner*), an action which is a fact and which does not require the subjunctive.

Practice

1 Buscando un lugar donde vivir *Looking for a place to live*

Look at the advertisements below placed by people looking for a flat or room to rent or let, or someone to share.

1.1 Can you give the contact name or telephone number for each of the following?
   a an English teacher wanting to share a flat
   b someone offering a room to a vegetarian and non-smoker
   c a student of French looking for accommodation with a French family
   d someone offering a large, sunny room to a female
   e someone looking for a two-bedroom flat to rent
   f someone looking for free accommodation for a weekend

INMOBILARIA

Pisos

▲ **Busco familia** francesa que viva en Francia y que me alquile una habitación durante diez meses. Soy estudiante de francés. T. 642 65 54 21. Luisa.

▲ **Busco piso** en alquiler. Zona Sagrada Familia. Dos habitaciones, sala, cocina y baño. Pago máximo 600 € /mes. Persona responsable. T. 94 418 50 05. Begoña.

▲ **Necesito sitio** gratis en Sitges, para pasar un fin de semana durante el Festival de Cinema Fantàstic. No molestaré. T. 644 30 65 96 (de 17 a 20 h.). Carlota

▲ **Profesora de** inglés busca habitación en piso compartido. Preferiblemente zona centro. T. 93 330 16 87 (horas de oficina).

○ **Busco chica,** para compartir piso. Zona Valle Hebrón. Habitación grande y soleada. Urge a partir de octubre. T. 93 357 26 71 (a partir 21h.)

○ **Busco chica** estudiante, para compartir piso junto Metro Marina. Precio: 290 € /mes+ gastos. T. 93 300 99 44 (de 21 a 22.30 h.).

○ **Llogo pis** zona Hospital de Sant Pau, 3 cambres, cuina, menjador, gran terrassa i assolejat. Preu: 640 € /mes. T. 973 44 04 57 (tardes).

○ **Sitges.** Alquilo habitación muy tranquila. Preferiblemente a persona vegetariana y no fumadora. T. 977 894 69 05 (noches).

1.2 One of the advertisements is in Catalan. Can you spot it? Give the contact number.

 2 Estudiante busca familia española *Student seeks Spanish family*

One of your friends is travelling to Salamanca to do a Spanish course and would like to stay with a family. His/her Spanish is not very good, and he/she needs help to compose the following advertisement. Try making sense of what he/she wants by changing the verbs in brackets into the appropriate form of the present subjunctive.

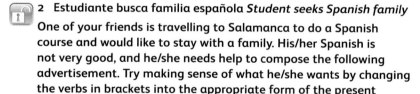

Estudiante busca habitación con familia española

Estudiante de habla inglesa de 20 años busca familia española que **(vivir)** en Salamanca y que me **(alquilar)** una habitación durante el mes de agosto. Prefiero una familia en la que **(hay)** otras personas de mi edad que **(poder)** ayudarme con mi español. Preferiblemente un sitio que **(estar)** cerca de la universidad. T. +44 (0)20 7741 3462.

3 Ahora tú *And now you*

You will be spending some time in a Spanish-speaking country in order to improve your Spanish, and would like to share a flat with someone. Write an advertisement like those in Activity 1, or a note like the one above, saying what you are looking for.

4 No creo que ... (*I don't think ...*), Espero que ... (*I hope that ...*)

dispuesto/a a	*a willing to*
los animales domésticos	*pets*
hacer la limpieza	*to clean (up)*
llevarse bien con	*to get on well with*

Raúl and his flatmates are trying to choose another person to share their flat. His friend Juan hopes the person they are discussing will be the right one, but Carmen is rather pessimistic. Follow the example and answer for Juan and Carmen.

Raúl	¿Pagará puntualmente?
Juan	Espero que pague puntualmente.
Carmen	No creo que pague puntualmente.

The future form in these sentences implies uncertainty and can translate with *will* or *I wonder*: **¿Pagará puntualmente?** (*Will he pay punctually?* or *I wonder whether he will pay punctually*).

a ¿Será sociable?
b ¿Estará dispuesto a hacer la limpieza?
c ¿Sabrá cocinar?
d ¿Tendrá sentido del humor?
e ¿Le gustarán los animales domésticos?
f ¿Se llevará bien con nosotros?

5 Los requisitos más importantes *The most important requirements*

imprescindible	*essential*
conducir	*to drive*
capaz	*capable*
la presencia	*appearance*
los estudios superiores	*higher education*
la informática	*computing*
contar (o>ue) con	*to have*
estar dispuesto/a a	*to be willing to*
incorporarse a	*to join*

Julio's company needs a new public relations employee and he has been asked to draw a list of possible requirements. Here are some notes he's jotted down. Give the English for each of the requirements listed by him and then complete the sentences using the present subjunctive in place of the infinitives.

a Es imprescindible que … (saber idiomas, tener carnet de conducir, tener experiencia y ser capaz de relacionarse bien con la gente).

b Es importante que … (ser creativo y dinámico, tener buena presencia y haber terminado sus estudios superiores).

c Es necesario que … (tener conocimientos de informática, contar con vehículo propio, estar dispuesto a viajar y poder incorporarse de inmediato a la empresa).

6 **¿Qué tipo de persona buscan?** *What kind of person are they looking for?*

veamos	let's see
preferiblemente	preferably

 25.03

6.1 Julio and Isabel are discussing the requirements for the new employee their company is seeking. Which of the requirements in Activity 5 are mentioned by them? Listen to the conversation and tick them as you hear them.

Think of situations in which you might find yourself establishing certain requirements even if it is only in your thoughts. Looking for the ideal partner for example. What sort of person would you look for? Here is a start. Can you fill in the missing words? **Busco una persona que …**

7 **Una historia personal** *A personal story*

(las ciencias) empresariales (f, pl)	*business studies*
conseguir (e>i)	*to get*
compañero/a de trabajo	*colleague*
aunque	*although*
el Instituto Nacional de Empleo (m)	*Department of Employment*
el anuncio de empleo (m)	*job advertisement*
pedir (e>i)	*to ask for*
el título	*qualification, degree*
recobrar	*to regain*

In Spain, as in other industrialized nations, the people most affected by unemployment, 'el desempleo', are the young, 'los jóvenes'. Read about José and about his experience with job hunting and, as you do, try answering the following questions.

a What are José's qualifications?

b How is he described?

c What actions has he taken in order to get a job?

d Why hasn't he been able to get one?

e How does he feel?

José tiene veintinueve años, hizo la carrera de empresariales en Madrid y tiene un máster de una universidad en los Estados Unidos. José habla y escribe perfectamente inglés y francés. Es extrovertido y simpático, pero nunca ha conseguido un empleo. Nunca ha trabajado en una oficina, no ha tenido jamás un jefe ni compañeros de trabajo. Simplemente, no encuentra empleo, aunque ha ido muchas veces al Instituto Nacional de Empleo, ha enviado su currículum docenas de veces y ha leído cientos de anuncios de empleo en los periódicos. Pero no ha tenido éxito. En unas empresas le piden experiencia, en otras le dicen que con sus títulos no pueden pagarle el salario que corresponde. José no sabe qué hacer, está desesperado. José espera que algún día su situación cambie y pueda conseguir un empleo que le permita recobrar su optimismo y seguridad.

Note that **la oficina** and **el despacho** both translate as office in English, but in Spanish they mean different things. **Oficina** describes an office in general terms, a place where a number of people work, while **despacho** refers to the actual room where someone works. In some Latin American countries the word **oficina** conveys both meanings.

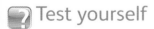 Test yourself

1 **Mercedes and Nicolás are each looking for the ideal partner. What sort of person does each want? Complete the sentences below with the appropriate form of the verbs in brackets.**

a Mercedes busca un novio que **(ser)** inteligente, que **(tener)** sentido del humor, que no **(fumar)** y que la **(querer)** de verdad.

b Nicolás quiere una novia que **(ser)** guapa, que **(saber)** varios idiomas, que **(llevarse)** bien con él y que **(estar)** dispuesta a casarse con él.

2 Complete each sentence with a verb from the list using the appropriate form.

tener   disponer   costar   aceptar   ser   estar

a Espero encontrar un hotel que ＿＿ cerca de la playa ...

b ... que no ＿＿ muy caro ...

c ... que no ＿＿ más de 50 euros ...

d ... que ＿＿ aire acondicionado ...

e ... que ＿＿ niños ...

f y que ＿＿ de servicio de Internet.

These are the last tests in your Spanish course. If you managed to get most answers right, ¡enhorabuena! (*congratulations!*), as the language covered in this unit can be a little tricky. Don't be discouraged if you made a few mistakes. Time and practice will help you to achieve the accuracy that you are probably aiming at.

Go back to this and previous units as many times as you think necessary, assisting yourself, if necessary, with a grammar book.

SELF CHECK

	I CAN...
○	... say what sort of place or person I want
○	... express hope
○	... express uncertainty.

Congratulations on finishing *Complete Spanish*!

We hope you have enjoyed working your way through the course. We are always keen to receive feedback from people who have used our course, so why not contact us and let us know your reactions? We'll be particularly pleased to receive your praise, but we should also like to know if things could be improved. We always welcome comments and suggestions, and we do our best to incorporate constructive suggestions into later editions.

You can contact us through the publishers at

Teach Yourself, Hodder Headline Ltd,

338 Euston Road, London NW1 3BH, UK

We hope you will want to build on your knowledge of Spanish and have made a few suggestions to help you do this in the section entitled **Taking it further**.

¡Buena suerte!

Juan Kattán-Ibarra

Taking it further

Sources of authentic Spanish

SPANISH NEWSPAPERS AND MAGAZINES

El País (http://www.elpais.es)

El Mundo (http://www.el-mundo.es/)

La Vanguardia (http://www.lavanguardia.es)

ABC (http://www.abc.es)

El Periódico (http://www.elperiodico.es/)

For general information, including Spanish current affairs and world news, try the following magazines:

Cambio 16

Tiempo

Tribuna

For light reading and entertainment you might like to look at *Hola*, *Quo*, *Mía*, *Pronto*, *Lecturas*, *Semana*, etc. These are by far the most popular amongst Spaniards and, as a beginner, you may find some of the articles easier to follow.

LATIN AMERICAN NEWSPAPERS AND MAGAZINES

Latin American newspapers and magazines will be more difficult to find outside each country, but if you have internet facilities you will be able to access their websites, although they may be special net versions. The following is a list of some main Latin American newspapers:

Argentina:

La Nación (http://lanacion.com.ar/)
Clarín (http://www.clarin.com)

Chile:

El Mercurio (http://www.elmercurio.cl/)

Colombia:
El Espectador (http://www.elespectador.com/)

Cuba:
Granma (http://www.granma.cu/)

México:
El Universal (http://www.el-universal.com.mx/)

Perú:
El Comercio (http:/elcomercioperu.com.pe/)
Correo (http://www.correoperu.com.pe/)

RADIO, TELEVISION AND INTERNET NEWS

An excellent way to improve your understanding of spoken Spanish is to listen to radio and watch television. On medium wave after dark (in Europe) and via satellite you will be able to gain access to *Radio Nacional de España, Televisión Española (TVE)* and other stations. For Spanish language news on internet you may like to go to *BBC Mundo.com*, or to *Podcast BBC Mundo Radio*, which offers a 15-minute world news summary from Monday to Friday, with a special focus on Latin America. The main website is http://www.bbc.co.uk/mundo/.

Travelling in Spain and Latin America

Travelling in a Spanish-speaking country is probably the best way to practise what you have learned and improve your command of the spoken language. If you are planning to do this, there are a number of good guidebooks which will help you to plan your journey. The well-known *Lonely Planet* covers not just specific countries, but also main regions and cities, including Spain and Latin America. For the latter, the *Mexico and Central American Handbook* and the *South American Handbook* have a long tradition among travellers in the region. *Time Out, Michelin, Fodor's,* among several others, have also become well established in the travelling market.

For travellers in Spain, the following websites may prove useful, with information such as tourist attractions, accommodation, travel, restaurants, etc:

Travelling to Spain: http://www.SiSpain/english/travelli/

Spain Today (local section of the *Europe Today* travel guide): http://www.wtg-online.com/data/esp/esp.asp

All about Spain: http://www.red2000.com/

Páginas amarillas del viajero (yellow pages for travellers): http://www.spaindata.com/data/1index.shtml

Spanish National Tourist Office: http://www.tourspain.co.uk

Railway Travel in Spain: http://horarios.renfe.es/hir/ingles.html

Madrid metro: http://www.metromadrid.es

Travellers in Latin America will find useful information in:
Travel.org – Latin America: http://www.travel.org/latin.htm/

Latin America – travel notes:
http://www.travelnotes.org/LatinAmerica/index.htm

Culture and history

Internet users interested in Spain may like to try the following sites:

España en la Red (Spain on the net):

http://www.msn.es/homepage.asp

Sí – Spain: http://www.sispain.org/spanish/index.htm/

Historia – Sí Spain: http://www.sispain.org/spanish/history

About.com – Spanish culture: http://spanishculture.about.com/

For Spanish language, the *Instituto Cervantes* a worldwide organization, offers courses in Spanish and promotes Spanish culture in general; the *Hispanic Council*, in the United Kingdom, based in London, may be able to help you with enquiries about Spanish language courses and aspects of life in Spain. For information on Latin American Spanish you can contact the *Hispanic Council* or the embassy of the country you are interested in.

For the *Instituto Cervantes* go to: http://cervantes.es

For other related information, including Latin America, go to:

http://www.spanish.about.com

http://www.spanish-language.org

http://www.spanishabroad.com

http://planeta.com/schoolist.html

Working in Spain and Latin America

For an overview of job prospects in Spain and Latin America, including teaching go to:

http://www.transitionsabroad.com/
listings/work/esl/teachingenglishinspain.html

http://www.transitionsabroad.com/
listings/work/esl/articles/workinlatinamerica.html

http://www.tefllogue.com/finding-a-job/
working-in-latin-america-an-overview.html

http://www.4icj.com/Latin-America

The publisher has used its best endeavours to ensure that the URLs for external websites referred to in this book are correct and active at the time of going to press. However, the publisher has no responsibility for the websites and can make no guarantee that a site will remain live or that the content is or will remain appropriate.

Glossary of grammatical terms

Adjectives Adjectives are used to provide more information about nouns, e.g. *That school is very _good_*. **Ese colegio es muy _bueno_**. *The _new_ hotel is _excellent_*. **El _nuevo_ hotel es _excelente_**.

Adverbs Adverbs tend to provide more information about verbs. *He left quietly*. **Salió _silenciosamente_**. But adverbs can also provide more information on adjectives: *It was totally unnecessary*. **Era _totalmente_ innecesario**. In English, adverbs often (but not always) end in **-ly**. The equivalent of this in Spanish is **-mente**.

Articles There are two types of articles, *definite* and *indefinite*. In English, the definite article is *the* – **el/la/los/las** in Spanish. *A*, **un/una**, are the indefinite articles.

Comparative When we make comparisons we need the comparative form of the adjective. In English this usually means adding *-er* to the adjective or putting *more* in front of it. *This shirt is cheaper than that one*. **Esta camisa es _más_ barata _que_ esa**. *This blouse is _more_ expensive _than_ that one*. **Esta blusa es _más_ cara _que_ esa**. See also **superlative**.

Demonstratives Words like *this* **este**, *that* **ese**, *these* **estos**, *those* **esos** are called **demonstratives**.

Gender In English, gender is usually linked to male and female persons or animals, so, for example, we refer to a man as *he* and to a woman as *she*. Objects and beings of an indeterminate sex are referred to as having neuter gender. So, for instance, we refer to a table as *it*. In Spanish, nouns referring to female persons are feminine and those referring to male people are masculine. But all nouns are either masculine or feminine in Spanish and this has nothing to do with sex. **La mesa** *table*, **la mano** *hand*, are feminine, while **el mes** *month*, **el día** *day*, are masculine. While there are some rules to help you, you have to accept that the gender of every noun has to be learned.

Imperative The imperative is the form of the verb used to give directions, instructions, orders or commands: *_Turn_ right at the corner*.

Gire a la derecha en la esquina. *First* *dial* 020. **Primero** *marque* **el 020.**

Infinitive The infinitive is the basic form of the verb. This is the form that you will find entered in the dictionary. In Spanish, infinitives end in **-ar**, **-er**, and **-ir**, e.g. **habl*ar*** *to speak*, **com*er*** *to eat*, **viv*ir*** *to live*.

Irregular verbs Life would be considerably easier if all verbs behaved in a regular fashion. Unfortunately, Spanish, like other European languages, has verbs which do not behave according to a set pattern and which are therefore commonly referred to as irregular verbs.

Nouns Nouns are words like *house* **casa**, *bread* **pan** and *wealth* **riqueza**. They are often called 'naming words'.

Number The term is used to indicate whether something is *singular* or *plural*. See singular.

Object The term *object* expresses the 'receiving end' relationship between a noun and a verb. So, for instance, the thief is said to be at the receiving end of the arrest in the sentence '*The policeman arrested the thief*'. **El policía arrestó** *al ladrón*. The thief is therefore said to be the *object* of the sentence.

In sentences such as '*My mother gave the driver some money*', the phrase '*some money*' is said to be the *direct object*, because the money is actually what the mother gave. The phrase '*the driver*' is said to be the *indirect object* because the driver was the recipient of the giving.

Plural See singular.

Personal pronouns As their name suggests, personal pronouns refer to persons, e.g. *I* **yo**, *you* **tú**, **usted**, *he* **él**, *she* **ella**, etc. See **pronouns**.

Possessives Words like *my* **mi**, *your* **tu**, **su**, *our* **nuestro** are called possessives. So are words such as *mine* **mío**, *yours* **tuyo**, **suyo**, etc.

Pronouns Pronouns fulfil a similar function to nouns and often stand in the place of nouns which have already been mentioned, e.g. *My girlfriend* (noun) *is twenty-five years old. She* (pronoun) *is very pretty.* **Mi** *novia* **tiene veinticinco años.** *Ella* **es muy guapa.**

Prepositions Words like *in* **en**, *for* **por**, **para**, *between* **entre**, are called prepositions. Prepositions often tell us about the position of something. They are normally followed by a noun or a pronoun, e.g. *The bank is* *between* *the school and the church.* **El banco está** *entre* **el colegio y la iglesia.** *This present is* *for* *you.* **Este regalo es** *para* **ti.**

Reflexive pronouns Words such as *myself* **me**, *yourself* **te**, **se**, *ourselves* **nos**, are called reflexive pronouns.

Reflexive verbs When the subject and the object of a verb are one and the same, the verb is said to be reflexive, e.g. *I washed myself before going out.* **Me lavé antes de salir.** *We enjoyed ourselves very much.* **Nos divertimos mucho.**

Singular The terms *singular* and *plural* are used to make the contrast between 'one' and 'more than one', e.g. *book/books* **libro/libros**, *city/cities* **ciudad/ciudades**.

Subject The term *subject* expresses a relationship between a noun and a verb. So, for instance, in the sentence *'My mother gave the driver some money'*, because it is the mother who does the giving, the mother is said to be the subject of the verb *to give*, **dar**.

Subjunctive mood The so-called subjunctive mood is used very rarely in modern English, but there are remnants of it in such sentences as *If I were you.* **Yo en tu lugar.** *I insist that he come.* **Insisto en que venga.** Spanish uses the subjunctive much more frequently than English.

Superlative The superlative is used for the most extreme version of a comparison. *This shirt is the cheapest of all.* **Esta camisa es la más barata de todas.** *This blouse is the most expensive of all.* **Esta blusa es la más cara de todas.** See also **comparative**.

Tense Most languages use changes in the verb to indicate an aspect of time. These changes in the verb are traditionally referred to as tense, and the tenses may be *present, past* or *future*, e.g., *They went out.* **Salieron** (*past*). *She is at home.* **Está en casa** (*present*). *We will go to the cinema.* **Iremos al cine** (*future*).

Verbs Verbs often communicate actions, e.g., *to play* **jugar**, states, e.g. *to exist* **existir**, and sensations, e.g. *to see* **ver**. A verb may also be defined by its role in the sentence, and usually has a subject, e.g. *My head* (*subject*) *aches* (*verb*). **Me duele la cabeza.**

Grammar summary

Essentials of grammar

1 DEFINITE ARTICLES (UNITS 2, 3)

	Masculine	Feminine
Singular	**el hotel** *the hotel*	**la habitación** *the room*
Plural	**los hoteles** *the hotels*	**las habitaciones** *the rooms*

2 CONTRACTIONS (UNIT 2)

a + el = al	Voy **al** estadio.	*I'm going to the stadium.*
de + el = del	Vengo **del** trabajo.	*I'm coming from work.*

3 INDEFINITE ARTICLES (UNITS 2, 11)

	Masculine	Feminine
Singular	**un coche** *a car*	**una casa** *a house*
Plural	**unos coches** *some cars*	**unas casas** *some houses*

4 NOUNS: MASCULINE AND FEMININE, SINGULAR AND PLURAL (UNITS 2, 3, 10)

a In Spanish, all nouns are either masculine or feminine. Nouns ending in **–o** are usually masculine, while those ending in **–a** are usually feminine: **el desayuno, la cena**.

b Words referring to males and females, such as occupations, must change. Change **–o** to **–a** or add **–a** to the consonant: el secretari**o** – la secretar**ia**, el doctor – la doctor**a**.

c Nouns ending in **–ista** and many of those ending in **–nte** do not change: el/la art**ista**, el/la estudia**nte**.

d Some nouns have different male and female forms: **el actor, la actriz**.

e Nouns ending in a vowel form the plural by adding **–s: el libro – los libros**.

f Nouns ending in a consonant add **–es: el hotel – los hoteles**.

g The masculine plural of some nouns may be used to refer to members of both sexes: **el padre** *father,* **la madre** *mother,* **los padres** *parents*.

5 ADJECTIVES: NUMBER, GENDER AND POSITION (UNITS 1, 8, 10)

a Adjectives **must** agree in *gender* (masculine/feminine) and number (singular/plural) with the noun they describe, but generally, those ending in a consonant or in **–e** change for number but not for gender: **un jersey negro, una camisa negra, unos pantalones negros,** but **un sombrero/una camisa azul, unos zapatos azules.**

b Adjectives of nationality add **–a** to the consonant: **un amigo español, una amiga española.**

c Adjectives normally follow the noun they describe but for emphasis, or to convey some kind of emotion, they are sometimes placed before the noun: **un hotel caro, un excelente hotel.**

d A few adjectives, among them **bueno, malo,** often precede the noun. Before a masculine singular noun, **bueno** and **malo** become **buen** and **mal,** respectively: **un buen/mal momento** but **una buena/mala educación.** Other adjectives with a shortened form are **primero, tercero, alguno, ninguno: el primer semáforo** but **la primera calle; ningún estudiante** but **ninguna persona.**

e Grande normally follows the noun when its meaning is 'big' or 'large', but it goes before it when it means 'great'. Before a *masculine or feminine* singular noun **grande** becomes **gran: un gran hombre/una gran mujer.**

6 COMPARATIVE FORM OF ADJECTIVES (UNIT 8, 10)

a Comparisons such as *smaller, more comfortable,* are expressed with the construction **más ... (que): Mi piso es más pequeño, pero más cómodo que el de Eva.**

b For forms such as *'fastest', 'most economical',* use **el/la/los/las más ...: Este coche es el más rápido y el más económico.**

c To say '*(not) as ... as*' use **(no) tan ... como: Madrid no es tan caro como Londres.**

d Bueno and **malo** have irregular comparative forms: **mejor(es),** *better,* **peor(es),** *worse,* **el/la/los/las mejor(es),** *the best,* **el/la/los/las peor(es),** *the worst.*

e The comparative forms for **grande** and **pequeño,** when they refer to age, are **mayor(es)** *older,* **menor(es)** *younger,* **el/la/los/las mayor(es)** *the oldest,* **el/la/los/las menor(es)** *the youngest.*

7 ADVERBS (18)

a Many adverbs can be formed by adding **–mente** to the feminine form of the adjective: **rápido – rápidamente.** If the adjective ends

in a consonant or **–e** add **–mente**: **fácil – fácilmente**, **amable –
amablemente**.

b Many adverbs are not derived from adjectives: **ahora**, **aquí**, **bien**,
etc.

8 SUBJECT PRONOUNS (UNITS 1, 3)

yo	*I*	nosotros/as	*we*
tú	*you* (informal, singular)	**vosotros/as**	*you* (informal, plural)
usted	*you* (formal, singular)	**ustedes**	*you* (formal, plural)
él, ella	*he, she*	**ellos, ellas**	*they*

Subject pronouns are usually omitted in Spanish, except for emphasis or
to avoid ambiguity (as with **usted**, **él**, **ella**, or **ustedes**, **ellos**, **ellas**, which
share the same verb forms).

Vosotros/as, and all forms related to it, are not used in Latin American
Spanish, where **ustedes** is used in formal and informal address.

9 OBJECT PRONOUNS (UNITS 5, 8, 9, 23, 24)

9.1 Direct and indirect object pronouns

In sentences such as *He gave it to me*, **Él me lo/la dio**, *John sold them to us*,
John nos los/las vendió, 'it' and 'me', in the first sentence, and 'them' and
'us' in the second one are known as *object pronouns*. 'It' stands for what was
given, for example 'the money', while 'them' stands for what was sold, for
example 'the books'. 'It' and 'them' are said to be the *direct object pronouns*
while 'me' and 'them', the recipients of the giving and the selling are said
to be the *indirect objects*. In the first and second person singular and plural
there is no distinction between direct and indirect object pronouns:

singular	plural
me *me, to me, for me*	**nos** *us, to us, for us*
te *you, to you, for you* (informal)	**os** *you, to you, for you* (informal)

In the third person singular and plural, direct and indirect object pronouns
differ:

Direct object pronouns	Indirect object pronouns
lo/le *you* (formal)/*him/it* (m, sing)	**le** (to) *you* (formal)/*him/her/it* (m/f,sing)
la *you* (formal)/*her/it* (f, sing)	
los/les *you* (formal)/*them* (m, pl)	**les** (to) *you* (formal)/*them* (m/f, pl)
las *you* (formal)/*them* (f, pl)	

In many parts of Spain now **le** and **les** are used as direct object pronouns instead of the standard **lo** and **los** to refer to human males, for example Le llamé *I called him*, with **lo** and **los** referring to masculine objects, as in **Lo compré** *I bought it*.

As indirect object pronouns, however, **le** and **les** are the norm among most speakers: **Le dije** *I told him/her*.

9.2 Position of direct and indirect object pronouns

a Object pronouns normally precede the verb: **Me invitaron** *They invited me* (literally, *Me they invited*).

b In sentences with two object pronouns, one direct the other indirect, the indirect one comes first: **Te lo/la daré mañana** *I'll give it to you tomorrow* (literally, *To you it I'll give tomorrow*).

c **Le** and **les** become **se** before **lo, la, los, las**: **Se lo/la traigo ahora mismo** *I'll bring it to you right now.*

d In constructions with a main verb followed by an *infinitive* (e.g. **escribir**) or a *gerund* (e.g. **escribiendo**), the object pronoun can either precede the main verb or be attached to the infinitive or gerund: **Voy a escribirle** or **Le voy a escribir** *I'm going to write to him/her.*

e Object pronouns must follow positive *imperative* or *command* forms, but they precede negative ones: **Dígale** *Tell him/her*, **No le diga** *Don't tell him/her.*

10 REFLEXIVE PRONOUNS (UNIT 12)

Reflexive verbs, for example, **levantarse** *to get up*, **irse** *to leave*, **divertirse** *to enjoy oneself*, are always accompanied by a reflexive pronoun, the Spanish equivalent of words like 'myself', 'yourself', etc. But note that many Spanish verbs which are used with a reflexive pronoun do not require a reflexive pronoun in English.

Reflexive pronouns are: **me** (for 'yo'), **te** (for 'tú'), **se** (for 'él, ella, Vd.'), **nos** (for 'nosotros/as'), **os** (for 'vosotros/as'), **se** (for 'ellos, ellas, Vds.'): **Me levanto a las 6:30** *I get up at 6.30*, **¿A qué hora te levantas tú?** *What time do you get up?*

The position of reflexive pronouns in the sentence is the same as for object pronouns (see 9.2 above): **(Yo) me levanto a las 7:00**.

11 PRONOUNS WITH PREPOSITIONS (UNIT 5)

With prepositions, that is words like **a**, **para**, **por**, **sin**, etc., use the following set of pronouns: **mí** (for yo), **ti** (for tú), and subject pronouns for all other persons, that is, **usted, él, ella, nosotros/as, vosotros/as, ellos, ellas**: **Para mí, una cerveza, para él/ella un café, ¿y para ti?.**

Con 'with' is a special case: **conmigo** *with me*, **contigo** *with you*, (inf) but **con él/ella/usted**, etc.

12 DEMONSTRATIVES (UNIT 7)

These are words like **este/esta** *this* (m/f, sing.), **estos/estas** *these* (m/f, pl). For the full forms see Unit 7.

13 POSSESSIVES (UNITS 2, 3, 20)

These are words like **mi** *my*, **tu** *your* (informal), etc., which are sometimes referred to as *short forms*, as apposed to **mío** *mine*, **tuyo** *yours* (informal), which are known as *long forms*. Short forms are treated in Units 2 and 3, and long forms in Unit 20.

14 USES OF 'POR' AND 'PARA' (UNITS 5, 6, 11)

14.1 Por is used:
 a To indicate cause or reason: **Lo hago por ti** *I do it for you.*
 b With expressions of time: **por la mañana/noche** in *the morning/at night*
 c To indicate movement through or along: **Pasé por Sevilla** *We passed through Seville*, **Anduvimos por el río** *We walked along the river*
 d To express means: **por email** *by email*
 e To indicate rate: **por hora/día** *per hour/day*
 f To express cost or value: **Pagué mucho dinero por él** *I paid a lot of money for it*
 g To introduce the agent of an action: **América fue descubierta por Colón** *America was discovered by Columbus*

14.2 Para is used:
 a To indicate direction: **un billete para Ecuador** *a ticket for Ecuador*
 b With expressions of time: **una habitación para dos días** *a room for two days*, **Déjalo para mañana** *Leave it till tomorrow*
 c To express destination: **para una persona** *for one person*, **para mí** *for me*
 d To express purpose: **Fue a España para aprender español** *He/she went to Spain to/in order to learn Spanish*

For other prepositions see Grammar section in Units 2, 5, 6, 11, 18.

15 QUESTION WORDS (UNITS 1, 2, 3, 6, 17)

a **¿Cómo?** ¿Cómo te llamas? *What's your name?*, ¿Cómo estás? *How are you?*

b **¿Cuál?** ¿Cuál quieres? *Which one do you want?*, ¿Cuál es tu email? *What's your email?*, ¿Cuáles son sus maletas? *Which are your suitcases?*

c **¿Cuándo?** ¿Cuándo vuelves? *When are you coming back?*

d **¿Cuánto/s?** ¿Cuánto cuesta? *How much does it cost?*, ¿Cuántos hay? *How many are there?*

e **¿Dónde?** ¿Dónde está? *Where is it?*, ¿De dónde eres? *Where are you from?* Note also ¿adónde? *where(to)?*

f **¿Por qué?** ¿Por qué no vienes conmigo? *Why don't you come with me?*

g **¿Qué?** ¿Qué desea? *What would you like?*

h **¿Quién?** ¿Quién es? *Who is it?*, ¿Quiénes son? *Who are they?*

Verbs

16 PRESENT TENSE (UNITS 1, 2, 3, 4, 12, 22)

The *present tense* is used to talk about actions taking place in the present, but it has a number of other uses, among them the following ones: to talk about timeless events and actions taking place regularly, to talk about the immediate future, etc.

¿Qué haces?	*What are you doing?*
Carmen es peruana.	*Carmen is Peruvian.*
Se levantan siempre a las 6:30.	*They always get up at 6.30.*
Nos vamos mañana.	*We're leaving tomorrow.*

For the *present tense forms* see the references above.

16.1 Stem-changing verbs (Units 3, 5, 12)

Some verbs undergo a vowel change in the stem in all persons but **nosotros**, **vosotros**, but their endings remain the same as for regular verbs. Such verbs are known as *stem-changing* or *radical-changing* verbs. The main types of changes are:

a *e>ie* (empezar, entender, pensar, etc.): **Empiezo a las 9:00** *I start at 9.00.*

b *o>ue* (volver, poder, acostarse, etc.): **Vuelven mañana** *They're coming back tomorrow.*

c *e>i* (seguir, pedir, servir, etc.): **¿Sigo todo recto?** *Shall I go straight on?*

16.2 Irregular verbs (Units 1, 2, 4, 12 and Irregular Verbs Section.)

A number of verbs form the present tense in an irregular way. Some, for example **salir** *to leave*, are irregular only in the first person singular, **salgo** *I leave*, while others, like **ser** *to be* or **ir** *to go*, are completely irregular. For a list of irregular verbs see relevant section.

17 PRETERITE TENSE (UNITS 15, 16, 17)

The *preterite tense* is used for talking about events which took place at a specific point in the past or which lasted over an extended period but ended in the past.

| Ayer hablé con él. | I spoke to him yesterday. |
| Viví dos años allí. | I lived there for two years. |

For the preterite tense forms see the references above.

18 IMPERFECT TENSE (UNITS 17, 18)

The *imperfect tense* is used to describe people, places and things known in the past, to talk about actions which occurred regularly in the past, to say what you were doing and, in place of the present tense, to request something in a polite way.

Era una persona maravillosa.	She/he was a wonderful person.
Nos visitaban a menudo.	They used to visit us often.
Iba hacia la oficina.	I was going to the office.
Quería una habitación.	I wanted/would like a room.

For the *imperfect tense* forms see the references above.

19 FUTURE TENSE (UNIT 20)

The *future tense* is used for talking about future events, especially in the written language. It is also used to express probability, certainty and uncertainty with regard to the present or the future, promises and predictions.

Este año iremos a México.	This year we'll go to Mexico.
¿Hablarán español?	I wonder whether they speak Spanish.
Lo haré esta tarde. Te lo prometo.	I'll do it this afternoon. I promise you.
Seguro que vendrá.	I'm sure he/she will come.

For the *future tense* forms see the reference above.

20 CONDITIONAL TENSE (UNIT 21)

Like the English 'would', the Spanish *conditional tense* is used for expressing conditions. It is also used for politeness, especially with **poder** and **querer**, but also with other verbs.

Yo iría con vosotros, pero no puedo.	*I'd go with you, but I can't.*
¿Podría Vd. volver mañana?	*Could you come back tomorrow?*
¿Querría acompañarme, por favor?	*Would you come with me, please?*

For the *conditional tense* see the reference above.

21 PRESENT SUBJUNCTIVE (UNIT 25)

The *present subjunctive*, like the subjunctive as a whole, has several uses, but only three have been discussed in this book: to express requirements with regard to something or someone, to express hope, to express uncertainty or doubt. The subjunctive normally occurs in a construction with a main verb, for example **quiero** *I want*, followed by **que** *that, which, who* and a subjunctive verb.

Busco una casa que tenga garaje.	*I'm looking for a house that has a garage.*
Quiero una persona que trabaje.	*I want someone who works.*
Espero que la encuentres.	*I hope you find her.*
No creo que sea difícil.	*I don't think it will be difficult.*

For the *present subjunctive* forms see the reference above.

22 PERFECT TENSE (UNIT 19)

The *perfect tense* is used for talking about the recent past and, generally, about past events which bear some relationship with the present.

He desayunado hace un momento.	*I had breakfast a moment ago.*
He visto esta película dos veces.	*I've seen this film twice (up until now)*

For the *perfect tense* forms see the reference above.

23 PLUPERFECT TENSE (UNIT 22)

The *pluperfect tense* is used much in the same way as in English, that is, to refer to what one had done or what had happened before another past event or situation.

Me dio un libro, pero yo ya lo había leído.	*He/she gave me a book, but I had already read it.*
Habíamos estado allí dos veces.	*We had been there twice.*

For the *pluperfect tense* forms see the reference above.

24 IMPERATIVE OR COMMAND FORM (UNITS 23, 24)

Expressions such as **¿Dígame?** *Hello?* (on the phone), **Deme** *Give me,* **Siga todo recto** *Go straight on,* **¡Mira!** *Look!,* **No nos esperes** *Don't wait for us,* correspond to the *imperative* or *command* form of the verb. Unlike English, Spanish uses different imperative forms depending on who you are talking to - *formal* or *informal form* - and whether you are speaking to one or more than one person, *singular* or *plural form*. In addition to that, the informal imperative has different *positive* and *negative forms*. For formal imperatives see Unit 23; for informal ones see Unit 24.

25 GERUND (UNIT 14)

Gerunds are forms like **hablando** *speaking,* **comiendo** *eating,* which are used with **estar** to refer to an action that is or was in progress, for example **Está hablando por otra línea** *He/she is speaking on another line,* **Yo estaba comiendo cuando llegaron** *I was eating when they arrived.* The gerund has a number of other uses which are beyond the scope of this book.

26 USING 'SER' AND 'ESTAR' (UNITS 1, 2, 3, 4, 6, 7, 10, 14, 16, 17)

26.1 Ser *is used:*

- a to give personal information such as who you are, your nationality, where you are from or your occupation: **Soy español** *I'm Spanish,* **Clara es mexicana** *Clara is Mexican,* **Agustín es estudiante** *Agustín is a student.*
- b to describe people, places and things: **Barcelona es una ciudad preciosa** *Barcelona is a beautiful city.*
- c with time phrases: **¿Qué hora es?** *What time is it?,* **Mañana es domingo** *Tomorrow is Sunday.*
- d to refer to the material something is made of: **Es de algodón** *It is made from cotton.*
- e to denote possession: **Es mío** *It's mine.*
- f to express cost: **¿Cuánto es?** *How much is it?* **Son cinco euros** *It's five euros.*
- g to say where an event will take place: **La reunión es aquí** *The meeting is here.*

For other uses of **ser** you may like to refer to a grammar book.

26.2 Estar *is used:*

- a *to express location:* **Buenos Aires está en Argentina** *Buenos Aires is in Argentina.*

b to express marital status: **Está soltero** *He's single* (in Latin America also **Es soltero**)

c to ask people how they are: **¿Cómo estás?** *How are you?*

d to denote a temporary state or condition: **Gloria está muy guapa hoy** *Gloria is/looks very pretty today.*

e to express cost when prices fluctuate: **¿A cómo/cuánto está el cambio?** *What is the rate of exchange?.*

f with *past participles*, to denote a condition resulting from an action **La puerta está abierta** *The door is open.*

g with *gerunds*, to talk about actions in progress: **Está lloviendo** *It's raining.*

h with *time phrases*: **Estamos a 15 de julio** *It's the 15th of July.*

For other uses of **estar** refer to a grammar book.

27 USING 'SE' (UNITS 3, 9, 12)

Se is used with the third person of the verb:

a to form impersonal sentences: **¿Cómo se va al aeropuerto?** *How do you/does one get to the airport?*

b to convey the idea that something 'is done': **Aquí se habla español** *Spanish is spoken here.*

c with reflexive verbs: **Se levantan tarde** *They get up late.*

d in place of **le** or **les** before **lo/la/los/las**: **Ahora mismo se lo traigo** *I'll bring it to you right now.*

Irregular verbs

The following list includes only the most common irregular verbs. Only irregular forms are given (verbs marked with an asterisk are also stem- or radical-changing).

abrir *to open*
past participle: abierto

andar *to walk*
preterite: anduve, anduviste, anduvo, anduvimos, anduvisteis, anduvieron

conducir *to drive*
present indicative: (yo) conduzco
present subjunctive: conduzca, conduzcas, conduzca, conduzcamos, conduzcáis, conduzcan
preterite: conduje, condujiste, condujo, condujimos, condujisteis, condujeron

dar *to give*
present indicative: (yo) doy
preterite: di, diste, dio, dimos, disteis, dieron
present subjunctive: dé, des, dé, demos, deis, den

decir* *to say*
present indicative: (yo) digo
present subjunctive: diga, digas, diga, digamos, digáis, digan
preterite: dije, dijiste, dijo, dijimos, dijisteis, dijeron
future: diré, dirás, dirá, diremos, diréis, dirán
conditional: diría, dirías, diría, diríamos, diríais, dirían
imperative (familiar, singular): di *(formal, singular):* diga
gerund: diciendo
past participle: dicho

escribir *to write*
past participle: escrito

estar *to be*
present indicative: estoy, estás, está, estamos, estáis, están
present subjunctive: esté, estés, esté, estemos, estéis, estén
preterite: estuve, estuviste, estuvo, estuvimos, estuvisteis, estuvieron
imperative (familiar, singular): está

hacer *to do, make*
present indicative: (yo) hago
present subjunctive: haga, hagas, haga, hagamos, hagáis, hagan
preterite: hice, hiciste, hizo, hicimos, hicisteis, hicieron
conditional: haría, harías, haría, haríamos, haríais, harían
past participle: hecho

ir *to go*
present indicative: voy, vas, va, vamos, vais, van
present subjunctive: vaya, vayas, vaya, vayamos, vayáis, vayan
imperfect: iba, ibas, iba, íbamos, ibais, iban
preterite: fui, fuiste, fue, fuimos, fuisteis, fueron
imperative: (Vd.) vaya, (tú) ve
gerund: yendo

leer *to read*
preterite: (él, ella, Vd.) leyó, (ellos, ellas, Vds.) leyeron
gerund: leyendo

oír *to hear*
present indicative: oigo, oyes, oye, oímos, oís, oyen
present subjunctive: oiga, oigas, oiga, oigamos, oigáis, oigan
preterite: (él, ella, Vd.) oyó, (ellos, ellas, Vds.) oyeron
imperative: (Vd.) oiga, (tú) oye
gerund: oyendo

poder* *to be able to, can*
preterite: pude, pudiste, pudo, pudimos, pudisteis, pudieron
future: podré, podrás, podrá, podremos, podréis, podrán
conditional: podría, podrías, podría, podríamos, podríais, podrían

poner *to put*
present indicative: (yo) pongo
present subjunctive: ponga, pongas, ponga, pongamos, pongáis, pongan

preterite: puse, pusiste, puso, pusimos, pusisteis, pusieron
future: pondré, pondrás, pondrá, pondremos, pondréis, pondrán
conditional: pondría, pondrías, pondría, pondríamos, pondríais, pondrían
imperative: (Vd.) ponga, (tú) pon
past participle: puesto

querer* *to want, love*
preterite: quise, quisiste, quiso, quisimos, quisisteis, quisieron
future: querré, querrás, querrá, querremos, querréis, querrán
conditional: querría, querrías, querría, querríamos, querríais, querrían

saber *to know*
present indicative: (yo) sé
present subjunctive: sepa, sepas, sepa, sepamos, sepáis, sepan
preterite: supe, supiste, supo, supimos, supisteis, supieron
future: sabré, sabrás, sabrá, sabremos, sabréis, sabrán
conditional: sabría, sabrías, sabría, sabríamos, sabríais, sabrían
imperative: (Vd.) sepa

salir *to go out*
present indicative: (yo) salgo
present subjunctive: salga, salgas, salga, salgamos, salgáis, salgan
future: saldré, saldrás, saldrá, saldremos, saldréis, saldrán
conditional: saldría, saldrías, saldría, saldríamos, saldríais, saldrían
imperative: (Vd.) salga, (tú) sal

ser *to be*
present indicative: soy, eres, es, somos, sois, son
present subjunctive: sea, seas, sea, seamos, seáis, sean
preterite: fui, fuiste, fue, fuimos, fuisteis, fueron
imperfect indicative: era, eras, era, éramos, erais, eran
imperative: (Vd.) sea, (tú) sé

tener* *to have*
present indicative: (yo) tengo
present subjunctive: tenga, tengas, tenga, tengamos, tengáis, tengan
preterite: tuve, tuviste, tuvo, tuvimos, tuvisteis, tuvieron
future: tendré, tendrás, tendrá, tendremos, tendréis, tendrán
conditional: tendría, tendrías, tendría, tendríamos, tendríais, tendrían
imperative: (Vd.) tenga, (tú) ten

traer *to bring*
present indicative: (yo) traigo
present subjunctive: traiga, traigas, traiga, traigamos, traigáis, traigan
preterite: traje, trajiste, trajo, trajimos, trajisteis, trajeron
imperative: (Vd.) traiga
gerund: trayendo

venir* *to come*
present indicative: (yo) vengo
present subjunctive: venga, vengas, venga, vengamos, vengáis, vengan
preterite: vine, viniste, vino, vinimos, vinisteis, vinieron
future: vendré, vendrás, vendrá, vendremos, vendréis, vendrán
conditional: vendría, vendrías, vendría, vendríamos, vendríais, vendrían
imperative: (Vd.) venga, (tú) ven
gerund: viniendo

ver *to see*
present indicative: (yo) veo
present subjunctive: vea, veas, vea, veamos, veáis, vean
imperfect indicative: veía, veías, veía, veíamos, veíais, veían
imperative: (Vd.) vea
past participle: visto

volver* *to come back*
past participle: vuelto

Listening comprehension transcripts

Antes de empezar (Introductory unit)

ACTIVITY 1.1

– ¡Hola!
– Hola, buenos días.
– Hola, ¿qué tal?
– ¡Hola!
– Buenas tardes.
– Hola, buenas tardes.
– Hola, buenas noches.
– Buenas noches.

Unit 1

ACTIVITY 2

a   Me llamo Silvia, soy española. Soy de Barcelona. Hablo español y catalán.
b   Me llamo Cristóbal, soy argentino. Soy de Buenos Aires. Hablo español e inglés.
c   Me llamo Sofía, soy norteamericana. Soy de California. Hablo inglés, italiano y un poco de español.

Unit 2

ACTIVITY 5

– ¿Dónde vive usted, Silvia?
– En Barcelona. Vivo en el Barrio Gótico, en la Plaza del Rey.
– ¿Dónde vives, Ana?
– Vivo en la Ciudad de México, en el Paseo de la Reforma.
– Y tú Julio, ¿dónde vives?
– Vivo en la calle de la Libertad.

a – Cero, cero, tres, información.
– Por favor, ¿el teléfono del hotel Sancho?
– El hotel Sancho tiene el número 965 122 018.
– Muchas gracias.
– De nada.

b – Información, ¿qué número desea?
– El número de teléfono del señor Martín Ramos, por favor.
– Martín Ramos. Un momento, por favor.
– Es el 947 925 436.
– Gracias.

Unit 3

ACTIVITY 2

a – ¿La habitación del señor Luis García, por favor?
– Es la número cuarenta y ocho.

b – Por favor, ¿el despacho de la señorita Sáez?
– El treinta y seis.

c – Buenos días, ¿cuál es la habitación de los señores Silva, por favor?
– Un momentito, por favor. Los señores Silva tienen la habitación número cien.

Unit 4

ACTIVITY 5

a
Señora Por favor, la avenida del Mar, ¿está muy lejos?
Señor Está a unos diez minutos de aquí. Sigue todo recto y luego toma la cuarta calle a la derecha. La avenida del Mar está al final de la calle.

b
Señor 1 ¿Para ir a la playa, por favor?
Señor 2 Está un poco lejos. En el autobús, entre diez y quince minutos. La parada del autobús está en la esquina, enfrente de la iglesia.

c

Señora 1	Perdone, señora, ¿sabe usted dónde está Correos?
Señora 2	Lo siento, no lo sé. No soy de aquí. No conozco muy bien la ciudad.
Señora 1	Por favor, señor, Correos, ¿dónde está?
Señor	Está en la calle de Picasso, al lado del museo. Sube usted por esta calle y coge la primera a la izquierda. Está a unos cinco minutos de aquí.

d

Señor	Los teléfonos, por favor, ¿dónde están?
Señorita	Están en la segunda planta, enfrente de los servicios. La escalera está al fondo del pasillo.

Unit 5

ACTIVITY 2

a Oiga, ¿nos trae otra botella de vino tinto, por favor?

b ¿Me pasas la sal?

c Por favor, ¿me traes dos aguas minerales sin gas del supermercado?

d ¿Me trae más azúcar, por favor?

e Por favor, ¿nos trae otros dos cafés y un té?

f ¿Me pasas una servilleta?

ACTIVITY 4

Camarero	Buenas noches. ¿Qué van a tomar?
Ramón	¿Qué tapas tiene?
Camarero	Hay champiñones, gambas, calamares y tortilla de patatas.
Ramón	¿Qué vas a tomar tú, Sofía?
Sofía	Para mí, una de calamares y una cerveza.
Ramón	¿Y para ti, Clara?
Clara	Yo quiero un bocadillo.
Camarero	Tenemos de jamón, queso, salchichón y chorizo.
Clara	De queso.
Camarero	¿Y para beber?
Clara	Un cortado.
Camarero	¿Y para usted?
Ramón	Yo, champiñones y un vino blanco.
Camarero	¿Algo más?
Ramón	No, nada más.

Unit 6

Buenos días. Soy Inés Suárez, de Iberiatur. Llamo para confirmar su vuelo a Lima, Perú, para el jueves diecisiete. El avión sale de Madrid a las veintitrés treinta y llega a Lima el viernes a las diez menos veinte de la mañana, hora local. La hora de presentación en el aeropuerto es a las veintiuna treinta.

Unit 7

Clienta	¿Cuánto es todo?
Vendedor	Son tres euros con veinte las fresas ..., un euro con noventa las manzanas ..., dos euros con diez las naranjas ..., tres euros con sesenta las uvas ..., un euro con setenta y cinco el melón y sesenta céntimos los ajos. Son trece euros con quince.

Unit 8

Dependienta	Hola, buenos días. ¿Qué desea?
Carmen	Por favor, quería ver esos zapatos.
Dependienta	¿Cuáles? ¿Esos?
Carmen	Sí, esos.
Dependienta	¿Qué número?
Carmen	Treinta y ocho.
Dependienta	¿De qué color?
Carmen	Los prefiero en negro.
Dependienta	En negro del número treinta y ocho no los tengo. Los tengo en marrón y en rojo solamente.
Carmen	Los prefiero en rojo.
Dependienta	Aquí tiene. ¿Quiere probárselos?
Carmen	No me quedan bien. ¿Tiene un número más grande?
Dependienta	Un momento, por favor.

Unit 9

– Buenos días. Quisiera cambiar libras a euros. ¿A cómo está el cambio? Tengo billetes.
– El cambio de la libra está a ... un euro con cuarenta. ¿Cuánto quería cambiar?
– Ciento setenta y cinco libras.

– ¿Dígame?
– Buenas tardes. Tengo unos cheques de viaje en francos suizos y quería cambiarlos a euros. ¿A cuánto está el cambio?
– Francos suizos ... un momento, por favor. Sí, mire, está a sesenta céntimos.
– Quiero cambiar doscientos cincuenta.
– Bien, ¿me permite su pasaporte, por favor?

– Por favor, quisiera cambiar ciento veinte coronas suecas a euros. ¿Puede decirme a cuánto está el cambio?
– La corona sueca está a diez céntimos.

Unit 10

Hola, me llamo Rodrigo Mora, soy ingeniero, tengo cuarenta y nueve años. Estoy casado y tengo cuatro hijos. El mayor, Raúl, tiene veintiocho años y la menor, Gloria, tiene veintiuno. Mi mujer se llama Pilar y tiene cuarenta y seis años.

Hola, yo soy Rosa, soy abogada, tengo treinta y dos años. Estoy divorciada y vivo con mi madre y mi hijo Rafael, que tiene siete años.

Unit 11

– ¿A qué te dedicas, Alfonso?
– Soy recepcionista. Trabajo en un hotel.
– ¿Cuánto tiempo hace que estás allí?
– Hace un año y medio.
– ¿Qué horario tienes?
– Bueno, durante el día hay dos turnos, uno de 8:00 de la mañana a 3:00 de la tarde y el otro de 3:00 a 10:00 de la noche.

– ¿Qué turno prefieres tú?
– Prefiero el turno de la mañana, porque durante la tarde tengo más tiempo para estar en casa, ver a mis amigos, hacer deportes...
– Y los sábados, ¿es igual?
– Sí, los sábados se trabaja igual, pero no trabajo los domingos.
– ¿Y cuántas semanas de vacaciones tienes al año?
– Tengo sólo quince días.

Unit 12

ACTIVITY 3

Los sábados suelo levantarme sobre las diez, me ducho y después tomo un café y unas tostadas y salgo a hacer la compra para la semana. A veces almuerzo fuera con algún amigo y por la tarde juego al tenis cerca de casa. Por la noche salgo con amigos al cine o al teatro, o a algún concierto. Los sábados me acuesto siempre muy tarde.

Los domingos por la mañana normalmente voy a algún museo para ver alguna exposición y a veces voy a casa de mi hermano que vive en el campo. Paso el día con él y su familia y vuelvo a casa por la noche. Ceno algo ligero y me acuesto.

Unit 14

ACTIVITY 2

Voz	¿Dígame?
Raquel	¿Está Lorenzo, por favor?
Voz	Está duchándose en este momento. ¿De parte de quién?
Raquel	Soy Raquel.
Voz	¿Quieres dejarle algún recado?
Raquel	Sí, dile que tengo las entradas para el concierto de esta noche.
Voz	Vale.

ACTIVITY 5

Voz	¿Dígame?
Sandra	Buenos días. Llamo por el anuncio para el puesto de diseñadora gráfica. Quería solicitar una entrevista.
Voz	Un momento, por favor. ¿Puede usted venir el lunes a las nueve y media?
Sandra	Sí, a las nueve y media me va bien.
Voz	Dígame, por favor, su nombre y su número de teléfono.

Unit 15

a Me llamo María, nací en México el 24 de julio de 1975. Llegué a España en 1998. Hace cinco años conocí a Antonio, un español con quien me casé.

b Me llamo Rafael, nací en Galicia el 4 de junio de 1935. Hace cincuenta años emigré a Argentina con mi mujer. Nuestros hijos nacieron en Argentina.

c Yo soy Fátima, nací en Marruecos el 16 de noviembre de 1986. Mis padres llegaron a España hace quince años. Estudié secretariado bilingüe en Barcelona y llevo un año trabajando.

d Me llamo José, nací en Argentina el 18 de mayo de 1979 y llegué a trabajar a España hace tres años. Primero trabajé en un bar y ahora estoy trabajando en un restaurante argentino. Llevo un año y medio allí. Estoy soltero y vivo con un amigo español.

Unit 16

ACTIVITY 7

Buenos Aires tuvo ayer un día de sol con temperaturas que llegaron a nueve grados la mínima y dieciséis la máxima. Para hoy se anunció nublado y lluvia por la tarde, con temperaturas extremas probables de cinco y doce grados. Perspectivas para mañana miércoles quince de julio, lluvia y fuerte viento por la mañana, y sol después del mediodía, con una temperatura mínima probable de siete grados y una máxima de catorce.

Unit 17

ACTIVITY 4

Roberto era un amigo extraordinario. Nos conocimos hace muchos años en un viaje a África y desde entonces fuimos amigos inseparables. Roberto era arquitecto y era un excelente profesional. Tenía una gran capacidad de trabajo y era muy creativo. Era un verdadero artista. Era alegre y extrovertido y tenía una muy buena relación con su familia y los amigos. Hace dos años Robertó dejó su trabajo, su familia y sus amigos y se fue del país. Un día me llegó una carta suya. Estaba en el Tíbet...

Unit 18

Begoña ¿A qué te dedicabas antes, Esteban?
Esteban Trabajaba en un restaurante. Era camarero.
Begoña Y ahora, ¿qué haces?
Esteban Soy programador. Trabajo en una empresa de programación.
Begoña Y tú Víctor, ¿qué hacías antes de llegar a España?
Víctor Era estudiante. Estudiaba lenguas. Ahora soy intérprete y trabajo para la Unión Europea. ¿Y tú, Begoña?
Begoña Yo era maestra. Trabajaba en un colegio, pero ahora estoy sin trabajo.

Unit 19

ACTIVITY 1

Buenos días. Soy María Bravo de México. Llamaba para informarles que ha sido imposible encontrar un vuelo para el 28 de marzo. Todos los vuelos están completos. He tenido que aplazar el viaje para el martes 2 de abril. Viajo en el vuelo 732 de Aeroméxico, que llega allí el miércoles a las once y media de la mañana. He reservado una habitación en el Hotel Intercontinental. Adiós, gracias.

ACTIVITY 3

Laura Buenas tardes.
Recepcionista Buenas tardes, señora. ¿Qué desea?
Laura Mire, mi marido y yo hemos pedido una habitación con vistas al mar, y usted nos ha dado una con vistas al aparcamiento. ¡Esto no puede ser! Además, la habitación no tiene ni baño completo ni terraza. Y el hotel no está a cien metros de la playa como ponía en el anuncio. Y no tiene piscina ni solarium. ¡Esto es el colmo! Hemos venido aquí varias veces y esta es la primera vez que nos pasa algo así.
Recepcionista Perdone usted, señora, pero ha sido una equivocación de su agencia de viajes. No es culpa nuestra. Yo no puedo hacer nada.
Laura ¡Es increíble!

Unit 20

a Hola Mónica, soy María. Te llamaba para confirmar que salgo de Madrid esta tarde en el tren de las 5:00. Llego a Sevilla a las 7:30. ¿Vendrás a la estación a recogerme? Tengo mucho equipaje. Hasta luego. Un beso.

b Mónica, soy Mark. Te llamo de Londres. Tengo un problema en el trabajo y me será imposible viajar el miércoles como tenía planeado. He cambiado el vuelo para el domingo. Saldré de Londres a las 9:30 de la mañana y llegaré allí al mediodía. Iré directamente a tu casa en un taxi. Adiós.

Unit 21

ACTIVITY 3

a – Oye, Lucía, ¿quieres venir a tomar una copa conmigo después del trabajo?
– Imposible, he quedado con María para ir de compras. Otro día, ¿qué te parece?
– Vale. Otro día.

b – Buenas tardes, señor Flores. Esta tarde hay un cóctel para darle la bienvenida al nuevo director. ¿Quiere usted venir?
– Lo siento, pero no puedo. Tengo hora con el dentista.

c – Hola Mario. ¿Tienes algún plan para el martes por la noche?
– No, ninguno.
– ¿Por qué no vienes a mi fiesta de cumpleaños? Voy a celebrarlo en casa.
– Encantado, gracias.

Unit 23

ACTIVITY 2

Al salir del hotel tome la calle Palacio que está aquí enfrente y doble a la derecha en la calle Triunfo. Siga por la calle Triunfo hasta la Plaza de Armas, cruce la plaza y después tome la calle Garcilaso. El hostal está una calle más arriba, a la izquierda.

Unit 24

a

Doctor	¿Qué le pasa?
Señora	Me siento muy cansada, doctor, y no duermo bien por la noche. Estoy constantemente nerviosa, intranquila. No sé qué hacer, doctor.
Doctor	Usted parece estar estresada. Tiene que descansar. Tómese unos días de vacaciones. Eso es lo que necesita.

b

Señor	Doctora, no sé qué me pasa. Desde hace dos días tengo un dolor de estómago horrible. No puedo comer nada. Me encuentro muy mal, doctora.
Doctora	A ver ... ¿Le duele aquí?
Señor	Ay, sí, doctora, me duele muchísimo.
Doctora	¿Ha tenido vómitos?
Señor	Sí, he tenido vómitos y fiebre.
Doctora	Bueno, probablemente se trata de una infección estomacal. Le voy a recetar unas pastillas. Tome dos cada seis horas. Con esto se le pasará.

Unit 25

Teresa	Veamos qué tipo de persona necesitamos para relaciones públicas.
Julio	Pues, tiene que ser alguien que sepa relacionarse bien con la gente. Eso es fundamental. Y que tenga dos o tres años de experiencia como mínimo. Que sepa idiomas ...
Teresa	Sí, sí, claro, que hable inglés y preferiblemente algo de francés.
Julio	Sí, creo que eso es muy importante. Y, por supuesto, que tenga conocimientos de informática y que tenga carnet de conducir. Queremos una persona que sea dinámica, creativa ...
Teresa	Sí, claro, y que esté dispuesta a trabajar en equipo. Espero que encontremos a alguien.
Julio	No creo que sea difícil.

Key to the activities and to 'Test yourself'

Antes de empezar (Introductory unit)

HELLO AND GOODBYE

a Buenos días **b** taking your leave

1.2 1 Hola, ¿qué tal? **2** Buenos días. **3** Buenas tardes. **4** Buenas noches.

2.2 1 ¿Cómo te llamas?, **2** ¿Y tú?.

2.3 1 ¿Cómo se llama usted?, **2** Me llamo Julia Montes.

2.4 1 Me llamo (*your name*). ¿Y tú?/Y tú, ¿cómo te llamas?
2 Me llamo (*your name*). ¿Y usted?/Y usted, ¿cómo se llama?/¿Cómo se llama usted?

3.2 1 ¿Qué significa *habitación*? **2** Más despacio, por favor. **3** Perdón/Perdone, no entiendo. ¿Puede repetir, por favor? **4** Perdone, no hablo muy bien español. ¿Habla usted inglés?

4.2 1 Adiós (buenas tardes). **2** Hasta luego. **3** Chao.

Check what you have learned llama – llamo – usted – entiendo – puede – hablo – habla.

TEST YOURSELF

a 3, **b** 7, **c** 5, **d** 1, **e** 8, **f** 2, **g** 4, **h** 6, **i** 10, **j** 9

Unit 1

SPANISH REGIONS

a Barcelona **b** Madrid **c** Málaga **d** Valencia **e** Canary Islands.

CONVERSATIONS

1.2 ¿De dónde eres?
2.1 a F **b** F **c** F **d** V
2.2 a Usted es español, ¿verdad? **b** ¿De dónde es usted?
3.1 a No. **b** Spanish.
3.2 a ¿Habla Vd. ...? **b** Hablo ...
4 Catalan, Spanish and some English.

1 a-6-E, **b**-4-D, **c**-5-F, **d**-7-G, **e**-1-C, **f**-3-B, **g**-2-A

2 a Española. Barcelona. Español y catalán. **b** Argentino. Buenos Aires. Español e inglés. **c** Norteamericana. California. Inglés, italiano y un poco de español.

3 a Me llamo Boris. Soy de Moscú. Hablo ruso. **b** ... Paco. ... de Granada. ... español. **c** ... Ingrid. ... de Berlín. ... alemán. **d** ... Marguerite. ... de París. ... francés. **e** ... Mark. ... de Nueva York. ... inglés. **f** ... Ma Ángeles. ... de Monterrey, México. ... español.

4 Me llamo ... soy ... Soy ..., hablo.

5 *Follow Activity 4.*

6 a Palma. **b** Guillermo. **c** Córdoba, España.

7 ¿Cómo se llama Vd.?/Me llamo ..., ¿de dónde es Vd.?/Soy de ... ¿Habla Vd. inglés?/Sí, hablo un poco de español.

a 4, **b** 3, **c** 1, **d** 2, **e** 6, **f** 5, **g** 9, **h** 10, **i** 8, **j** 7

Unit 2

INTRODUCTIONS

a shake hands and maybe give a friendly pat on the shoulder. **b** give a kiss on each cheek.

CONVERSATIONS

1.1 Are you Mr Peña?; Yo soy Cristina Dueñas.

1.2 Sí, soy yo.

1.4 1 ¿Es usted el señor Santana? **2** Yo soy (*name*). Encantado/a *or* Mucho gusto.

2.1 ¿Cómo está?, Muy bien, gracias. ¿Y usted?

2.2 Le presento a (name), Esta es la señora (*name*).

3.1 ¿Cómo estás?, ¿Y tú?, Te presento a ...

3.2 1 un compañero de trabajo **2** pero vivo en Madrid.

3.3 1 Te presento a Luis/a, mi marido/mujer. **2** Esta es Isabel, una compañera de trabajo.

4.1 Home Tel. number: 981 54 63 72. Mobile phone: 696 00 19 82.

4.2 1 ¿Cuál es tu número de teléfono? El teléfono de mi casa es el (*number*) **2** ¿Tienes correo electrónico?

1 a eres/soy/soy/estás. **b** es/es/está/está/es.
2 a – **b** la **c** la **d** el **e** – **f** una **g** un
3 ¿Vd. es el señor Barrios?/Yo soy …/ Encantado/a, señor Barrios./Le presento a John, un compañero de trabajo.
4 a Te presento a mi marido/mujer. **b** … mi novio/a. **c** … mi padre/madre. **d** … mi hermano/a. **e** Esta es … **f** Este es … **g** Este es … **h** Esta es …
5 a la Ciudad de México, en el Paseo de la Reforma. **b** … la calle de la Libertad. **c** … Barcelona, en el Barrio Gótico, en la Plaza del Rey.
7 a 965 12 20 18 **b** 947 92 54 36.
8 a Vivo en (*city*). **b** Vivo en (*area*). **c** Vivo en la calle (*name of street*). **d** (*Your telephone N°*). **e** Sí/No tengo teléfono. **f** (*Telephone N° at work*). **g** Sí/No tengo. **h** (*Extension N°*) **i** Es el (*number*)/No tengo teléfono móvil/celular. **j** Es (*your email*)/No tengo correo electrónico/email.
9 Horizontales: 1 tiene 2 tienes 3 usted 4 vivo 5 eres
Verticales: 1 vive 2 mi 3 tengo 4 su 5 tu

a Soy Pat Johnson. **b** Mucho gusto. **c** Encantado/encantada. **d** ¿Cómo estás? **e** Le presento a Mario. **f** Esta es Ana, una compañera de trabajo. **g** ¿Dónde vives? **h** Vivo en Londres. **i** ¿Cuál es su número de teléfono? **j** ¿Tienes correo electrónico/email?

Unit 3

a a double room. **b** Is breakfast included?

1.1 She wants a single room for six nights.
1.2 1-b, 2-d, 3-a, 4-c.
1.3 Para dos personas. Una habitación doble. Para tres noches.
2.1 They want a double room with two beds. The rooms have a bathroom, television and air conditioning.
2.2 1 ¿Tienen baño las habitaciones? 2 ¿Está incluido el desayuno?
2.3 1 Somos dos, – Quisiéramos una habitación doble con cama de matrimonio. – Sí, claro, (tienen) baño, teléfono, aire acondicionado, televisión y minibar. – Sí, está incluido.
3.2 1 Tenemos una habitación reservada. **2** ¿A qué nombre? **3** Tienen la habitación treinta y cinco. **d** Pueden cambiar aquí mismo.

1 Treinta y seis, cuarenta y cinco, cincuenta y nueve, sesenta y cuatro, setenta y seis, ochenta y ocho, noventa y tres.

2 **a** Habitación 48. **b** Despacho 36. **c** Habitación 100.

3 **a**-5 **b**-1 **c**-6 **d**-3 **e**-4 **f**-2

4 C: Buenas tardes/noches. Quisiéramos una habitación doble con baño, por favor. R: ¿Para cuántas noches? C: Para cinco noches. ¿Está incluido el desayuno? R: No, es sin desayuno. El desayuno es aparte. C: Vale. ¿Se puede aparcar en el hotel? R: Sí, claro. Sus pasaportes, por favor. Gracias. Tienen la habitación setenta y ocho.

5 **a** tengo **b** tienen **c** son **d** tienen **e** tiene/tenemos **f** son/somos.

6 **a** Air conditioning in the dining room and bar, telephone, bar, fire exit. **b** Individual safe deposit box. **c** In four- and five-star hotels/In all hotels.

8 Check alphabet on page 55.

9 Check alphabet on page 55.

TEST YOURSELF

a 6, **b** 4, **c** 7, **d** 1, **e** 8, **f** 2, **g** 5, **h** 3, **i** 10, **j** 9

Unit 4

FINDING YOUR WAY

a the cathedral. **b** a chemist's. **c** a supermarket. **d** the castle.

CONVERSATIONS

1.1 She's looking for a bureau de change and a hotel. ¿Hay una oficina de cambio por aquí? ¿Y dónde hay un hotel?

1.2 1-b, 2-d, 3-a, 4-c.

1.4 **1** ¿Hay un banco por aquí? **2** Hay uno en la calle Bandera, la cuarta a la izquierda, al lado de la oficina de turismo.

2.1 It's at the end of this street, on the right, five minutes away.

2.3 **1** ¿Sabe (Vd.) dónde está la catedral? **2** Lo siento, no (lo) sé. No conozco muy bien Granada. **c** Está lejos. Al final de la calle, a la izquierda, está la parada del autobús.

3.1 ¿Dónde están los servicios?

3.2 They are on the first floor. Go straight on to the end, then take the corridor on the left and go up the stairs. The toilets are opposite the café.

PRACTICE

1 **a** hay **b** está **c** hay **d** está **e** están **f** hay

2 **a** ¿Hay un restaurante por aquí cerca? **b** ¿ ... una librería ...? **c** ¿ ... una

tienda de ropa ...? **d** ¿ ... una tienda de comestibles ...? **e** ¿Dónde está la
estación de autobuses? **f** ¿ ... la iglesia? **g** ¿ ... la biblioteca? **h** ¿ ... la Plaza
Mayor?

3 sabes; sé; conozco; conozco; conoces; conozco.

4 *Possible answers:* **a** Hay dos, uno detrás de la plaza de la Luz y otro
detrás del cine. **b** Hay uno en la esquina, al lado de un restaurante.
c Está entre el museo y la estación de metro. **d** Hay dos, uno delante de
la gasolinera y otro delante de la estación de metro. **e** Está en la primera
calle, a la derecha, al final de la calle. **f** Hay una al lado de la parada de
autobuses, a la izquierda. **g** Hay una en la primera calle, a la derecha, al
lado de un restaurante. **h** Está detrás de la iglesia/Correos.

5 a The avenida del Mar is about ten minutes from here. Go straight on
and then take the fourth street on the right. The avenida del Mar is at
the end of the street. **b** The beach is a bit far. On the bus, between ten
and fifteen minutes. The bus stop is at the corner, opposite the church.
c (The first person doesn't know where the post office is, as she's not from
there and doesn't know the city very well) It's on calle Picasso, next to
the museum. Go up this street and take the first (turning) on the left. It's
about five minutes from here. **d** The telephones are on the second floor,
opposite the toilets. The stairs are at the end of the corridor.

6 *Possible answers:* **a** Está en (*name of street/area*). **b** Hay una parada
de autobús a cinco minutos de mi casa. **c** Hay un supermercado, tiendas
de ropa, una panadería, etc. **d** Hay un museo, una biblioteca, un parque.

TEST YOURSELF

1 a ¿Hay un hotel por aquí? **b** ¿Dónde hay un banco, por favor? **c** ¿Sabe
usted dónde está el museo? **d** Perdone, la oficina de turismo, ¿está muy
lejos? **e** ¿Dónde están los servicios, por favor?

2 a There's one on Lorca street, the second street on the right.
b It's at the end of this street, next to the church. **c** Go straight on as far
as Plaza Mayor (the main square) **d** I'm sorry, I don't know. I don't know
the city. **e** They are on the second floor, opposite the cafe.

Unit 5

EATING OUT

a ensalada mixta (mixed salad which, as well as the normal salad
ingredients, will have others such as hard-boiled egg, tuna flakes, onion);
b sardinas a la plancha (grilled sardines); **c** peras al vino (pears in wine).

1.1 1 Gazpacho, and grilled hake and salad. **2** Peas and ham, and chicken and chips. **3** Still mineral water. 4 Red wine.

1.2 Queremos el menú del día. Para mí ... , ¿Y para usted ...?, De primero/ segundo.

2.1 Javier wants some more bread, and Ángeles another mineral water. Ángeles orders a chocolate ice cream and Javier a creme caramel and coffee.

2.2 What do you have for dessert?

2.3 1 ¿Nos trae (un poco) más (de) vino? **2** ¿Me trae otro café? **3** ¿Nos trae la cuenta?

3.1 Silvia: 2, 5 Gloria 3, 6 Paco 1, 4.

3.2 1 ¿Y para ti ...? 2 Para mí ...

3.3 1-c, 2-a, 3-b.

1 R: para – de – de – de – con. C: para. F: de – con – de – a – con. C: para. F: de. C: con – sin. F: con – sin.

2 a Vd. **b** tú **c** tú **d** Vd. **e** Vd. **f** tú.

3 Tú: Queremos el menú del día, por favor. P: Yo quiero una ensalada mixta de primero, y de segundo quiero paella. Tú: Para mí sopa, y de segundo quiero cordero asado con puré de patatas. Tú: Vino tinto para mí, por favor. ¿Y para ti Pepe? ¿Qué quieres beber? P: Quiero un vaso de vino blanco. Tú: ¿Nos trae también una botella de agua (mineral) sin gas? Tú: ¿Qué tiene(n) de postre? P: Yo quiero fresas con nata. Tú: Arroz con leche para mí. ¿Y nos trae dos cafés y la cuenta, por favor?

4 Sofía: squid/a beer. Clara: cheese sandwich/white coffee (with a dash of milk). Ramón: mushrooms/white wine.

5 Pescado: atún, merluza. Carne: pollo, cordero, cerdo. Verdura: lechugas, ajos, cebollas. Fruta: piñas, uvas, manzanas. Utensilios: cuchillo, cuchara, tenedor, plato.

6 a F **b** F **c** V **d** F.

a ¿Qué van a tomar? **b** Queremos el menú del día. **c** Para mí, sopa de primero. **d** De segundo quiero cordero asado con patatas fritas. **e** ¿Y para beber? **f** Un vino tinto y dos aguas minerales sin gas. **g** ¿Me trae un poco más de pan? **h** ¿Qué tienen de postre? **i** Quiero una cerveza y un bocadillo de jamón/Quiero un bocadillo de jamón y una cerveza **j** Por favor, ¿me pasa la sal?/¿Me pasa la sal, por favor?

Unit 6

a two **b** the airport.

CONVERSATIONS

2.1 **1** 9.15 a.m., 11.30 a.m., 2.30 p.m., 4.15 p.m. **2** a single ticket **3** business class.

2.2 **1** para Sevilla **2** para el domingo **3** por la tarde

2.3 **1** Quería hacer una reserva para Barcelona, para el sábado.
2 Hay un tren que sale a las trece cuarenta y cinco, otro a las quince quince y otro a las diecisiete veinte. **3** El tren de las quince quince, ¿a qué hora llega a Barcelona? **4** Quiero un billete de ida y vuelta. **5** ¿Cuánto cuesta la clase turista? **6** Ciento treinta y cinco euros.

3.1 **1** They run every hour. **2** An hour and a half. **3** It leaves in half an hour (9.05) and it arrives in Ronda at 10.35. **4** She gets a return ticket.

3.2 **1** cada hora **2** ¿Cuánto tarda el viaje? **3** El próximo sale ... **4** ¿Cuánto es?

PRACTICE

1 ¿Qué hora es en (*name of city*)? **a** Son las seis de la tarde.
b Son las cinco de la tarde. **c** Es la una de la mañana. **d** Son las nueve de la mañana. **e** Es la una de la tarde. **f** Son las doce/Es mediodía.

2 **a** A las ocho menos diez, a las doce y veinte, a las siete menos veinte de la tarde. **b** A las once menos dos, a las cuatro y diecisiete minutos de la tarde, a las diez y tres minutos de la noche.

3 *Destination:* Lima, Perú *Departure:* Thursday 17th, 11.30 p.m. *Arrival:* Friday, 9.40 a.m., local time. 21.30 at airport.

4 100, 299, 500, 900, 3500, 100.000, 1.000.000, 2.000.000.

5 cuatrocientos cuarenta euros, cuatrocientos cincuenta y ocho, mil quinientos noventa, mil ochocientos setenta y siete, mil doscientos treinta y tres, mil setecientos ochenta, dos mil quinientos noventa y tres.

6 Buenos días. Quería hacer una reserva para Cartagena para el viernes por la mañana. ¿A qué hora hay vuelos? – ¿A qué hora llega a Cartagena? – Para el domingo por la noche. ¿A qué hora sale el último vuelo de Cartagena? - ¿Cuánto cuesta el billete/boleto (LAm) de ida y vuelta? – Está bien. Deme un billete/boleto de ida y vuelta, por favor.

TEST YOURSELF

1 **a** ¿Qué hora es? **b** Es la una. **c** Son las cinco y cuarto. **d** Son las siete y media. **e** Son las nueve menos cuarto.

2 a (1) billetes, (2) para, **b** (1) que, (2) de, **c** de ida y vuelta,
d (1) cuánto, (2) horas, **e** (1) a, (2) a, **f** (1) hacer, (2) para, (3) por

Unit 7

GOING TO THE MARKET

a a kilo of oranges **b** half a kilo of strawberries **c** two tomatoes and a lettuce **d** How much does the pineapple cost?

CONVERSATIONS

1.2 One kg bananas, one and a half kg oranges, 2 kg tomatoes, one lettuce, 2 kg potatoes.
1.3 1 ¿Qué quería? **2** ¿Cuánto cuestan estas …? **3** ¿(Quiere) algo más?, ¿Alguna cosa más? **4** ¿Cuánto es todo?
2.1 a quarter kg cheese, one hundred and fifty grams of ham, half kg olives, one packet of butter, a tin of tuna, a loaf of bread, half a dozen eggs, one litre bottle of olive oil.
2.2 1-b, 2-d, 3-a, 4-c.
2.3 1 doscientos gramos de jamón serrano **2** un kilo de azúcar
3 un paquete de galletas de chocolate **4** una lata de salmón **5** un cuarto de chorizo **6** una barra de pan integral.

PRACTICE

1 1-d 2-e 3-a 4-f 5-b 6-c
2 Quería un kilo y medio de tomates. - ¿Cuánto cuestan/valen las fresas? *or* ¿A cómo/cuánto están las fresas? – Me da/pone un kilo. *or* Deme/ Póngame un kilo. - ¿Tiene pimientos verdes? – Quiero cuatro. – Sí, quiero perejil también. – Eso es todo, gracias.
3 a plato **b** botella **c** lata.
4 a 3.20 € **b** 1.90 € **c** 2.10 € **d** 3.60 € **e** 1.75 € **f** 0.60 €
5 a i esto ii estas iii este iv esta v estos **b** i esas ii ese iii eso iv esos v esa.

TEST YOURSELF

a 4, **b** 8, **c** 7, **d** 1, **e** 6, **f** cuarto, **g** 5 and 9, **h** 3 and 2 **i** 12 **j** 11

Unit 8

FASHION

a ¿Puedo probármelos? **b** ¿Puedo probármela?

1.1 1-c 2-f 3-d 4-a 5-e 6-b. She's buying a (red) jacket and a (black) sweater.

1.2 **1** ¿De qué color la quiere? **2** La prefiero en rojo. **3** Me queda grande. **4** ¿Tiene una más pequeña? **5** Esta me queda bien. **6** Me la llevo.

2.1 He's buying (grey) trousers and a (medium-size white) shirt.

2.2 **1** forty-six, for the trousers and medium for the shirt. **2** at the back, on the right **3** ¿Puedo probármelos? **4** ¿Cómo le quedan? **5** Me quedan muy bien. Me los llevo.

PRACTICE

1 **a** (*See model*) **b** ... esos zapatos marrones - ¿Estos? – Sí, esos - ¿... probármelos? - ¿... le quedan? – Me quedan pequeños. **c** ... esa camiseta amarilla - ¿Esta? – Sí, esa - ¿... probármela? - ¿... queda? - Me queda ancha. **d** ... ese vestido gris - ¿Este? – Sí, ese - ¿... probármelo? - ¿... queda? – Me queda estrecho.

2 **a** más corta **b** más baratas **c** más pequeña **d** más largos **e** más anchos **f** más grande.

3 **a** ¿Puedo probármelos? **b** Me lo llevo. **c** Me quedan bien. Me las llevo. **d** Me los llevo. **e** ¿Puedo probármela? **f** No me queda bien. No me lo llevo.

4 **a** size 38 **b** black **c** brown and red **d** red **e** They don't fit well. She wants a larger size.

TEST YOURSELF

1 **a** las, **b** probármelos, **c** (1) le, (2) me, **d** (1) me, (2) la, **e** lo.

2 **a** Quisiera ver esas botas, por favor. **b** ¿Tiene esta camisa en la talla 16? **c** La prefiero en blanco. **d** ¿Puedo probarme estos zapatos? **e** Esta falda me queda grande. ¿Tiene una más pequeña?

Unit 9

CHANGING MONEY

a £200 **b** by credit card

CONVERSATIONS

1.1 She's changing 250 dollars. The rate of exchange is 0.79 cents.

1.2 **1** ¿Me permite ...? **2** Aquí tiene.

1.3 ¿Qué desea? – Quería cambiar ... – ¿Tiene cheques de viaje ...? – Tengo billetes. ¿A cómo está ...? – Está a 540 ... ¿Cuánto quería cambiar?

– Cien dólares – Muy bien. ¿Tiene su pasaporte? – Sí, aquí tiene. – ¿Cuál es su dirección aquí? – Calle Moneda 842.

2.1 **1** F **2** F **3** V **4** F.

2.2 19 € per day.

2.3 **1** ¿Qué nos recomienda? **2** Les recomiendo ... **3** Se lo recomiendo. **4** ¿Podemos pagar ...?

3.1 She wants to go to the airport and she wants the taxi right now.

3.2 1 ¿Me lo puede enviar ...? 2 Se lo envío ...

3.3 Quería un taxi para ir a la Estación de Atocha, por favor. ¿Me lo puede enviar a las 11:00?/Lo quiero para las 11:00. Pues, se lo envío a las 11:00. (*No other changes in dialogue apart from address and telephone number*).

PRACTICE

1 Libras: 1.40 €, 175 pounds; Swiss francs: 0.60 €, 250 Swiss francs; Swedish crowns: 0.10 €, 120 Swedish crowns.

2 Tú Quisiera cambiar dólares a pesos. ¿A cuánto/cómo está el cambio? E ¿Tiene billetes? Tú No, tengo cheques de viaje. E Está a catorce pesos por dólar. ¿Cuánto quiere cambiar? Tú Quisiera/ Quería cambiar doscientos dólares./Y el cambio de la libra, ¿a cuánto/cómo está? E La libra está a 21 pesos. Tú Quisiera/Quería cambiar 180 libras. E ¿Qué dirección tiene en México? Tú (*address*).

3 me – le – lo – lo – lo.

4 (*Possible questions*) a Queríamos un coche económico. ¿Qué (coche) nos recomienda? b ¿Cuánto es/cuesta el alquiler? c ¿Está incluido el seguro obligatorio?/El seguro obligatorio, ¿está incluido? d Y los impuestos, ¿están incluidos?/¿Están incluidos los impuestos? e ¿Va con gasolina o con gasóleo? f ¿Podemos pagar con tarjeta de crédito?/¿Se puede pagar con ...? g ¿Podemos llevarlo ahora mismo?/¿Lo podemos llevar ahora mismo?

5 **a** Queríamos/Quisiéramos el desayuno en la habitación, por favor. Estamos en la habitación 12. **b** ¿Puede enviárnoslo ahora mismo?/¿Nos lo puede enviar ...? Queremos un té y un café, un zumo/jugo (LAm.) de piña y un zumo/jugo (LAm.) de naranja, y pan integral, por favor. **c** ¿Puede enviarnos un periódico inglés?/¿Nos puede enviar ...? **d** También quisiéramos/queríamos un taxi para ir al aeropuerto. **e** El avión sale a las doce y media. Lo queremos para las diez y media. **f** ¿Nos da la cuenta, por favor? Quisiéramos/Queríamos pagar con tarjeta de crédito.

6 *Horizontales:* 1 efectivo 2 alquilar 3 quisiera 4 tarjeta 5 incluidos 6 gasolina 7 recomiendo *Verticales:* 1 alquiler 2 cuánto 3 firmar 4 cambiar 5 billetes 6 viaje 7 casa (LAm usage).

a ¿A cuánto está el cambio? **b** Queríamos un taxi para ir a la estación. **c** ¿Para qué hora lo quiere? **d** ¿Me lo puede enviar ahora mismo/Puede enviármelo ahora mismo? **e** ¿Me dice su nombre? **f** En seguida se lo envío. **g** Quería alquilar un coche para el fin de semana. **h** (1) Es un coche excelente. (2) Se lo recomiendo. **i** Quería cambiar doscientas libras. **j** ¿Qué dirección tiene en Barcelona?

Unit 10

FAMILY LIFE

I am an only child but I have lots of cousins.

CONVERSATIONS

1.1 **1** F **2** V **3** V **4** F.
1.2 **1** Estás casada, ¿verdad? **2** Tú estás soltero, ¿no? **3** Tengo veintidós años. **4** el mayor/la menor.
2.1 bathroom, neighbourhood/area, heating, kitchen, bedroom/ room, flat, sitting room; **1** It's not bad. It has four bedrooms, a large sitting room, a fitted kitchen, two bathrooms, and it's very bright.
2 It's very good and quieter than the centre. **3** His flat is not as big as María's but it's very comfortable. It has three bedrooms, a sitting room, a large kitchen, independent heating.
2.2 **1** Gracia **2** Génova.

PRACTICE

1 **a** llamo **b** tengo **c** estoy **d** vivo **e** padres **f** mayor **g** llama **h** tiene **i** que **j** menor
2 **a** se llama **b** tiene **c** está **d** vive con su madre, sus tres hermanos y su abuela. **e** Sus padres ... **f** Él es el menor. **g** llama **h** tiene **i** que **j** menor es su hermana ...
3 *Possible answer:* Me llamo Luisa, tengo cuarenta y cinco años, estoy casada. Mi marido se llama Pedro y tiene cuarenta y siete años. Tengo tres hijos. La mayor se llama Teresa y tiene veintitrés años, después viene Raquel, que tiene veinte, y el menor es mi hijo Felipe, que tiene diecisiete años.
4 **a** Tiene cuarenta y nueve. **b** Tiene cuatro. **c** El mayor tiene veintiocho y la menor veintiuno. **d** Tiene cuarenta y seis. **e** Tiene treinta y dos. **f** Está divorciada. **g** Vive con su madre y con su hijo de siete años.
5 *Follow models:* dialogue 1, key to Activity 3, and transcript for Activity 4.

6 a Tiene dos. **b** Es estupendo, mucho mejor que el anterior y más barato. **c** Es muy tranquilo. d Tiene calefacción y aparcamiento.

7 a *See example.* **b** El piso de la calle Lorca es más grande que el piso de la avenida Salvador. **c** ... Salvador es más céntrico que ... Lorca. **d** ... Lorca es tan cómodo como ... Salvador. **e** ... Lorca es más seguro que ... Salvador. **f** ... Lorca es tan tranquilo como ... Salvador.

8 Use Elena's letter in Activity 6 as a model.

TEST YOURSELF

1 a tengo, **b** estoy, **c** tengo, **d** es, **e** tiene, **f** está, **g** es, **h** es, **i** es **j** estoy

2 a La casa de Mónica es más grande que mi casa. **b** Este hotel es mejor que el otro. **c** Pablo es menor/más joven que su hermano. **d** Londres es más caro que Los Ángeles. **e** María es la más guapa/bonita y la más inteligente. **f** Barcelona es tan interesante como Madrid.

Unit 11

THE WORLD OF WORK

a I work long (*literally*, many) hours, from eight to eight. **b** I don't have a job, I'm unemployed.

CONVERSATIONS

1.1 Elena is a nurse and works in a hospital. Álvaro is a student. He's studying history.

1.2 1 Cristina **2** Cristóbal **3** Ángeles.

1.3 1 ¿Qué estudias? **2** Trabajo en un hospital. **3** ¿Cuánto tiempo hace que trabajas allí? **4** Doy clases de inglés. **e** Estoy jubilada. **5** Estoy sin trabajo.

2.1 1 He works from 8.30 to 1.00 and from 2.30 to 6.30, Monday to Friday. He doesn't work on Saturdays. **2** Three weeks. **3** She works at home.

2.2 1 ¿Qué horario de trabajo tienes? 2 No tengo horario fijo.

2.3 Isabel: Trabajo de 9:00 a 5:00 (de la tarde), de lunes a viernes, y de 10:00 a 2:00 (de la tarde) los sábados. Tengo un mes de vacaciones. Hugo: Trabajo de 9:00 a 2:00 y de 4:00 a 7:00 de la tarde, de lunes a sábado.

PRACTICE

1 a-4 **b**-9 **c**-6 **d**-1 **e**-8 **f**-7 **g**-3 **h**-10 **i**-5 **j**-2

2 a-2 **b**-4 **c**-1 **d**-3

3 a Es recepcionista. Trabaja en un hotel. **b** Un año y medio

c Durante el día hay dos turnos, uno de 8:00 a 3:00 de la tarde y otro de 3:00 a 10:00 de la noche, de lunes a sábado. **d** Prefiere el turno de la mañana. **e** Quince días.

4 a Mónica **b** Victoria **c** María Ángeles **d** Juan Carlos **e** Eugenio **f** Adela.

5 *Follow Activity 4 as a model.*

6 a ¿Cuánto tiempo hace que estás aquí? Estoy aquí desde hace dos meses y medio *or* Hace dos meses y medio que estoy aquí. **b** ¿ ... que estudias inglés? Estudio inglés desde hace ... /Hace ... que estudio inglés. **c** ¿ ... que vives en este barrio? Vivo en este barrio desde hace .../Hace ... que vivo en este barrio. **d** ¿ ... que conoces a Paul? Conozco a Paul desde hace .../Hace ... que conozco a Paul.

7 *Possible answers:* **a** Soy (*occupation*), Trabajo en (*place of work*), Trabajo allí desde hace (*number of months/years*), Trabajo de (*time*) a (*time*), de (lunes) a (viernes). Tengo tres semanas de vacaciones al año. **b** Estudio (*lenguas*) en (*un colegio/una universidad*), Hace (*un año*) que estudio español, Tengo clases de (9.00 a 1.00) de (lunes) a (viernes)/No tengo un horario regular.

TEST YOURSELF

1 a 4, **b** 6, **c** 1, **d** 5, **e** 2, **f** 3

2 a ¿A qué se dedica usted? **b** Trabajo en un colegio. **c** Hace dos años que viven en Bilbao. **d** Soy periodista, pero ahora estoy sin trabajo. **e** Los sábados trabajo sólo por la mañana. **f** ¿Cuál es tu horario?

Unit 12

DAILY LIFE

a in a bar near her work **b** She goes to the gym and on Wednesdays to an English class as well.

CONVERSATIONS

1.1 1 siete **2** nueve **3** una hora/la oficina **4** autobús/el coche **5** un restaurante/la oficina **6** cinco/seis **7** once/once y media.

1.2 te levantas/me levanto, empiezo, tardo, vas/voy, almuerzas/almuerzo, sales/salgo, vuelvo, te acuestas/me acuesto.

1.3 1 Me levanto a las siete y cuarto. **2** Empiezo a trabajar a las nueve y media. **3** Voy al trabajo en tren. **4** Almuerzo en la oficina. **5** Nunca salgo de la oficina antes de las cinco y media.

2.1 Joaquín: a, b, d, f, g Amaya y Ramiro: i, j, l, n

1 a 2, 6, 8, 9 **b** 3, 4 7 **c** 1, 5
2 a Me levanto a las seis. **b** Me ducho. **c** Me afeito. **d** Me lavo los dientes.
e Me peino. **f** Me visto/pongo la ropa. **g** Desayuno. **h** Leo el periódico.
3 a She takes a shower, has a coffee and toast and goes out to do the
week's shopping. **b** She plays tennis near her home. **c** She goes out with
friends to the cinema, theatre, or a concert . **d** She normally goes to a
museum to see an exhibition.
4 a ¿A qué hora te levantas? **b** ¿Cómo vas al trabajo? **c** ¿A qué hora
empiezas a trabajar? **d** ¿Dónde almuerzas? **e** ¿A qué hora sales del
trabajo? **f** ¿Qué haces por la noche?
5 *Use Conversations and Activities in the Practice section as a model,
including the transcript of the listening comprehension text for Activity 3.*
6 a Completely quiet. He doesn't accept any engagement and does
absolutely nothing. He stays at home, he rehearses, studies, reads ... **b** He
eats a very light meal, a little bit of chicken or some veal and soup. **c** Eight
hours on a normal day, but when he has a performance he sleeps up to
eleven hours. **d** Most of the time by the seaside.

TEST YOURSELF

1 a me levanto, **b** me ducho, **c** desayuno, **d** salgo, **e** llego, **f** como,
g trabajo, **h** vuelvo, **i** leo, **j** veo
2 a 3, **b** 3, **c** 1, **d** 4 and 5 **e** 2

Unit 13

SPORT AND LEISURE

Me gusta ver la tele (watching telly).

CONVERSATIONS

1.1 Nieves, 3. Miguel, 2, Eduardo, 1.
1.2 1 Voy a ir al cine. **2** ¿Vas a salir? **3** ¿Te gusta el cine? **4** Me gusta
mucho. **5** A Raquel le encanta bailar.
2.1 1-c, 2-e, 3-a, 4-f, 5-b, 6-d.
2.2 Eduardo: 1, 2, 3. Nieves: 4, 5, 6.
2.3 1 New York **2** She likes it very much **3** Travelling by plane **4** They are
going to spend ten days in Ibiza.

PRACTICE

1 vamos, pensamos, quieres, vamos a ir, me encanta, le gusta.
2 *Follow Activity 1 as a model.*

3 a ¿Adónde vas a ir este verano? **b** ¿Con quién vas a ir? **c** ¿Cuánto tiempo vas a quedarte? **d** ¿Dónde vas a alojarte? **e** ¿Qué te gusta hacer en tus vacaciones? **f** ¿Te gusta nadar? **g** ¿Cuándo vas a volver?

4 *Examples:* Me encanta escuchar música, me gusta ir al cine, no me gusta (nada) trabajar, detesto realizar tareas domésticas.

5 me gusta - me encanta – detesto - me fascina - me gusta - me gusta - nos gusta - nos encanta - le gusta - no me gusta nada.

6 a Cristina **b** Elvira **c** Elvira **d** David **e** Daniel **f** Daniel **g** Cristina **h** David.

7 *Follow models above.*

TEST YOURSELF

1 a me encantan **b** le gustan **c** les fascina **d** nos encanta **e** te gusta

2 a ¿Qué vais a hacer el sábado por la noche? **b** ¿Quieres venir conmigo? **c** Estoy un poco cansado. Quiero acostarme pronto. **d** A Rafael le encanta el fútbol. **e** A nosotros el fútbol no nos gusta nada.

Unit 14

ON THE TELEPHONE

a ¿Dígame? **b** Al habla.

CONVERSATIONS

1.1 He's speaking on another line (2).

1.2 Sí, ¿diga? - ¿Está María? – No, no está en este momento. ¿De parte de quién? – De José Luis. - ¿Quieres dejarle algún recado? – No, luego la llamo.

2.1 1 Quisiera hablar con ... **2** Es la tres, sesenta y ocho. **3** Su extensión no es esta. **4** ¿Me puede poner con ...?

2.2 1-b, 2-d, 3-a, 4-c.

3.1 1 For tomorrow **2** Thursday **3** 9.30 a.m. or 4.15 p.m. **4** 9.30 a.m.

3.2 1 Quisiera pedir hora con el/la dentista para el lunes. **2** No hay hora disponible hasta el miércoles a las diez y veinte o por la tarde a las tres menos cuarto. **3** A las tres menos cuarto me va bien.

PRACTICE

1 ¿Está Leonor? – ¿De parte de quién?/¿Quién la llama? – ¿Quiere dejarle algún recado?

2 a 3 **b** She says she's got the tickets for tonight's concert.

3 ¿Dígame? – La señora Smith no puede ponerse en este momento. Está almorzando con un cliente. ¿De parte de quién?/¿Quién la llama?

– ¿Quiere dejarle algún recado? – Muy bien, señor Calle. Le daré su recado. – Sí, el señor Roberts está. No se retire, por favor. En seguida se pone.

4 a pones – necesita **b** atendiendo – quiere **c** se pone **d** se retire – pongo **e** cuelgue **f** comunicando.

5 a Llamo por el anuncio para el puesto de diseñadora gráfica. **b** Quería solicitar una entrevista. **c** Sí, a las nueve y media me va bien.

1 a Se ha equivocado de número. **b** Quisiera hablar con el señor Julián. ¿Me puede poner con él? **c** ¿De parte de quién?/¿Quién le/la llama? **d** En seguida/Ahora le pongo. **e** En seguida/Ahora se pone. **f** ¿Quiere dejar(le) algún recado?

2 a Gloria can't come to the phone now. She is taking a shower. **b** Mrs Martínez is speaking on another line. **c** Just a minute, please. Don't hang up. **d** Hello? Señor Mella's extension is engaged. **e** There are no appointments available until tomorrow afternoon. **f** Have you got an appointment?

Unit 15

WHO LIVED HERE?

Cervantes died on the same day and in the same year as Shakespeare. (In Spain, 23 April is **el día del libro**, a day when people gift one another books and the men may give women red roses in recognition of it also being St George's Day.)

CONVERSATIONS

1.1 1 I arrived in December 1997. **2** I met her a year and a half ago. **3** We got married in October of last year.

1.2 1 llegaste **2** ¿Cuánto tiempo hace …? **3** Nos casamos …

2.1 She's been there for three years. She lived and worked in Seville before.

2.2 ¿Cuánto tiempo llevas trabajando aquí?

2.3 1 Llevo cinco años en España. **2** Trabajé dos años en Salamanca. **3** Estudié español allí.

3.1 She was born in Santander on 15th March 1983.

3.2 1 ¿Dónde naciste? 2 ¿Cuándo naciste?

3.3 1 Nací en (place). **2** Nací el (date).

1 **a**-6, **b**-3, **c**-1, **d**-4, **e**-2, **f**-5.

2 terminé – trabajé – me trasladé – ingresé – desempeñé – ocupé – perdí.

3 **a** ¿Dónde nació? **b** ¿Cuándo nació? **c** ¿Qué estudió? **d** ¿Cuándo terminó sus estudios? **e** ¿Dónde trabaja ahora? **f** ¿Cuánto tiempo lleva trabajando allí? **g** ¿Dónde trabajó antes?

4.1 **a**-4, **b**-3, **c**-1, **d**-2.

4.2 **a** ¿Cuánto tiempo llevas viviendo en Londres? – Llevo dos años (viviendo en Londres). **b** ¿... estudiando inglés? – Llevo un año y medio. **c** ¿... haciendo atletismo? – Llevo tres años. **d** ¿... trabajando como enfermera? – Llevo un año.

5 **a** María: 24th July 1975; Rafael: 4th June 1935; Fátima: 16th November 1986; José: 18th May 1979. **b** five years ago **c** fifty years ago **d** in Argentina **e** fifteen years ago **f** one year **g** three years ago
h He worked in a bar and now he's working in an Argentinian restaurant.

6 Antonio Banderas; nació – filmó – dejó – triunfó – se casó – tuvieron – fue – realizó – actuó – obtuvo.

7 nació – llegó – es – está – tiene – estudió – terminó – conoció – se casaron – su (primer hijo) – su (hija Francisca) – su (marido).

a nací, **b** llegué, **c** me casé, **d** nos conocimos, nos casamos, **e** llevo un año y medio dando clases ... **f** lleva tres años trabajando **g** vivimos **h** nació **i** pasamos **j** le gustó

Unit 16

THE RAIN IN SPAIN

It was sunny and quite hot. It only rained one day.

CONVERSATIONS

1.1 2, 3, 5.

1.2 estuve/estuvimos, pasé, gustó, hicisteis/hice, fuiste/fui, fueron, encantó, me quedé, pareció.

1.3 interesantísimo, muchísimo.

2.1 The weather seemed very pleasant to her. It's not very warm, although in July it often rains. They were lucky because it only rained once.

2.2 no hace mucho calor, llueve a menudo, sólo llovió una vez, hizo muchísimo calor.

1 salió – fue – hice – cené – me acosté – tuve – estuve – me gustó – fui – hice – vinieron – fuimos – pasé – conocí – parecieron.

2 a-3, salió **b**-5, fue **c**-1, nadó **d**-4, conoció **e**-6, hizo **f**-2, tomó

3 a fuimos **b** estuvimos **c** vimos **d** anduvimos/nos parecieron **e** hicimos **f** tuvimos.

4 a ¿Dónde fuiste? **b** ¿Cuánto tiempo estuviste allí? **c** ¿Te quedaste con amigos? **d** ¿Qué hiciste allí? **e** ¿Qué te pareció el lugar? **f** ¿Hizo mucho calor?

5 *Follow the models in the previous activities.*

6.1 a-6, **b**-2, **c**-8, **d**-1, **e**-7, **f**-4, **g**-3, **h**-5.

6.2 a Hace sol. **b** Hace viento y está nuboso. **c** Está lloviendo/llueve. **d** Está nuboso.

8 a It was a sunny day **b** It will be cloudy in the morning and there'll be rain in the afternoon. **c** There'll be rain and strong wind in the morning. **d** It will be sunny after midday. **e** Minimum temperature, 7 degrees, maximum, 14.

TEST YOURSELF

1 a fuimos, estuvimos, **b** gustó, pareció, **c** hizo, llovió, **d** fueron, fue e vimos, gustaron

2 a No pudo venir a la fiesta. **b** Tuvo que trabajar. **c** ¿Qué hiciste ayer por la noche? **d** Fui al cine con Raúl. Vimos una película muy buena. **e** Teresa vino el lunes. Estuvo aquí con su novio.

Unit 17

TELL ME WHAT IT WAS LIKE

He did not have many friends because his parents were very strict with him.

CONVERSATIONS

1.2 1 Rocío's boss: insoportable, agresivo, antipático, feo, horrible.

2 Santiago: guapo, inteligente, divertido, irresponsable, machista; Daniel's mother: reservada, tímida, trabajadora, generosa, estricta.

3 mis compañeros de trabajo, todo lo contrario, un gran sentido del humor.

2.1 Hotel Don Quijote.

2.2 1 ¿Qué tal era el hotel? **2** Estaba a cien metros de la playa **3** Las habitaciones eran muy cómodas.

2.3 It was very good. It was a 4-star hotel, a hundred metres from the beach, it had a swimming pool, a good restaurant, seaview and parking. The rooms were comfortable and they had air conditioning and cable TV.

PRACTICE

1 **a**-3, **b**-4, **c**-6, **d**-1, **e**-2, **f**-5.
2 **a** aburrido/a **b** alegre **c** tímido/a **d** inteligente **e** arrogante **f** descortés **g** pesimista **h** antipático/a **i** débil **j** agradable **k** perezoso/a **l** responsable **m** maduro/a **n** seguro/a
4 **a** They met while travelling in Africa. **b** He was an architect. **c** He had great capacity for work and was very creative. He was a real artist. He was cheerful and extrovert and had a good relationship with his family and friends. **d** He left his job, family and friends and left the country to go to Tibet.
6 **a** era **b** era **c** tenía **d** estaban **e** estaban **f** había **g** habían **h** estaba **i** era **j** había **k** eran **l** era.

TEST YOURSELF

a era, **b** estaba, **c** estaba, **d** tenía había, **e** era, tenía, **f** era, tenía, **g** había, había, **h** tenía, eran, eran, **i** eran, tenía **j** tenía, era, estaba, había.

Unit 18

THE *PASEO*

He went out every night when he lived in the town. In the city he gets home late and is very tired.

DIALOGUE

1.1 She was there for five years. She worked as a sales manager in a travel agency.
1.2 antes de llegar, vivía en, trabajaba en..., compartía un piso.
2.1 She had good friends there and used to see them practically every day. They used to go out for drinks or to dinner, and at weekends they used to go dancing.
2.2 The job wasn't bad. She didn't earn much: No estaba mal. No ganaba mucho.

PRACTICE

1 1-e me levantaba a las 8.00, 2-c iba a la escuela, 3-f comía con mi madre, 4-a dormía la siesta, 5-d hacía los deberes, 6-b jugaba con mi pelota.

2 vivía, trabajaba, iba, empezaba, salía, ganaba, estaba, tenía, se llamaba, nos veíamos, dábamos, hablábamos.

3 *Example:* Vivía en... Mi padre era (*occupation*) y trabajaba en (*place*). Mi madre era ... y ... trabajaba en ... Mi madre me llevaba a la escuela. Me gustaba/encantaba ir a la escuela. Pasaba mis vacaciones en ... Allí nadaba, jugaba, salía con mis amigos, etc.

4 Esteban: **c** trabajaba/era, **f** es/trabaja; Víctor: **e** era/estudiaba, **a** es/trabaja; Begoña: **b** era/trabajaba, **d** está.

5 a Contestaban ... **b** Leían ... **c** Mandaban ... **d** Trabajaban ... **e** Atendían ... **f** Servían ...

6 a Contestábamos... **b** Leíamos ... **c** Mandábamos ... **d** Trabajábamos ... **e** Atendíamos ... **f** Servíamos ...

7 a ¿A qué se dedicaba antes?/¿En qué trabajaba antes?/¿Qué hacía antes? **b** ¿Cuánto tiempo trabajó allí? **c** ¿Cuánto ganaba? **d** ¿Por qué dejó su trabajo?

a conocí, tenía, **b** estaba, **c** era, tenía, vivía, trabajaba, **d** vi, iba, volvía, **e** vi, hablé, **f** fue, estuve, **g** fuimos, **h** salíamos, terminaba **i** íbamos **j** besé.

Unit 19

SPANIARDS ON THE WORLD STAGE

Studied a bit of Spanish.

CONVERSATIONS

1.1 1 He estado dos veces aquí. **2** Es la primera vez que vengo. **3** He ido al museo, pero todavía no he visto la catedral. **4** Por la tarde he salido con unos amigos a comer.

1.2 1 ¿Has visitado ...? **2** he ido a ... **3** no he visto ...

1.3 1 Esta es la segunda vez que vengo a España. **2** Hoy he ido al mercado. **3** Todavía no he visto las ruinas. **4** Me han dicho que son muy interesantes.

2.1 It's a blue-checked umbrella.

2.2 1 He comido aquí **2** ¿Es este su paraguas? **3** Sí, es ese.

3.1 They had asked for an outward-facing room and they have been given one facing a central patio. The air conditioning doesn't work and there aren't enough towels.

3.2 1 llamo de ... **2** no funciona **3** usted perdone **4** ahora mismo les doy otra habitación.

1 María Bravo from Mexico has phoned. She says it has been impossible to find a flight for the 28th of March. All flights are full. She has had to put off her journey until Tuesday 2nd of April. She's flying on Aeromexico flight 732, which arrives on Wednesday at 11.30 a.m. She has booked a room at the Intercontinental hotel.

2 a ha hecho **b** han pasado **c** ha viajado **d** ha vuelto **e** se han mudado **f** me he quedado **g** hemos pintado **h** han abierto

3.1 Hotel Condes

3.2 a V **b** F **c** F

4 a The heating, the air conditioning, the television, the hot/cold tap ... isn't working. **b** The toilet, the washbasin, the bath ... is blocked. **c** There isn't any soap, shampoo, toilet paper. **d** There aren't enough towels/ blankets.

5 a La calefacción no funciona. **b** El lavabo está atascado. **c** Falta/No hay jabón en el baño. **d** Necesito más mantas en mi cama.

6 She left a briefcase with some documents. She says it is a black leather briefcase.

7 *Possible answers:* Perdone, he estado aquí al mediodía y he olvidado/ dejado un libro un jersey amarillo de manga larga/un bolso azul.

8 a See example. **b** See example. **c** ¿Ha pedido hora con ...? Sí, ya la he pedido. **d** ¿Ha escrito a ...? Sí, ya les he escrito. **e** ¿Ha hecho el pedido de ...? No, todavía no lo he hecho. **f** ¿Ha visto a ...? Sí, ya la he visto. **g** ¿Ha abierto la ...? No, todavía no la he abierto.

1 b 3, **c** 5, **d** 1, **e** 8, **g** 7, **h** 2, **i** 4, **j** 6

2 b Ha hecho ... **c** Ha respondido ... **d** Ha hablado ... **e** Ha asistido ... **g** Han escrito ... **h** Han entrevistado ... **i** Han ido ... **j** Han vuelto ...

Unit 20

Eating paella at the beach.

1.1 He's leaving this afternoon and will be arriving in Madrid at 8.30 tomorrow.

1.2 1 She offers to pick him up at the airport. **2** Rafael's, because her car is too small. **3** He'll phone Ana. **d** Seguro que mañana hará calor.

2.1 1 Llamaba por ... **2** una reserva a nombre de ... **3** No podremos viajar. **4** Tendremos que anularla.

2.2 Buenas tardes/noches. Llamaba por una reserva que hice a nombre de ... para el 20 de agosto. No podré viajar en esa fecha y tendré que anularla. Lo siento mucho.

PRACTICE

1 saldré, llegaré, me quedaré, llamaré, llevaré.

2 a María is calling to confirm that she's leaving Madrid this afternoon on the 5 o'clock train and will be arriving in Seville at 7.30. She asks Mónica whether she can come to the station to pick her up, as she has a lot of luggage. **b** Mark is phoning from London to say that it will be impossible for him to travel on Wednesday as planned. He has changed his flight for Sunday. He will leave London at 9.30 in the morning and will arrive there at midday. He will go straight to Mónica's house in a taxi.

3 a – 4, **b** – 5, **c** – 1, **d** – 2, **e** – 3.

4 a See example, **b** ... te entrevistarán, **c** ... te lo ofrecerán, **d** ... será muy bueno **e** ... te lo darán.

5 a See example, **b** ... vendrá solo, **c** ... tendrá nuestra dirección, **d** ... sabrá cómo llegar aquí, **e** ... entenderá algo de español.

6 a su – mío - el mío, **b** sus – mías – las mías.

TEST YOURSELF

1 a iré, **b** saldré, **c** viajaré, **d** hará, **e** llegaré, **f** me quedaré, **g** volveré, **h** tendré

2 a irá, **b** saldrá, **c** viajará, **d** hará, **e** llegará, **f** se quedará, **g** volverá, **h** tendrá

Unit 21

EL PUENTE

She could visit her sister but she would rather do a bit of travelling. She would love to go to Paris.

CONVERSATIONS

1.1 1 She suggests going to the cinema tonight. **2** In front of the cinema, about 9.30. **3** Because he has to work.

1.2 1 ¿Qué te parece si vamos ...? **2** ¿Qué te apetece ver? **3** Podríamos quedar ...

1.3 1 ¿Qué te parece si vamos al teatro mañana? **2** Me gustaría ver ...
3 He visto la obra, pero me encantaría verla otra vez. **4** Podríamos quedar aquí mismo sobre las ocho menos cuarto.

2.1 Antonio accepts it: Yo, encantado, gracias. Santiago doesn't accept it: A mí me encantaría, pero no puedo. Tengo un compromiso. ¿Otro día quizá?

2.2 ¿Queréis venir a cenar?

2.3 1 ¿Queréis/Os gustaría venir a mi casa el sábado? Tengo una fiesta y he invitado a otros amigos. **2** Me encantaría, pero no puedo. Tengo un compromiso con unos/algunos amigos de la oficina. ¿La próxima vez, quizá?

PRACTICE

1 a haría **b** lavaría **c** escribiría **d** llamaría **e** saldríamos **f** veríamos
g tendríamos **h** podríamos

2 Soy (*your name*). ¿Tienes algún plan para esta noche? ¿Qué te parece si vamos al teatro? Me gustaría ver (*play*). ¿La has visto? La ponen en el Olimpia y empieza a las 7:00. Podríamos quedar en el café enfrente del teatro a las 6:30. ¿Qué te parece?

3 Lucía is being invited to have a drink with someone after work. She doesn't accept the invitation because she's going shopping with María. Señor Flores is being invited to a cocktail party to receive the new Director, but he can't accept because he has an appointment with the dentist. Mario is being invited to a birthday party, and he accepts the invitation.

4 He's inviting me to see Joaquín Cortés and he suggests we meet in the bar next to the theatre at 7:30.

5 *Follow Activity 4 as a model.*

6 The Chamber of Commerce of Santa Cruz has pleasure in inviting you to the inauguration ceremony for our new offices. The opening ceremony, which will be attended by the local authorities will take place/be held on Avenida del Libertador, 52, on Tuesday 25th May at 19.30.

TEST YOURSELF

a trabajaría, **b** haría, **c** compraría, **d** pondría, viviría, **e** me casaría, tendría/tendríamos, **f** podríamos, **g** enviaríamos, **h** ayudaríamos, **i** nos mudaríamos, **j** sabríamos.

Unit 22

No, gracias. De verdad. (*No, thank you. Really.*)

CONVERSATIONS

1.1 She had never been to Mérida. She thinks it is a very beautiful city.

1.2 **1** ¿Había estado aquí antes? **2** Nunca había venido a ...

1.3 **1** ¿Había estado en España antes? **2** Había estado en Barcelona, pero nunca había venido a Granada. **3** ¿Qué le parece el hotel? **4** Me gusta. Es un hotel buenísimo/muy bueno.

2.1 **1** buenísimo **2** delicioso **3** un poco más **4** un poco más de

2.2 **1** La paella está buenísima. **2** El pollo está delicioso. **3** ¿Le sirvo un poco más de postre? **4** ¿Quiere un poco más de café?

3.1 **1** c, d **2** a, b.

3.2 **1** ¡Qué tarde es! **2** Debo irme. **3** Gracias por haber venido. **4** ¡Que tenga un buen viaje!

PRACTICE

1 **1-d**: había aprendido **2-c**: había viajado **3-e**: había hecho **4-f**: había estudiado **5-a**: había escrito **6-b**: había terminado.

2 **a**-2 **b**-4 **c**-1 **d**-3.

3 No había estado nunca aquí antes. Es un país muy bonito. /Los mariscos están buenísimos./Están deliciosos./Sí, pero sólo un poco./No, gracias./Sí, de verdad, gracias. No puedo beber más porque tengo que conducir.

4 Possible answers: **a** ¿Le sirvo otra taza de café?/¿Quiere otro café? **b** ¿Quiere/Le sirvo un poco más de tarta? **c** ¿Quiere/Le sirvo un poco más de coñac? **d** ¿Quiere/Le sirvo más agua mineral?

5 **a** por tu regalo **b** ha sido **c** mucho de **d** conocerla.

6 agradecer – marido – estancia – placer – poder – visita.

TEST YOURSELF

a El pescado/la carne está delicioso/a. **b** ¿Le sirvo un poco más? **c** '¿De verdad?'- 'De verdad, gracias'. **d** ¿Quiere un poco más de vino? **e** Sí, gracias, pero sólo un poco. **f** Muchas gracias por la invitación. **g** Han sido ustedes muy amables. **h** Me alegro mucho de haberla conocido (*haberlo* or *haberle* for a man). **i** Gracias por haber venido or Gracias por venir. **j** ¡Que tenga un buen viaje! (informally, '¡Que tengas ...!')

Unit 23

Carry straight on and at the end of the street, turn left, then take the first on the right.

CONVERSATIONS

1.1 He's looking for the Post Office. He needs to go straight on and when he reaches Mijas Avenue, the fourth on the right, he has to turn right. The Post Office is on Bailén Street, the second on the left.

1.2 1 ¿Podría decirme ...? 2 la segunda a la izquierda c la cuarta calle a la derecha.

1.3 ¿Podría decirme dónde está el museo? – Siga todo recto y al llegar a la calle (de) Cervantes gire a la izquierda. El museo está en la avenida San Alfonso, la tercera a la derecha.

2.1 1 F 2 V 3 F.

2.2 por – hasta – de.

3.1 1 de 9:00 a 11:30 de la mañana y por la tarde de 4:00 a 6:00 2 al 952 642 21 09 c 952 759 55 32.

3.2 1 marque 2 llame 3 indique 4 haga.

PRACTICE

1 1-d 2-g 3-a 4-f 5-h 6-c 7-e 8-b

2 He/she is staying at Hotel Monasterio and is looking for the Hostal Los Marqueses.

3 siga – gire – tome – siga – suba – pregunte

4 Sí, siga todo recto/de frente y tome/coja la tercera (calle) a la izquierda, luego tome/coja la primera a la derecha y siga todo recto/de frente hasta el final de la calle. El banco está enfrente de la estación.

5 *Possible answer:* Siga todo recto/Siga por la calle San Antonio, después tome/coja la primera (calle) a la izquierda y luego la primera a la derecha. Esa es la avenida de Bailén. La estación está pasada la avenida de Mijas a la izquierda.

6 **a** Envíelo **b** Llámela **c** No lo haga **d** Pásemelas **e** No lo conteste **f** Enséñemelo

TEST YOURSELF

1 **a** ¿Podría decirme dónde está la estación? **b** Perdone (or 'Por favor'), ¿sabe usted dónde está la estación? **c** ¿Dónde están los servicios, por favor? **d** ¿Dónde hay un banco, por favor? **e** ¿Puede decirnos dónde está

el hotel Granada? **f** ¿Sabe usted si hay un supermercado por aquí?
2 a Go straight on along this avenue and then take the fourth street on the right. Continue along that street until you get to a church. The Condor hotel is next to the church. **b** Go up the stairs to the third floor and then take the corridor on the left. Mrs Castro's office is number 310 and it's at the end of the corridor. **c** The bar is on the second floor, past the restaurant. The lift is next to the reception. **d** This is doctor Palma's surgery. To ask for an appointment with the doctor dial one, to change or cancel your appointment dial two, for other enquiries dial three, to go back to the main menu dial zero.

Unit 24

MINOR AILMENTS

A cold and a headache.

CONVERSATIONS

1.1 1 tráeme **2** tengo **3** espera
1.2 1 ¿Qué te pasa? **2** Vuelvo en seguida.
2.1 1 She's not feeling well. **2** Because she's too hot. **3** To rest for a while, to try to sleep and not to get up.
2.2 1 No me encuentro bien. **2** Me duele la cabeza. **3** Por favor, abre la ventana. **4** ¿Por qué no descansas ...?

PRACTICE

1 Germany, the Netherlands (Low Countries) and Spain.
2 a Fatiga, ansiedad/insomnio/problemas digestivos. **b** To rest and take a holiday/Some tablets, two every six hours.
3 a me encuentro/siento **b** me duele **c** tengo dolor **d** tengo
e me duele **f** me siento
4 No me encuentro/siento bien. – Tengo un dolor de cabeza horrible y tengo fiebre. – Por favor, tráeme un vaso de agua mineral. Tengo mucha sed. – ¿ Podrías abrir la puerta? Tengo mucho calor. – No, gracias, no tengo hambre.
5 Isabel: She doesn't manage to lose weight. Sometimes she goes on a diet for a few days and loses a few kilos, but she's not persevering and so gains weight again. Ricardo: At the end of the day he suffers from terrible headaches which prevent him from doing anything. He also has nausea which usually ends up in vomiting.
6 Isabel: **b, c, f**. Ricardo: **a, d, e**.

1 **a** 3, **b** 6, **c** 5, **d** 1, **e** 4, **f** 2

2 **a** No cierres la puerta. **b** No enciendas la luz. **c** No lo pongas sobre la mesa.
d Por favor, no lo hagas. **e** No se lo digas ahora. **f** No toméis el autobús.

Unit 25

Not far from the shops.

1.1 She's looking for a flat near the centre, with three or four bedrooms,
and not too expensive. She doesn't want to pay more than 800 euros.
And she prefers it furnished.

1.2 The one which costs 650 € or the one which costs 700 €.

1.3 Example: Busco una casa que esté cerca de la playa, que tenga dos o
tres dormitorios, que tenga garaje y jardín, y que no cueste más de 1200
€. La prefiero sin amueblar.

2.1 **1** V **2** F **3** V **4** F.

2.2 Espero que encuentres a alguien, No creo que sea fácil.

2.3 *Example:* Quiero una persona que sea joven/mayor, que sea
estudiante o profesional, que sea tranquila, que tenga sentido del humor
y que le gusten los deportes (como a mí).

1.1 **a** 93 330 16 87 **b** 977 894 69 05 **c** Luisa **d** 93 357 26 71 **e** Begoña
f Carlota.

1.2 973 44 04 57.

2 viva – alquile – haya – puedan – esté.

3 Follow *activities 1 and 2 as a model.*

4 **a** sea **b** esté **c** sepa **d** tenga **e** le gusten **f** se lleve.

5 **a** to know languages, to have a driving licence, to have experience, to
be able to relate to people well/sepa, tenga, tenga, sea. **b** to be creative
and dynamic, to be presentable, to have finished higher education/sea,
tenga, haya. **c** to be familiar with computers, to have own vehicle/car, to
be willing to travel, to be able to join the company immediately/tenga,
cuente, esté, pueda.

6.1 sepa relacionarse ... , tenga experiencia, sepa idiomas, tenga
conocimientos de ... , tenga carnet de ... , sea dinámica, sea creativa y que
esté dispuesta a trabajar en equipo.

7 **a** He did Business Studies in Madrid and has a Master's degree from a university in the United States. He also speaks and writes English and French perfectly. **b** He's extrovert and nice. **c** He has been to the Department of Employment many times, he has sent his curriculum dozens of times, and he has read hundreds of job advertisements in the newspapers. **d** Some companies require experience, others tell him that with his qualifications they can't pay him an appropriate salary. **e** He doesn't know what to do, he's desperate.

TEST YOURSELF

1 **a** sea – tenga – fume – quiera **b** sea – sepa – se lleve – esté
2 **a** esté **b** sea **c** cueste **d** tenga **e** acepte **f** disponga

Index to grammar

If the reference starts with a number, this always refers to the unit number. The abbreviations following the unit number are:

'G' for *(Grammar) Language Discovery* section
'P' for *Practice* section
'HS' for *How do you say it?*

The following refer to sections at the end of the book:

'GS' to *Grammar Summary*
'GGT' to *Glossary of Grammatical Terms*
'IV' to *Irregular Verbs*

Credits